Plays for an Imaginary Theater

Judson Jerome

PLAYS FOR
AN IMAGINARY
THEATER

University of Illinois Press

Urbana, Chicago, London

For Paul and Jessie Treichler

Acknowledgments

The following poems, essays, and play were first published, sometimes in a slightly different form, in the periodicals and books listed below and are used here with the permission of those publications.

"Vera's Blaze," *Prairie Schooner*, Summer, 1957.

"Instructions for Acting: Improvisation," in *Light in the West*, Golden Quill Press, 1962.

"Revival," *Epoch*, Winter, 1961.

"The Unchosen," *Saturday Review*, April, 1968.

"Candle in the Straw," *Religious Theatre*, no. 1, Fall, 1964.

"Edenitis," *Ante*, 3, no. 2, Summer, 1967.

"Eden Revisited," *Prairie Schooner*, Spring, 1965.

"Gull at Play," *Colorado Quarterly*, Winter, 1958.

"A Storm Time," *Chicago Review*, Summer, 1957.

"Descent of Man," *Coastlines*, Autumn, 1960.

"Love, the First Decade," *Saturday Review*, April, 1958.

"Go East, Young Man," *Chicago Review*, Winter, 1965.

"The Alchemist," *Ladies' Home Journal*, September, 1963.

"The Superiority of Music," *Chicago Review*, 17, no. 1, 1964.

"Alcoholic" (poem), *Prairie Schooner*, Spring, 1960.

"On Mountain Fork," *Poetry*, November, 1968.

"Alcoholic" (essay), *Colorado Quarterly*, Winter, 1965.

Contents

Plays for an Imaginary Theater

I

An Attic in Muskogee:
Introduction

Ｍy theatrical experience began, I believe, when Jimmy, a sailor who had picked up my cousin during a vacation in Galveston in 1931 (I was a miniature four), this otherwise mesomorphic and natural enemy Jimmy gave me a cut-down sailor suit, including a yard-square black silk scarf. For me, for the next ten years, this was cape, turban, loincloth, or skimpy toga. Jimmy carried me on his shoulder through the echoing passageways of his cruiser, which seemed an elaborate mock-up. It was seeing up close something in a show. It was going backstage. My cousin was skinny and glamorous, about eight feet tall from my point of view, with a dark tempest of long curls. Those lithe giants would gambol on the sand and disappear into the shadowy beach cabin leaving me blinded. I learned to be rolled by the sea until all night the salt and sand would grind and the bed tilt and curtains belly into the room like houris and dreams were only the long crushing collapse of surf (like applause) and salty swaying of the island. Nothing was securely attached.

In fact, Texas was to me, an Oklahoma boy, all rather artificial. Christmas of 1933 (I remember the year because my mother took me on the train without fare, exploiting my small size, and kept snatching books out of my hands when the conductor came down the aisle) we went again—to Houston, to Aunt Orpha's, and as the car moved down the strangely humid, warm, and silent residential street, I saw the bearded oaks. No sooner was I out of the car than I ran across the street to a grove of them, jumped up, and pulled a nest of the stuff into my hands. It was like damp excelsior, dyed a purply grey. I nodded my head sagely: so that's how they do it. Aunt Orpha's house was tall and brick, full of adults, with a maid, impeccable actress who seemed to share the secret with me that this was all put on.

We went off (leaving my new baby brother in Houston with the maid) across the oleander-lined causeway to Galveston, across the drawbridge (I saw it! Saw the highway tilt up, still with its white line, into the air like stacked scenery!), and onto the island where they say Jean Lafitte once lived. (I wore my sailor-scarf as a pirate's kerchief around my head.) There was crab gumbo with okra which made me vomit. There was surely the swiftest and loudest merry-go-round in the world, with real brass rings which only adults seemed able to reach as we whirled past. A fun house with distorting mirrors reduced adults to stocky midgets and pulled my pencil legs out like salt-water taffy. There were shifting walls and floors that pitched menacingly underfoot. It was all a show and it scared hell out of me.

My theatrical experiences are chiefly associated with aunts, houses of aunts, especially aunts on my mother's side. Home necessarily seems real—though if you turned chairs over, blocked doors, draped bedclothes, and moved lamps you could make it strange enough. I remember my mother telling me it was not nice to play Virgin Mary when I must have been very young, sitting in a Palestine of upholstered pillows, a desert of sheets, with a magazine-rack manger and a puppy playing an uncooperative Jesus. (How deliciously theatrical is blasphemy!) When my father's father was alive, smelling of pipesmoke and woodfinish, my grandparents' house offered some possibilities. (I remember hearing on the radio shaped like a Tudor arch that President Hoover had been defeated, just as my grandmother switched off the Hoover and I watched its fat black stomach graphically collapse with a diminishing whine.) Her youngest daughter, Aunt Bonita, adolescent and demonic, took me to see *King Kong,* against orders, and I was sick for several days. That fright was useful. Bonita also read me "The Raven" in a horrifying voice from a limp leather book with scrolled etchings of the bird on the bust of Pallas, and she could sometimes be induced to play doctor with me on the porch swing, providing something of the terror and titillation of make-believe I yearned for. Aunt Tubby taught me poems; Aunt Marie taught me songs—with a view to public performance at family gatherings. But these aunts were too familiar, too sentimental, too obviously playing with a child, to have any convincing dramatic effect. They were more like big sisters or extra mothers.

It was my mother's sisters who were most utterly beyond belief. Aunt Audrey had a mansion in Muskogee with plate-glass windows like sheets of ice blanking the grey stone. Her husband was suitably terrifying—blind, fat, bald, with a dent in his forehead; he seemed coarse and cruel to me, and I do not remember that we ever exchanged even greetings. Luckily he couldn't see me. He sat in a den with huge leather chairs and a wolf at his side. (This police dog was probably very

gentle: I never got close enough to find out.) Or I would see
him feeling his way down the hall in a satin dressing-gown, and
I would streak off through the endless corridors which led to
rooms which led to rooms which opened embarrassingly into
bedrooms, beyond which were bathrooms with exaggerated
fixtures, which opened onto sun porches. Panting, I would find
the teak-smelling room with the exerciser, rest myself in the
wide canvas strap like a swing, turn the switch, and jiggle myself to insensibility.

Old Rob, who remembered the Civil War, stepped off the
sidewalk when a white person approached, doffed his hat, and
bowed his head. The only inhabitant of that house who knew I
was there, he would take me through the garden (in which I
could easily get lost) and toothlessly tell me stories which
were all the more frightening because I could not understand
his dialect. His wife Lilly, the cook, would sometimes let me
into their quarters above the garage where a large, luminous
cardboard skeleton hung on the wall. She churned in the base-
ment, and the knock, knock, knock of the stick on the keg
would echo through the cool, summer, adult, and darkly shaded
house. I would go to the attic, where there were steamer trunks
and souvenirs of Egypt and my aunt's old hats—a yard wide,
velvety with great arched ostrich plumes. There were a helmet
and dented canteen from the War, a bayonet, a sword, a dressing dummy standing with dignity, no head, and an undefined,
swelling bust. There were postcards from the Orient, sachet
and sandalwood and ivory, tall boots like broken soldiers and
strange bottles drunkeningly sweet, an endless attic with unlit
gables, except for dusty, stained-glass, round windows. There
I was safe from my uncle and his dog.

Audrey would take me to the country club in her long, black
Pierce-Arrow with lights on the fenders. While she played golf
I would swim or, better, sneak around the locker-rooms (of
either sex: I was young enough to be neutral) and lounges,
watching adults in their endless performance. I remained
hushed so as not to spoil the show, the scandalous stories and
mannered gestures, the remarkable clothing and mysterious

moods. Audrey, a handsome horse of a woman with bunions like granite and removable teeth, loved me with hearty indifference. She thought I should get more sun. But she didn't really give a damn. She let me watch and knew she was a show.

VERA'S BLAZE

Aunt Vera had it: Oh, I was convinced
nothing would wear like gold, the way she blazed,
a wheel fluttering, strung with electric dance;
but she turned fifty—and was reappraised.
I know. I peeked in the bedroom, saw her peel:

her shinbones stood like poles above her dress,
and how I started at my first sight of Woman—
bosoms like symbols of all fishiness
swinging upon her ribcage like the lanterns
forsaken on lattice after carnival,

and flesh, in fact, appeared to stream in tatters
of crepe, wind-whipped, and too entwined to fall.
Gay oranges and purples, now rain-spotted;
lime streaked the buttery pennants of her hair,
and chalky pink were now the cheeks that waited

like posters for another day of fair,
that would not come (she knew it), or that *would* come,
blaring and bannering, fun for young and old,
with desperate paint to banish any mood one
might have, reflecting, how has peeled the gold.

I had other aunts of the same muscular and heroic breed with hair of pewter sheen—Orpha in Houston, Peggy in Dallas (much the most civilized, with Lawrence of Arabia on her bookshelves, a badminton court, and an English husband with the crisp bearing and grey moustache of his military ancestors who lined the walls). Holidays when the four sisters came on stage together, usually around a bridge-table with a 20,000-piece picture puzzle, husbands sanely and dully off in other rooms discussing automobiles and real estate (the old blind one fortunately dead), I would sit on the couch, pretending to read, and eavesdrop on the ladies' unselfconscious madness and mystery.

When we moved to Texas it was to become part of the
show. The Texas Centennial and Pan-American Exhibit,
Dallas, 1936–37, enlarged tremendously my vision of the possibility of display and spectacle. In the lot behind our garage
apartment in Houston we staged an Outdoor Panoramic Cavalcade of the History of the State of Texas. I remember particularly a fifteen-foot carpenter's bench which we stood on end.
I would climb to the top and shoot at my brother Stew, now
about five with thick brown curls. He wore a cowboy hat
turned inside out to look Mexican, hooted like a tribe of
Mexicans, went *kggh, kggh* in his throat, like hawking to spit,
and finally pushed the bench, which toppled as I stood to ride
it screaming to the ground. That was the Fall of the Alamo,
about Act 7 of the Cavalcade. I have a purple scar on my leg
from getting hung on a nail as a memento of that war. (The
scar on the back of my head is from slipping during a bike
trick when the Jerome Brothers' Circus went on in the rain—
for a couple of miserable adults, our loyal public, huddled on
the back porch.)

With experience of these back-yard spectaculars, supple-
mented by marionettes in the winter, we went on to launch our
first and last real theater, the Garage Playhouse. There we had
a six-inch platform, a proscenium arch (one of the joists of the
garage) which held a curtain of sheets, and a backstage ceiling
light which we could use for special effects, like blinking to
indicate lightning. Some family death enlarged our wardrobe,
and I had acquired a girlfriend, Helen, too shy for acting, who
cadged make-up. In our production of "The Pit and the Pendulum" I would lie writhing for half an hour while Stew blinked
the light, pushed the cardboard walls closer, and lowered a
swinging curtain rod over me (by means of two threads, one
to control its height, another to make it swing). When the curtain rod grazed my ropes, I would roll to my knees on the
stage, the walls driving me toward the pit; then, suddenly, the
walls would fly back (usually falling completely), and Stew,
cowboy hat turned inside out to look French, would leap in,
grab my arm as I toppled fainting into the abyss. He was to
explain in a ringing voice (which never quite rang: he was a

timid six-year-old) that he was General La Salle, and the French army had entered Toledo, and the Inquisition was over in Ohio. (We Texans imagined a terrible history for Yankees.)

Stew was not always stagehand and supporting actor. He played the title role in our production of "Rip Van Winkle." He would walk on stage, stretch, yawn, and slump to sleep while, for twenty minutes, I performed twenty years of American history—the Boston Tea Party, Bunker Hill, Benedict Arnold, George Washington, and Nathan Hale, Yorktown and the Constitutional Convention. Then I would disappear behind a primitive scrim of cheesecloth, and Stew, who had surreptitiously fastened on a cotton beard during his nap, would yawn, stretch, get up, and walk off. Curtain. We simplified stories somewhat because our cast was small and I could never depend on Stew to say lines loud enough to be heard.

The scarf of Jimmy was in every play—and during the long summer afternoons, Mother working, I was Sabu, the black scarf bound on my head, and a folding bed was my elephant. I was lying on the bed eating grapes, the scarf laving my crotch, reading *Ben Hur,* when a neighbor lady yelled across the drive that Italy had gone into the war. Those Romans, I thought— and played them awhile. Reading *A Tale of Two Cities,* I found the scarf most useful as a sling. For *Treasure Island* days it was the Jolly Roger. It was slithery to the skin, opaque, wild, bad, elegant. I terrorized the neighborhood with it when I was a reincarnated Indian prince, mystifying the guys with a Joy-Buzzer I had ordered from the back of a comic book, wearing the scarf as a hood or cape. I learned to snap it like a whip at Stew's bottom, and it would be my muleta if Stew would be the bull.

I don't know that I ever saw a play—except Thanksgiving programs at school assemblies—until, in the eighth grade, I acted in one. It was a detective story called *Danger at the Door,* and it seems to me that I was the detective although that may be romantic exaggeration. Anyway, before a crowd of thousands, we began forgetting lines in the first scene. The ending must have occurred three times. Familiar passages kept recurring like Grape-Nuts burped all day from breakfast. We

were hysterical, terrified, dared not look across the lights at our
patient schoolmates, and saw no possibility of the thing ever
ending as each line seemed to bring on an entrance of a new
character or a response (from Act I) which swung us always
right back into the misty mid-regions of Weir. Somehow we did
manage to bring it to a conclusion and the applause was thun-
derous. I won a prize, a volume entitled *101 Famous Poems,*
inscribed to me as "Best Boy Actor in *Danger at the Door."*
There it was, you see, that poetry and theater came together in
my life.

There was no "legitimate" theater in Houston that I knew
of. Occasionally the motion picture theaters would have personal appearances (I remember seeing Zazu Pitts on the street,
looking, as an earlier dramatic character described herself,
"like an old peeled wall") or special performances by people
like yo-yo artists or magicians. Thurstone made a great difference in my life because he talked too much. He said, for instance, that when he pointed, an adult looked to see what he
pointed at, but a child watched his hand. I thereafter watched
his hand, and the illusion of magic was replaced by the much
more exciting recognition of skill. I went up on stage with a
gang of kids and all of us put our hands on a birdcage which
he held in his hands. There was a presto and violent jerk and
our hands all smacked together. All I knew was that wherever
the cage had gone, the bird had been smashed, and learned
the expendability of canaries. He levitated a girl with a sheet
over her, walked her all around the stage, floating in mid-air,
and then said, "And now I am going to show you something
you will remember all the days of your life." He jerked the
sheet off and she was gone. I learned that people will never
forget things you tell them they will never forget. *Hellzapoppin'*
with Olsen and Johnson came to our high school auditorium
and tore down some assumptions about the relation between
performers and audience. I loved the puppet shows they
brought around from time to time. If there was a class play,
I knew nothing of it, for I graduated in absentia, sixteen, the
war on, eager to get as much college as I could before being
drafted.

That is when my career as playwright began. I started by writing a five-minute narrative radio program for the campus station at the University of Oklahoma called "Today in History," involving much research to document obscure historical events which occurred on a given date in the past. This was soon changed to a weekly, fifteen-minute show, "Know Thou This Land," about events in American history. With no more research than a five-minute narrative required, and much dramatic padding and sound effects (I loved sound effects—to the exasperation of the production crew), I could fill out fifteen good solid minutes of patriotic corn. I was reading Norman Corwin and Arch Obler and Archibald MacLeish and getting a taste for unusual ways of telling stories and the possibilities of poetry. The productions were casual. Scripts were sometimes handed to actors on the way into the studio. The director would whisper "You're Joe," in your ear as you entered, and you were on, all over Oklahoma.

College, though, comes at the wrong time. You are supposed to be learning just at the age when you are eager, above all, to demonstrate that you know everything. Five feet tall, weighing a hundred pounds, looking eleven years old, I had a terrible need to be the bantam cock of the walk and must have been insufferable. I don't remember impressions coming *in* to my consciousness at all; everything was going out. I think I must have tried to keep talking so that I would never find out what was expected of me. I was overproductive—as I have always been: by the time I went into the army at eighteen I had a couple of years of scripts behind me, plus four or five stories in two campus magazines, plus a poem which I blush to own in an Oklahoma poetry magazine called *Red Earth*. And all had that makeshift quality about it suggesting this-would-do and who-would-know and on-with-the-show.

Was this because I never quite believed in life? I carried an imaginary theater with me, a kind of portable proscenium for framing what I saw. I got my chills, got my laughs, but they were those of an audience. I think I never looked close, supposing that if I were to I would find the moss-dyed excelsior. My immaturity qualified me for the role of Jake in *Papa Is*

All, a university theater production, and this first experience
with real flesh and blood theater, where you do not forget your
lines, confused me all the more. Now I was *in* (at least for
a while) the real world backstage, seeing how it was done,
knowing the clever people, and seeing the props assembled. I
learned to paint to look more natural. I saw what it was like to
put on the show, to steal a glance at the crowd, to hold a
grimace while they laughed, to labor with all sincerity to make
them believe my lie. I was not much of an actor, but I began to
have a sense of how it felt to walk in another's skin. We took
this show to several army and navy bases and relished the roar
of response. How they needed us! How they needed illusion,
and how much more real was our hour upon the stage than,
for example, KP, close-order drill, the facts of life.

I will probably never be a real playwright—I mean one of
those Broadway fellows with three wives and a yacht—but
writing will always mean to me writing drama. Poetry is the
medium—the way the language is arranged—but the product
is drama, the interchanges of imaginary personalities in imaginary situations. An individual poem is something someone
says on some occasion: even if the speaker is most sincerely
me and the occasion is as general as I can make it, I will
change, circumstances will change, and the poem remains as
what might have been said then, like a speech from a play.
Fiction adds description to dialogue, but I am impatient with
that, as background can always be more easily done with a set.
I prefer to give the reader a few words to permit him to imagine
the setting and get on with the talk and action. Thus though
my experience with the theater has been chiefly mooning
around the wings, though I cannot pretend to be a pro, I prefer
to write in the dramatic form. I like the discipline of not being
permitted introspection (except as it is expressed externally in
words and movement), in frankly recognizing that words are
always those of a given personality at a given time. I like
the clean form of a play where the setting and description are
clearly distinguished from what people say and do. I like the
swiftness of drama, its condensation and economy. And I like
the conscious artificiality—for a novel pretends to be a history,

but a play pretends only to be a performance. Writing in dramatic form, I feel much more strongly than I do writing fiction the obligation to get on with it, to entertain. My bad dreams are of an audience restless in the dark.

But a play in actual production—on stage, film, or television—requires a collaborative art of overwhelming complexity, and I cannot imagine being very good at it. The script itself must become a piece of property handled by directors, actors, agents, publicists, musicians, designers, and stagehands. I have never been one for team play (my sports are swimming and figure skating), not because of any ferocity for independence but because of a kind of impatience and clumsiness in cooperation.

From this dilemma comes this volume. As I write a play I dream of production—and these plays may actually be workable on stage (some have had amateur productions). But on reflection, with perspective, I see that production is not really my goal. I have written imaginary episodes for an imaginary theater. I have written for readers, perhaps, more than for playgoers. Much as I love the theater, I recognize that actually attending a play, dulled by dinner, sitting still (I am not very good at sitting still), worrying about the abilities of the actors, trying to hear (I am not very quick at picking up talk), observing the details of lighting, costume, scene design, make-up, I do not get as much from other people's plays as I would like them to get from mine. When all works, of course, nothing can equal the theatrical experience, the communal feeling, the forgetting of details and coming to believe. It is especially difficult to appreciate comedy when one is reading alone—and what is enormously funny on stage (when one may laugh freely, anonymously in the dark with all the others) oftens looks very silly or corny in print. One especially misses comic "business," which can never be described or put into the script.

On the other hand, even comedy is bound to suffer in some ways in production. When an earlier version of *Winter in Eden* was produced I noted night after night that the biggest laughs came on the most blatant lines—the ones which would be most painful in print. There is a kind of democratizing effect resulting from the pace of theatrical production and the difficulty of grasping spoken words which makes it very hard for a playwright to say certain kinds of things. I enjoy the fun of the overtly farcical, but hate to see that element of comedy obscure the others. These plays were not written *for* reading (as was, say, *Samson Agonistes*), but I think their best production may be, after all, in the imaginary theater of the lone reader's mind. If he approaches the book as he would a novel or work of (abominable term) nonfiction, that reader will not, I think, find the dramatic form or the poetry getting in the way of his entertainment and stimulation.

The people in these plays are imaginary: they are a little simpler, less idiosyncratic, a little more abstract than so-called real people like aunts. Ultimately they are abstractions of myself, and keep recurring in different costumes. Harper is Satan is the Princess is me, in one respect, interacting with other aspects of my own personality. I have to assume that they are aspects of your personality, too, and will permit your harmonious identification. We chuckle to see Punch and Judy battle out that endless war our right side carries on against our left through all our days.

Some genius of the theater such as John Cage is in music should mount the following show: the curtain rises, a family walks into a living room, sits down, turns on the television set (a real, live television set), and watches it for a couple of hours. Let the restless audience make of it what they will. That would be the ultimate in realism—just as John Cage is the ultimate in musical realism, letting noise and silence, unplanned, knockabout as they occur in the world, do for music. All this is to say I do not see the point of realism.

My theatrical moments have been those which induced fear or laughter because they gave me some perspective on my experience. I had to go to the spooky home of an aunt to see life. (One cannot see and live life at the same time, and seeing it is theatrical.) Elegant, bizarre, gaudy, phony, distorted, and spectacular experiences give me a sensation at the base of my spine which lets me know that the world and I are real—then

I go back into it and am absorbed as Lassie (who pants through her, or his, performance without a thought of grooming or artifice). One of my daughters once asked if we were on someone's television set—and while part of me cried, oh god I wish we were (wish that someone were watching), another part recognized that at the moment one asks such a question he is most truly alive, conscious, and human. The beasts know life is not a show, and we are, like them, bound to practical needs and mortality. But what excitement and fulfillment in illusion! Frame it for a moment in an imaginary proscenium arch and life seems to have some point. The fact that we can so frame it may indicate that we may be able to give it meaning.

We have our moment in the air. Before cracking my head on the board a few times I used to be a fairly fancy diver, and having sprung from the board, knowing that the water was certainly below, I relished the moment of contortion, of performance, and hoped to enter with grace. We are called upon to act, not simply to be, but to make a bit of show, not "showing off" but using the instant, achieving an artful goal, defying and then learning to get along with gravity (for the dive would have no meaning if we could suspend ourselves in the air and contort at leisure). It is not the most efficient way to get into the water. It is not—except finally, beautifully, and incredibly—realistic. It is best done nearly naked.

That figure may serve for these plays, which are artificial complexities resolved, I hope, with grace. They are plays more of idea than of character, not representations of life but ways of playing with it. (One of my daughters mispronounced the word *clay* as *play*—and had a great sense of its significance. What are people made of? I would ask her. "Play." What are houses, trees, ideas, feelings, foods, and families made of? And she would answer, with the single-mindedness of Poe's raven, "Play." She was, of course, right.)

The plays employ verse and rhyme because I believe these means of order and pleasure render language more memorable —and because I am much concerned to regain for poetry the larger forms (narrative and dramatic), to enlarge the audience

for poetry. I have provided stage directions to accommodate
your private imaginary theater (which has no stage-left and
right and moves as quickly as a movie).

Interwoven with the plays are prefaces, autobiographical
essays which explore the reality from which the plays emerged.
Today the line between documentary and art has been almost
obliterated as we have come to realize that personal vision,
values, style, and shaping are inseparable from what we call
truth. The myth of objectivity has been exploded in the sciences and in the arts; with it must go the notion that anything
is ever completely "made up." Fiction is simply another way of
talking about fact. In thinking about these plays I was
increasingly fascinated by the relationships I discovered between them and my own life—and thought you might like to
share such discoveries. The essays have appeared in magazines
as separate publications, but they were written specifically as
background for the plays.

The theater you are entering is a Muskogee attic, with
mustiness and mystery and slanting orange light and piles of
darkness and unlikely props. May you see life with new strange-
ness. May you be entertained through the long afternoon.

INSTRUCTIONS FOR ACTING: IMPROVISATION

We have no prompter for this show. In fact,
I have never seen a script, although, of course,
all surely know the general story line:
it gripped us young, continues to intrigue
in spite of its familiarity.
A kind of dazzle from the klieg glare makes
us unaware, performing, of the fact

that no one sits out there in the dark house.
No intermission follows any act.
No gun fires blanks. We laugh at our own jokes.
Although not many of us have studied lines
and almost none is very strong or wise,
the show goes on: the curtain already has risen.
Fear silence. Look alert. And improvise.

II

A Brickbat for the Belfry:
Notes on *Candle in the Straw*

REVIVAL

Sermons from Science! Reverend Moon, a man
from Moody Bible Institute, began
in Houston to convince us of his view:
the Bible, word by word, was scientific,
a world not good nor beautiful, but true,
the myth all tucked away, the soul aloof
from mysteries reduced to certain proof,
for agitated youth, a soporific.

His stage was full of beakers, tubes and wires.
He could prove anything with a slide or movie.
He prayed demonstrably; his hymns were groovy.
He handled all the elemental fires
and in a week did most of Genesis.
He could extrapolate a wife for Cain,
explain what Noah didn't know (for he
founded the Flood on sound geology).
His sparks jumped gaps, chemicals made a hiss,
and time-lapse films showed vines grope toward the light.
His climax was to stand on a coil one night,
a million volts spurting from his finger tips.

My sins poured forth from adolescent lips.
I cried, I cried, for fear I would not be saved—
Even my yearning for goodness was depraved:
I finally lied to be saved with the rest,
claiming I felt the spirit in my breast
and that I heard a Voice I could not hear.
I wrestled with the worm beneath my skin,
then, worm and all, I joined. They let me in.

I did not stay revived. The flesh is weak.
My Youth Group, so impassioned, throbbed out of church
in spiritual adventure. Mostly my search
was one of kissing every other cheek.
We listened to the sermons with our legs
crossed tight and sang our hymns like troubadors.
Oh halleluja! how emotion begs
for any outlet, turn it out-of-doors.

Science, meanwhile, bequeathed the true to faith
and took up beauty and goodness. So did I.
Our times are cool—and Reverend Moon may boil
with certainty and passion, like a wraith
with fiery fingers on his surging coil,
but he looks foolish. I can verify
neither my friendly worm nor my damnation.
One can be burned by mere spark-gap salvation.
Electrons are uncertain; so am I.
For any act, I know not any cure;
more facts, above all, make me more unsure,
and though they would forgive me, I will not
permit my sins—my self—to be forgot.

A ctually that doesn't give all the facts. I began attending the
Sunday School of the Riverside Baptist Church in early adolescence at the insistence of my buddy Edwin, who was already
saved. Occasionally he would persuade me to stay for the
sermon (those days I had to have two nickels), where in the
barnlike church with walnut pews, with sliding doors behind
the altar concealing the tub (that's where they *do* it, explained
Edwin, and described how the preacher in a white gown stood
in the water and ducked the saved, in white gowns, and how
you could see through the girls' gowns when they were wet), we
sat listening to the incomprehensibly winding rhetoric of guilt. I
was never sure of the line of argument, but I understood the
central truth (which only needed to be pointed out to me) that
I was slimy, and that I could step outside the church and be
hit by a car, unredeemed. The final hymn was endless. Just one
more chorus, the preacher would call, and we all stood singing
with our heads bowed, peeking right and left to see if anyone
would buckle.

Sometimes they did, explosively—with a shout of Lord save me! and palms flying and tears running as they moved up to the altar in a state of exaltation. These were mostly the old timers, who had been saved again and again, and had had a wild time the night before. When the new ones went (as I felt I would surely go some day), it was shyly, with a kind of guilty embarrassment, as though they were planning to slip in by fraud. I could never get it out of my head that perhaps they were, that they weren't saved at all, but were so afraid of the imminent automobile accident on the church steps that they figured they might as well gamble on a lie. (I learned later about Pascal's wager.)

THE UNCHOSEN

I guess I have a deficiency. God never
said boo to me when as a boy I stood
straining in church with muscular endeavor
for the sweet squirt of Salvation. I never could
see why He spoke to this and that old lady,

sending them, hallelujah, down the aisle.
Was I alone in the congregation vile?
Or was their claim of spirit something shady?
And now, when I read poets who simply Know,
drinking their imagery from God's own cup,

whose poems "just come" and then, like Topsy, grow,
whereas I always have to make them up
with never a tremor saying, "Break this line,"
or "Save this phrase, regardless of its beat,"
hear no obscurities which seem Divine,

and knowing not God's Measure, still count feet,
I yearn that reason give me some relief
(besides those lapses when my mind—not soul—
is not so much inspired as out of control).
Non-Linear God, help Thou my unbelief!

The preacher explained repetitively what the feeling would be when it came. He put much emphasis on believing *on* Jesus Christ as opposed to believing *in* Him. It would be a sensation of sweet certainty slightly left of center of the rib cage. (I kept feeling the spot; nothing was happening.) When they passed around trays with little glasses of grape juice and crackers, I was not allowed to take any because I was not a Christian. I always developed a terrible thirst as the tray came down the row—each standing person, head bowed, taking a shot with a head jerk, returning to piety and passing on the tray, being careful not to rattle it too much—and I nearly joined the church just to get refreshments. The mystery of grape juice which symbolized wine which, in turn, symbolized blood teased me out of thought, as did the attitude of my friends and neighbors toward cannibalism. Was a simple want, an obsessive desire for that magic swallow, salvation? I especially resented that children younger than I went up to the altar, were paptized (a typographical error, but I'll leave it), and could participate in communion. I added suspicion of their motives to my sins.

I wish I could say that I refrained from joining because of sincere doubt or honesty, waiting for the true sensation of salvation to overpower and compel me, but I was such a sinner I would have done anything to get in if it hadn't required walking down that aisle to the front of the church, everyone watching beneath lowered lids, and having that waxy-handed minister make a fuss over me. I detested him instinctively, in spite of the truth of his message; he had the toneless earnestness of a salesman, a flat-faced East Texan type of young man with an unctuous twang. He made mistakes in grammar and used words I didn't know. I would not let *him* triumph—and I especially wouldn't do it in front of a lot of self-righteous, floury-breasted, and mealy-minded grown-ups and kids I didn't trust. It is hard to sort out my feelings, but the strongest seems to have been a horror of public exposure.

Thus I was deeply agitated by the problem when Reverend Moon came to the First Baptist Church, downtown, with a one-week, nightly series of Sermons from Science. Edwin, tall (I came to his waist), shuffling, ugly, continually whistling through his teeth in sheer spiritual contentment, was an initiate of science as well of religion. He was building a ham radio, was an amateur chemist—he was saved no matter which side won. The two of us would take the bus downtown each evening, wait on a windy corner (by a Catholic church looming sinister and dark) for the 11:35 bus to take us home. Though I was fifteen I could still get by for half-fare—most of the time. When the bus driver questioned my age I would explode in lofty indignation that I was *ob*viously eleven and a half because I had dropped only a nickel in the glass box. I would sit in that church for a couple of hours of agony and fear for my soul, imagining that blinding moment to come on the church steps, the drunken driver veering around the corner, bumping right over the curb and hideously climbing the church steps, the grate and bang of metal and shatter of glass and then Hell Fire—then I would make it safely off the steps (which *did* seem to be the most dangerous spot), and cheat on the bus. I was impossible.

Whether Genesis was absolutely, scientifically, word-for-word the literal truth did not much concern me. We learned that when the earth cooled the water all remained in the atmosphere, like a great steamy canopy enveloping the ball, and that was why it rained upwards before the Flood. But then a spark of lightning or something caused sudden condensation, and woosh, all the water fell at once, or, rather, for forty days and nights. We learned how widespread were stories of the Flood in other religions, heard the geological and anthropological evidence that this Flood actually occurred, supplying all the water to form the glaciers. I accepted all such information with weary wonder. Didn't science beat all? But the gimmickry of science fascinated me. He carried a kind of telephone dial around his neck, and when he dialed a particular number sparks would fly on the other side of the stage, or the lights would go out, or flasks would start bubbling with colored liquid. How I would like to have had one of those telephone dials!

This seemed to be a long way from salvation, which was what we were there for, but by scaring us, he got us jumpy enough to visualize that careening car (was I wearing clean underwear?) and preparing the ground generally for violent emotional experience. The climax was the business on the coil. He climbed barefooted on what looked like a great cable drum, took all metal objects off his body, then they darkened the auditorium and turned on the juice—literally, he said, a million volts—lighting up Reverend Moon like a giant sparkler, sizzling and popping and streaming light. He said it had something to do with purity of spirit. When the endless final hymn came they streamed up in dozens. Each day he would announce the score for the preceding evening. "Now while we sing that chorus one more time I want to see you turn to your neighbor there in the pew and introduce yourself, and ask him, 'Brother, are you saved?' and if he isn't, won't you tell him kindly to come forward and speak for Jesus?"

This would mean several frightening moments, singing like a stuck record, eyes burning the floor, wondering whether that sweet-smelling, lard-fleshed, pillow-bosomed lady next to me would turn and ask me whether I were a Christian. Edwin's fist suddenly appeared before my eyes, thumb extended, the gesture of a traffic cop, indicating I should get the hell up front. I looked up at him and his face was grim. I never expected it of Edwin. I looked down the long aisle, at one after the other of the congregation succumbing like fruit dropping from a tree. Moon was down in the aisle, his telephone dial still on a strap around his neck, sweating and singing like it hurt, shaking the hand of each as he came forward and sending the sobbing sucker backstage where, no doubt, a team of assistants performed some weird initiation rites. I could not do it.

That night I cried by the Catholic church, waiting for the bus. I was furious with Edwin. I was scared, and though I was still wiping tears when I got on the bus, the driver caught me dropping only a nickel and added shame and expense to my misery. The next day I went around the corner to the Epworth Methodist Church, a dignified brick building (much tonier than the clapboard Riverside Baptist) and talked to the Nordic, handsome minister, a soft-voiced, educated man of reason. I quizzed him in detail about the ritual of joining. No, I would not have to come forward after a service. All I had to do was sign a card. Sometime later there would be a baptism ceremony —a sprinkle of water—but this could be done privately, at my convenience, perhaps with my family present. Well, okay! I hadn't realized there were churches you could join in the back room.

So I saw less of Edwin, going now to a different Sunday School, meeting a more prosperous and refined class of people, listening to sermons like lectures in the Anglican dignity of a thin, sedate chapel. I even persuaded my mother to go to the back room and sign up. But I here record that Reverend Moon, wherever he may be, should chalk up one more (two, if you count Mother) on his scoreboard. It was he who scared me into it—with the help of Edwin's imperious thumb.

I was soon drawn back to the Baptists on Sunday nights, though, to attend their Youth Group, whose activities were much more interesting than anything the Methodists had to offer. The "teacher" was a rather stupid, stumpy man, interested in boys and girls, who owned a moving van in which he would take us all to neighboring towns for revival meetings. Closed in the dark cavern of the truck, we would pull down the comforters used to pack furniture, spread them on the floor, and neck (as we used to call making out above the shoulders) while the truck rumbled to Jesus. Thirty miles away in a tiny village we would sit on benches in a shack or tent while the preacher bellowed, eyes like running sores, throat knotting and bulging like a spastic python.

The revival meetings one can find on AM radio Sunday mornings are much the same, but on a grander scale. After a reasonably coherent beginning, the preacher begins pounding the pulpit to emphasize his *words,* and gradually the rhythm becomes more *reg*ular, and is answered by scattered shouts of *a*men from the congregation, and with this en*cour*agement the preacher begins to suck *air* and blast it *forth* in the rhythm of copu*la*tion, his body *sway*ing, the fist *slam*ming, the words becoming indis*tinct,* but with frequent clear *ref*erences to the terror of *Hell* and the sins of the *wick*ed, which are generally *i*temized and luridly con*sid*ered, how these young boys and *girls* in the drive-ins and *honk*ey-tonks permit their tender *bod*ies to be abused and *de*filed; and with the preacher's hair swinging loose around his sweating face, which was gasping and twisting in tortuous ecstasy, a sob in his chanting, the

rhythm laborious with pumping, we could easily imagine what
he was referring to, crossed our legs and squirmed, pulsing
with his rhythm, until the last sinner for the night was saved
and we could go streaming back into the groaning hell of the
moving van. When we reached Houston we insisted that the
amiable dope drive around and around the block to delay
getting out.

The next year, when I was sixteen, I started as a freshman
at the University of Oklahoma (in those days one squeezed in
as much college as possible before submitting to the inevitable
draft), and I called myself an atheist—as was fashionable. It
was my French period. I identified with Rimbaud and Marat
("the little radical"). But in the Army, at eighteen, I was
drawn again to religion, as the chaplains seemed the most un-
military people around with the possible exception of the
absolutely terrifying Red Cross girls. On Okinawa I shopped
around the quonset churches. There it was the Catholic chaplain who most appealed to me, a rotund friar out of Chaucer.
I went to his quarters one day weeping, sick of the crudity and
stupidity of my fellow soldiers, feeling that I, refined, delicate,
was born for better company. He disillusioned me by asking a
lot of personal questions about my sex life (which seemed to
me irrelevant, particularly as I wasn't having one). I thought
he had a dirty mind.

Religion, sex, science—these were all getting confused in
my mind. They had in common a kind of zeal, sense of obligation, exploration of the forbidden, shame. Of the three, theol-
ogy and science seemed least attractive and most alike. Both,
in their way, were concerned with God, or what immutably
Is. They attempted to understand reality and learn its implica-
tions for behavior. They seemed to be pursued by ascetic men
in monkish garb (black or white) with an inclination to symbols and abstruse and intricate reasoning. Both assumed that
whatever reality (or God) was, it was to some extent know-
able, had its underlying principles, was predictable. And salvation, for either, was recognizing (with a rush of blood and
hallelujah) that reality is bigger than we are, that our private
unpredictability was subject to the control of something firmer,

more factual, more enduring, something pure and white and bloodless. Maturity and salvation seemed much the same sort of thing—the discovery that action is circumscribed by circumstance, that in God's (or nature's) will is our peace—which is the peace of beasts, whose life is very factual. Intuitively I felt that such salvation, such surrender of self to conditions, such relinquishment of the sins, errors, creativity, and aspiration of the individual will should be put off as long as possible. The Army, the church, and the university (at least that part of it devoted to "the exact sciences") seemed extensions of the voice of my stepfather, telling me, without love, to buckle down, stop squirming, stop picking my nose, shut up, and perform the bidding of the Machine.

When I entered the Humanities Division of the University of Chicago at twenty, it was with a highly developed case of God-allergy and science-allergy. I have overcome both in subsequent years, but I can still describe them. God-allergy is a closing of the mind to any question framed in theological terms, and since some of these questions have been framed *only* in theological terms, God-allergy is a very serious limitation of a questioning mind. Science-allergy is a deep-seated resentment of facts and logic. One builds a fence around precious concepts to prevent prying. Now mystery is a very good thing: love, for example, would be nothing without it. But to be authentic, mystery must be what is left *after* examination, that which stubbornly refuses to be reduced to fact and logic, not that which is protected from them. Hamlet knew "There are more things in heaven and earth . . . Than are dreamt of in your philosophy," but he didn't, on that account, stop research.

I began focusing on English cultural history of the mid-seventeenth century (now in a doctoral program at Ohio State University) as the point at which something changed critically —perhaps went deeply wrong—in our civilization, and I began to sense an alliance between the cause of poetry and the cause of religion. I was studying the process by which the infinite variety of Protestant sects merged into a monolithic Church of Reason (coming at Marat, now, by the back door), and

became particularly interested in the history of the Quakers.
I went to a few silent Meetings in Columbus—my first church
experience since that of the Catholic chaplain (not counting
a few moments in a chapel to be married). It was strange
coming from the library, which throbbed with those vigorous
preachers in leather breeches, to the silent communion of
middle-class Ohio burghers. I felt very silly, sitting there in a
square trying to stare at the infinite. I kept wondering what
George Fox, who felt exactly as I do about steeple-houses,
only more violently, would have thought of those erected by
modern Quakers.

All that was nearly twenty years ago, during which time I
have gone to various churches, for various reasons—most
recently to one which did not call itself a church at all, but a
Community. Its burlap-covered walls were splashed with joyous
and saucy posters in the style of Sister Corita. We sat around
tables with gay decorations and were served coffee and sweet
rolls for communion. A man in a purplish plaid sports jacket
popped in and out of a control booth, where he played folk
and rock hymns on the stereo. A long-haired youth strummed
"He Has the Whole World in His Hands" on a guitar—and we
sang with him, exuberantly clapping our hands. Bible readings
and prayers emerged in a planned, random fashion from
various spots around the tables—grey ladies whining words
of wonder and joy. And the preacher sat in the middle of the
room on a leather-upholstered bar stool. But still he preached
—a method, a discipline, an insistence on God's authority—in
the flat, driving cadence of one who has achieved certainty
and order and who will not rest until all of us share his illu-
mination.

I tried to remember why it was once (briefly) so important
that I go to church several times a week and at least twice on
Sunday. It is hard for me to realize that every Sabbath morning such a large proportion of the population, to the tolling of
bells, participates in that old-fashioned parade to sit on benches
under stained glass and play the international game of Simon
Says, complete with kneeling, standing, sitting, squatting, and
other group calisthenics, memorized and meaningless prayers,

mumbled readings, sonorous unintelligibility, passionless and tuneless singing—now a number from the choir of ladies whose thin and scratchy voices twist past the notes like skiers avoiding flags in a slalom race—children piping recitations, acolytes swinging incense, priests decked out as uncles used to be for lodge meetings, salad bowls of offerings passed down the aisle of bowed heads (gone are the days when you could go to church for a nickel!), organs churning, children squirming, husbands dozing, deacons monitoring the back rows, and the preacher's clammy hand at the door.

It doesn't seem to matter what you believe, so long as it is in "Something," so long as you have a "religious affiliation" (albeit United Atheists) to put on forms, so long as you dress up and go to some kind of meeting at eleven on Sunday mornings. Protestantism, which began in noble questioning, controversy, and refusal to conform, seems to have resulted in a kind of rosy indifference—as though metaphysical and ethical issues were, after all, a matter of taste—a cozy but misguided brotherhood which dulls the mind and eases the conscience. A great Cease Fire embraces Christian and non-Christian sects like a fog. The churches seem to have done exactly what Dostoevsky's Grand Inquisitor said it was their job to do—relieve man of his freedom, ease his agony of doubt, protect him from the terrible demands of the prophets with solace of mystery, miracle, and authority.

This prevalent attitude is a dangerous threat to any piece of writing which attempts to deal seriously with religion. I would hate to think my play satisfied anyone's pietistic urge—and I also hate to think that some will automatically close their minds to it because it is about a seventeenth-century preacher, religion and all that. So far as I know, the play has no moral and promulgates no doctrine. I am not trying to interpret modern or historic Quakerism; I am trying to find out what matters and what to do about it. The resulting play tosses and turns with my own uncertainties, as I have not freed myself from the tangles of emotion I experienced in the First Baptist Church of Houston hearing the sermons of Reverend Moon.

There were a dozen small sects, antinomian in one degree or another, in seventeenth-century England which might have given rise to the episode which provides the focus of this play. But it did occur, in a very vivid fashion, in the Society of Friends under the leadership of George Fox. Essentially it is the story of a man who took Fox's teachings too seriously and found himself a blasphemer. James Naylor was a beautiful and gentle man whose immense personal attractiveness inspired overwhelming enthusiasm, particularly among his women followers. They believed, and he did not sufficiently discourage them, that Christ lives in any, and that the way of the Lord is Love.

Naylor's popularity in the movement came to be such that it threatened to divide the Society. It culminated in the Bristol ass ride (the beast may have been a horse), Naylor being led into the town by zealots chanting "Holy, Holy, Holy," scattering the way with clothing, branches, and other articles. Black Friday followed Palm Sunday. Fox rejected his Friend (the foot-kissing represented in the play is fairly well substantiated) for "running out into imagination." Naylor was condemned by Parliament after a fascinating and frustrating trial in which he made quite plain the blasphemous implication of what most antinomian Christians believe. He was branded with a B for blasphemy, forced to re-enter Bristol riding backwards on an ass before a reviling crowd, his tongue was bored with a red-hot iron, and he was imprisoned. After he was released there was some reconciliation with the movement and with Fox, and Naylor wrote pamphlets for the Friends with considerable effect.

Finally he started off from London, over a year after his release from prison, to join his long-neglected family in Wakefield. He was set upon by thieves, beaten, and died in the house of a Friend. On his deathbed he is reputed to have made the following statement—which gives a clue to the quality of mind I hoped to create in the play:

> There is a spirit which I feel that delights to do no evil, nor to revenge any wrongs, but delights to endure all things, in hope to enjoy its own in the end. Its hope is to outlive all wrath and con-

tention, and to weary out all exaltation and cruelty, or whatever is of a nature contrary to itself. It sees to the end of all temptations. As it bears no evil in itself, so it conceives none in thoughts to any other. If it be betrayed, it bears it, for its ground and spring is the mercies and forgiveness of God. Its crown is meekness, its life is everlasting love unfeigned; and it takes its kingdom with entreaty and not with contention, and keeps it by lowliness of mind. In God alone it can rejoice, though none else regard it, or can own its life. It's conceived in sorrow, and brought forth without any to pity it, nor doth it murmur at grief and oppression. It never rejoiceth but through sufferings: for with the world's joy it is murdered. I found it alone, being forsaken. I have fellowship therein with them who live in dens and desolate places in the earth, who through death obtained this resurrection and eternal holy life.

There is great eloquence and warmth in the statement—also passivity, submissiveness, and obsessive gloom, surely deriving from the experiences of his last years and probably not characteristic of the way he preached at the height of his power. I have speculated that the humane tradition in the Society of Friends may be owing to Naylor's influence whereas Fox's is more felt in the ascetic tradition. Of course it is not that simple, but I have used the very different leaders to symbolize traits which complement one another and are at times in conflict.

Though I cannot imagine myself joining any cult, I find it easy to identify with both Fox and Naylor. I admire their physical courage, facing sticks and stones in their root-and-branch attack on the indifference, insincerity, and conformity of institutional religion. I am even more impressed by the spiritual courage which enabled them to deny easy answers and open themselves to the terrible springs of the heart. The Inner Voice is a joker in the deck—wild and dangerous, and utterly necessary as a concept to help me survive in a universe which seems otherwise so determined.

I call this a verse tragedy in two acts. I use the term *verse* for all the plays in this volume to describe a rhythmic texture of the language, like the grain of a canvas; the term does not refer to imagery, symbolism, to the imaginative or poetic quality of the play—which quality it may or may not have in your judgment. I call it a tragedy because I hoped to represent an individual brought to a serious and defeating encounter with ultimate reality in which the self gains dignity in the process of the recognition of the inevitability of the self's defeat.

Imagine not seventeenth-century England, but a theater— a very fluid stage with quickly assembled, partial sets—a wall, a bench, a desk, a door, the bars of a jail. The action in each act is continuous: lights go down on one side of the stage and up on another simultaneously, our attention moving to a new group of characters discovered in action. They are dressed very simply. Their speech is very neutral, not characterized by dialect or mannerism. Nothing about the way you stage this play in your mind should permit you to hold it off at arm's length, to say to yourself that this is how it was with those people, way back then, over there.

III

Candle in the Straw

ACT I

*I*n *the darkness we hear a passionate, spine-tingling chant of mixed voices shouting in unison:*

HALLELUJAH! KING OF ZION!

We see by spreading, dim light a knot of worshippers in the distance, gathered around a small knoll on which Clay Harper

*stands, his head inclined humbly and lovingly, his hands ex-
tended slightly at his sides, a shaft of light illuminating long,
soft curls and beard, a beautiful face of a man of about forty.
He is dressed in a simple, rustic tunic; the people of the crowd
wear similar clothes, those of the peasant class of seventeenth-
century England. They are huddling near him, kissing his hands
and the hem of his tunic. Suddenly a woman stands 'and
screams, beating her chest, shouting:*

HALLELUJAH! HALLELUJAH!

*And a trembling seizes her, shaking her whole body. Others
in the crowd turn adoringly to her as she quakes. The crowd
shouts in unison:*

> THE SPIRIT SEIZES HER, THE SPIRIT
> OF THE LORD

Individuals cry: HALLELUJAH!
> THE LORD MOVES!
> WITNESS THE SPIRIT OF THE LORD!

*As they are shouting, an old, crippled blind beggar moves away
from them and comes forward, a crutch under one arm, the
other tapping ahead with a walking stick. He is, in spite of
his age and bad leg, a spry, wiry man, twinkling with humor.
Over his shoulder is a lute on a thong. As he separates himself from the crowd a hush falls and all freeze in tableau. As
he begins to speak, the crowd and Clay disappear.*

BLIND MAN: Such burning you get in a dry season!

> Clay Harper, that preacher there, whom I can't see,
> but whose flame I can feel the heat of, and hear the
> crackling of, like in August grass, that has such a
> need of burning, is a sweet singer of the Lord. Me?
> I'm a reedy old singer of sin, but, like the Devil, I
> mean well.
>
> (*Strums lute.*) And who is to say, in a world of deaf-
> ness, what singing is finer? (*Confidentially*) Now
> Clay Harper's friend, the leader of this sect of

Seekers, Mr. Lemuel Thomas . . . well, *he* sings
like a bull-frog by comparison. But among frogs,
you know, such resonance is relished. Mr. Harper,
though, chirping sweetly as a cricket in milady's
hearth, tends to be more popular. (*Accompanying
himself he begins to sing, meditatively, as to himself.*)

A frog and a cricket, I tell you,
once sat on a lily pad, one and two,
on a summer night, with an ivory moon,
and each sang out his own sweet tune.

The frog was more of a baritone:
he yodeled with a painful moan.
The cricket had a treble range
and a single note he could not change.

"Harumph!" said the frog, "you pipsqueak you!
That twiddling racket will not do!
Why don't you shut your tiny face
and listen to my velvet bass?"

"It's not my face. I fiddle my feet—
and make a note both tart and sweet.
Stop creaking and you soon will see
you can learn how to sing from me!"

At this the frog took a bite of air
and belched it back with a trombone blare.
"How's that, you cousin of a bumble bee?"
"It has volume—but lacks quality."

The cricket, then, put his leg to his cheek
and made this makeshift fiddle squeak
till through the swamp bugs raised a limb
and a million crickets answered him.

The frog confessed the cricket won.
He wished the duel had not begun.
His head was drilled by the twittering tune
and he looked up sadly at the moon . . .

and let his long black tongue unroll,
and swallowed down the cricket whole—
thus put his music to a stop—
and jumped from the pad with a great loud plop!

Now wait! the moral of this tale
shall be appended, never fail!
Popularity, a winning start,
is not the *last* test of good art.

(*Our vision of the beggar drifts away with the last words of the song, and we see Lemuel Thomas sitting facing the desk of General Friar. Lemuel has his head in his hands, elbows on the desk. Some open letters are spread before him—a ruddy, ham-faced, powerful man, quick-tempered, passionate, with an incredible, stocky dignity. He is dressed in leather breeches and jerkin, his straight, cheek-length hair is falling forward over his face. When he speaks his eyes are round with frankness, his great lips form the words with massive integrity.*

His dejection, which we see now, is as passionate as his other moods. The General is standing on his side of the desk, resplendent in his uniform and wig, wearing a sword—a tall, severe man of aristocratic bearing, clever, speaking with thin-voiced, insidious irony, less capable of anger than of hate.)

FRIAR: Look at these letters, Mr. Thomas! Addressed
      to "Everlasting Son of Righteousness,"
      to "Prince of Peace," to "Fairest Among Ten Thou-
        sand." . . .
      Then read their words of love—the giddy endear-
        ments
      of women itching with a sentiment
      I would not call quite pious! Parliament
      instructs me to distinguish now and then
      reverence from lechery, praise from blasphemy.
      Your people are polluting faith with love.
LEMUEL (*weakly*): I say I did not know of this. . . .
FRIAR: Not know?
      Your friend, your partner, the man who next to you

is thought of as the leader of the Seekers . . .
who in some parts of England, Mr. Thomas,
is recognized in*stead* of you as leader. . . .
You are not easily duped, now, Lemuel Thomas.
I must believe that you have spurred him on.

LEMUEL (*quietly*): I have been betrayed.

FRIAR: *Eng*land has been betrayed—
or, at least, God. Not only by you and Harper.
You and your squirming kind, these fertile sects
of Brownists, Baptists, Ranters, Come Outers, Shak-
        ers,
Family of Love, and wild Fifth Monarchy Men,
all led by rebel saints in leather breeches—
in the name of freedom undermining law,
in the name of inspiration turning loose
all howling madness, nudity and vice,
a holy name for every debasing impulse,
the jabbering puppets to their Inner Voice . . . !
You are not guiltless, Mr. Thomas. No!
You are a partner in your partner's crime!

LEMUEL (*pulling himself together*): I will restrain him, General
                Friar. You may
rely on my distaste for such cavorting. . . .

FRIAR: Too late—and not enough. I will report
all, all of this to Parliament—in hopes
they will permit me to suppress you utterly,
to cleanse religion of the pus of zeal.

LEMUEL: Cromwell will see it otherwise.

FRIAR: I know
you charm him, somehow, into blind indulgence—
But Cromwell has not seen these letters! No
official, after this, will trust in you. . . .

LEMUEL (*rises, furious*): Trust me?
Recall those words, you silk magnifico,
you strutting soldier, noisy ass, offense
in the eye of God, you blowing fool, you tool
of the steeple-houses, counting-houses, houses
of vanity, corruption, hypocrisy and sin. . . .

FRIAR (*contemptuously*): Restrain your preacher's tongue. . . .
LEMUEL (*shouts*): I will not hold my tongue! *You* will not
                smirch
                the value of my word! Oh! Will not trust *me!*
                There may be two or three men in this kingdom
                who can be trusted: I am one. I challenge
                any exalted military fop
                to find me false!
FRIAR (*calmly*):   Falseness is not the charge.
                Rather, unsoundness of mind, fanaticism. . . .
LEMUEL: You lead an army, General. That requires
                some soundness of mind, I warrant? I command
                an army of peace, the twenty thousand Seekers,
                with every day more order in their ranks.
                Ask those who trust their lives to me if I
                am some unhinged fanatic. . . .
FRIAR (*matter-of-factly*):   This I have done.
                Corporal!

(*A soldier enters and salutes.*)

                Bring in that lady from the hall.

(*Soldier leaves.*)

                I move against you armed, you may be sure.
                You know, I think, the wife of Harper? She
                agrees with us the rabble's prince of peace
                is hardly safe at loose among the women.
                She will persuade him to return to farming.

(*Soldier re-enters with Sarah Harper, then leaves. She stands
at the door a moment, gathering her strength to assume the
righteousness of Judas. She is a thin, intelligent woman with
a sharp beauty subdued by the modesty and plainness of her
dress and manner. She bristles at Lemuel's gesture of kindness.*)

LEMUEL: Sarah! We once were friends. . . .

SARAH (*bitterly*):   Four years ago
    I thought that Lemuel Thomas was a saint. . . .
LEMUEL: But now you have turned witness for the Army?
SARAH: It takes awhile to tell some saints from witches.
    Oh, I can tell of Seekers I have seen
    raging, in tremors, stripping off their clothes,
    of one man who walked nude with a pot of coals
    smoking on his head through the streets of
        Lichfield. . . .
LEMUEL: That was no Seeker. You know he was a Ranter!
SARAH: I know it was your sermon set him off!
    I've seen them foam at the mouth and gag and fall,
    and gangs set out against the churches, seen
    the women shriek against the soldiers marching. . . .
LEMUEL: You have so shrieked yourself. . . .
SARAH: I know I have!
    I was demented!
LEMUEL: To cry for peace? To protest our kingdom's building
    a military state in the name of God?
SARAH (*suddenly crying*): Can you deny you drove my hus-
        band mad?
LEMUEL (*disgusted*): Foh, Sarah!
    Clay left you, Sarah, to toil with me for God
    in perfect sanity. I cannot say
    what wild imaginations taint him now!
SARAH: For God?
    (*spitefully*) Why is it only women write him letters?
LEMUEL (*roars*): What, Sarah, do you think I *am?* Did I
    set women after him? Am I a witch
    because he's learned to preach in some soft way
    that sounds like making love?
                  I'm through with him.
    You will not need an Army, Sarah; I
    have seen those letters, too. I soon will send
    your overstimulating husband home.
    I thus save you your treachery.
                 Or, better,
    fetch him yourself. The movement has a cause

that cannot be contaminated by
domestic squabbles. If your wifely heart
demands an Army drag him to the post,
why drag him there—but, Sarah, do not drag
the Seekers down with him, or I will turn
a flood of holy fury loose to crush
all petty picking of Parliaments and wives!

(*Starts to leave.*)

FRIAR (*to Lemuel*): Wait!
(*to Sarah*) Mrs. Harper, would you step outside?

(*She leaves, sobbing. The General circles his desk watching Lemuel, who stands taut, suspicious. The General approaches him insinuatingly.*) I welcome your suggestion, Mr. Thomas. (*Nearer, now, he lays a conspiratorial hand on Lemuel's hunched shoulder.*)

LEMUEL (*jerking loose*): No hands on me, General Friar. I am no ally.

FRIAR (*unruffled*): But yet you might be. You have shown me how.
One way to rid the Seekers of Clay Harper
would be to let our soldiers apprehend
him in an overt act of blasphemy.
Just now he is at Bristol, where the people
adore him and, besides, are easily
stirred into flagrant demonstrations of
their holy moods. Should you arrange a time
when Harper might whip up an ecstasy—
we would move in. These letters we have seized
and one such incident would be enough. . . .

LEMUEL (*red in the face, fists clenched and raised, sputters*):
May . . . God . . . restrain me from . . .
Beware the day of wrath, oh General,
spirit aroused and singeing Hell in England,
Westminster crackling as a house of straw,
for the flame breaks forth and shall not be confined,
flame of the heart, flame of the fist, flame

>   of the telling tongue that cries aloud, for truth
>   gathers heat, oppressed, and finding issue, licks
>   along the streets of stone to seek out Generals!

(*He wheels and leaves. We discover the interior of a cottage
on the outskirts of Bristol where Susannah Potter, all in a
bovine dither, is lifting cushions, going down on her knees to
look under furniture, slapping her hands along high shelves.
She is an earthy, meaty woman in her forties, rich-voiced,
courageous, honest. She calls her husband:* Clarence! *and
a thin, obedient voice answers from another room:* Yes,
Susannah? *Clarence enters, a thin, gentle, rather clownish
man, with the wisdom of the weak.*)

SUSANNAH: The Bible, now!
>   What kind of Christian home have I and cannot
>   find even a Bible? Have you seen a fat
>   black book about—perhaps turned red with shame
>   for its neglect? Clay is to preach today.
>   We must, at least, provide him with a Bible.
CLARENCE: It's in your bed.
>   You said a week ago that you would sleep with it.
SUSANNAH: I did! I did! I *knew* I had a vague
>   and unaccountable sense of having studied!
CLARENCE: But why a Bible? You don't think that Clay
>   is one of those new exegetical kind
>   who preach like rabbits, ever ready to dive
>   into a burrow for quotations—or
>   who face the meeting with their ears and eyes
>   above the book, their noses under. . . .
SUSANNAH (*matter-of-factly*): No. But he should have it to
>   wave and slap.
CLARENCE: Oh my! Now you would make him out to be
>   like dissenters fantastical, those fiery-eyed
>   and fuzzy-minded progeny of the new
>   translation who think that no one yet has read
>   the true Lord's word but them, and take plain English
>   through all their vertigo until it comes
>   regurgitated out more like the Latin!

(*A knock at the door. Clarence admits Lemuel, whose tension makes him abrupt, awkward.*)

> Why, Lemuel! Returned from London? What
> is the word from General Friar now?

(*Lemuel kisses Clarence's cheek perfunctorily, crosses and does the same to Susannah. He takes a seat while they wait expectantly. He ignores Susannah.*)

LEMUEL: We've blots upon us, Clarence, that call for quick
> scrubbing. Has Clay come here?

SUSANNAH: Why, yes, he has!
> He's in the barn—doing the milking for me.
> Why, if you stay, you'll hear him preach today.

LEMUEL (*not looking at her*): Get him.

SUSANNAH (*leaving*): Now aren't we friendly, love?

LEMUEL: He won't be preaching, Clarence. Spread that word.
> Have there been movements of the Army here?

CLARENCE: They say a coach came frothing in from London,
> middle of the night. The clatter in the streets
> woke Benjamin the tapster, who looked out
> and thought the French were coming to restore
> the King—but I said surely not in Bristol.
> Why would they come clear round to Bristol?
> He . . .

LEMUEL: That was your General Friar. I've raced him here—
> but he could change his horses and come on.
> The Cartwright coach is also on its way,
> Seth bringing Sarah Harper. The London road
> burgeoned with us, all descending here
> in honor of that milking preacher, Clay.

(*We move to a public square, where to the strumming of the blind beggar's lute people are engaged in a lively round dance. Others are watching, clapping out the rhythm, but there is some worry among them, as from time to time they look down the streets nervously. The dance ends to more applause and general laughter which is self-consciously hushed, the dancers taking turns drinking from a large jug. One of the women wipes her mouth, passes on the jug, and says:*)

FIRST WOMAN: La! I am winded. I do hope there's preaching today.

SECOND WOMAN (*smugly*): If this were London, we could go to the bear-pits.

FIRST MAN: That's evil on a Sunday.

SECOND MAN: You and your London! Preaching's more exciting, anyway.

FIRST WOMAN: Besides, I hear that Cromwell closed the bear-pits.

SECOND WOMAN (*still smugly*): Not last summer, he hadn't. And they sold ices there, in the middle of summer.

FIRST WOMAN: You can be sure he's closed them down since then.

FIRST MAN (*piously*): It's for the best: bear-baiting is more evil than theaters.

BLIND MAN: Now why is that? The bears play themselves in their roles, and the dogs play themselves. Why, it's all natural as eat and sleep the way the dogs come snarling at the bear and tear him to shreds so long as he's chained. If they are going to close the bear-pits, they'd better close down commerce, war, and marriage. They'd better close down the public square!

SECOND WOMAN (*saucily*): You're right! Oh, I prefer the bear-pits to a sermon any day.

SECOND MAN (*craning to see if anyone is coming*): And the troops find us here, we will be in the pits ourselves.

THIRD WOMAN: Troops? That sleepy Bristol company never stirs out on a Sunday.

SECOND MAN: But a coach-load of officers arrived in the night. Something's afoot.

THIRD MAN: Some say we are at war again.

THIRD WOMAN: La! They don't fight wars with officers.

SECOND MAN: No, but they do form press gangs.

BLIND MAN (*improvises song*): Oh, peace of heart in war I find to be a man lame, halt, and blind!

(*We see the exterior of the Potter house, Clarence coming out the door. As he does, Sarah, wearing a traveling cloak, approaches, looking about apprehensively.)*

SARAH: Is that Clarence Potter?

CLARENCE (*turning, delighted*): Why, Sarah! Sarah Harper!

(*He starts to open the door to invite her in—but thinks better of it. He takes her hands and kisses her on the cheek in greeting.*)

It's been . . . how many years?

SARAH (*relaxing a little*): Four, Clarence,
                since we worked together, since those meetings
                at our home. Since the day that Clay was moved
                to abandon home and me. . . .

(*She glances uneasily at the shutters, then sits on a bench beside the door, loosening the cloak on her shoulders.*)

CLARENCE (*sympathetically*): He *has* become a traveler. . . .

SARAH: He never once came back!

CLARENCE: The call, in his case, *did* come rather strong.

SARAH (*bitterly*): The call of what? Oh, I am not a shrew—
                I can forgive men for conviction. Some
                can fly with faith and sense of duty, fly
                right off this brown domestic earth, and reach
                with anxious hands the fabric of the night. . . .

CLARENCE (*quietly*): And sometimes pull it down and smother
                all.

SARAH (*protesting*): No, Clarence. I believe his call was true:
                he was inspired. . . .

CLARENCE: They say the very spirit shines from his eyes. . . .

SARAH: And so I thought—resigned myself. My boys
                and I then healed our widowed home: their cheeks
                stayed bright, their breeches mended, minds grew full
                of manly thoughts, their knuckles scarred; their dogs
                were faithful. They fathered one another, husbanded
                their mother, and we lived as a lonely woman
                and children live, potatoes more than meat,
                more stories than adventures, and, at night,
                clung tight together, making up for manhood.

CLARENCE: Oh, you have more patience than my wife would
    have. . . .

SARAH (*fiercely*): *Your* wife! But I am coming to your wife.
    I heard reports of how the movement swelled,
    how Clay grew famous as a preacher, great
    as Lemuel himself, how he was loved. . . .
    Then soldiers came to the farm one day. A General
    told me in more detail—and showed me letters—
    that made explicit *just* how he was loved!
    He named your wife, Susannah, as the one
    who led them all in passionate adoration.

CLARENCE (*sadly*): Well, the plain fact is, religion seems to be
    rather too much for Susannah. . . .

SARAH: Or not enough?

CLARENCE: Well, some can saddle their convictions, ride
    them sedately to and fro. They gallop off
    with her. A notion in her head just skips
    like a nervous horse and takes her with it. I,
    now, take productions of the brain like signs
    of addling. If I get one, I am quick
    to quell it. . . .

SARAH (*affectionately*): Quell those of Clay and of your wife
    and you will be for me a kind of hero.

CLARENCE: No hero, Sarah. A traveling tinker, safe
    from highway men because I look so sickly
    no cut-throat would risk stopping me for fear
    of scaring me to death and being charged
    for murder when he meant not that, but only
    harmless thieving.

SARAH (*bitterly*):   Susannah, though, is holy!

CLARENCE: Oh, I'm not sure she sorts her urges
    according to the best theology.
    These preachers, like your husband (no offense)
    have love so often on their tongues I think
    the ladies come to want it on their lips. . . .

SARAH: So I understand from General Friar.

CLARENCE: I do not say that Clay obliges. No.
    There's not yet scandal, Sarah. Holy people

tend always to express themselves, it seems
to me, in rather muddled terms, but innocent,
or so it seems to me. I judge it not.
The issue is too fine for brains like mine.

SARAH: They tell me Clay is staying here.

CLARENCE: He is—
but Lemuel, an hour ago, came raging
from London, his face like knots of grapes, and Clay
took him out walking in the fields, I think,
to cool. . . .

SARAH (*tensely*):   Susannah?

CLARENCE (*reluctantly*):   She's inside . . . But, Sarah—
(*kind irony*) Seekers believe in peace!

SARAH (*friendly*):   I am no Seeker,
Clarence, any more. The movement is
all foul with flowing human sores, miscalled
the gush of inspiration. But, please trust me,
peace will attend my freeing you all of Clay.

(*As Clarence leaves, Sarah knocking on the door, we move to Lemuel and Clay, walking in a field.*)

CLAY (*passionately*): Where have I erred? I have, a thousand
        hours,
besides this hour with you, carded my soul
with iron teeth to find whatever burr makes me im-
        pure.

LEMUEL (*putting his arm around Clay's shoulder*):
Oh, Clay . . . I am no bewigged judge to name
your crime. I'd be an ass to try. I must,
you know, be honest if I speak. Such things
I've had made clear to me . . . that, well, if I
just named them now it would wipe out somehow
our years together—and the love we've shared.

(*He pulls away, sits on log.*)

Sarah . . . I saw in London. She is coming,
I hear, to Bristol. I want you, Clay, to take

her home . . . and farm again. We'll keep a fond
thought of your service. That's all we can want.

CLAY (*stunned*): But Lemuel—I cannot turn off God
like the sluice of a dam: my preaching is not only
for you, for the Seekers. *You* have taught me: God
flows inescapably through my passive tongue.

LEMUEL (*mutters*): His message, lately, seems to have been
blurred.

CLAY: Then tell me how I sin! What must I do?

LEMUEL (*kindly*): A wobbling wheel will wobble all the more
for all its earnest turning. Oh, I am tired—
talk . . . talk mends nothing. You are not a fool.
If you but *think* you will discover how
you've lost . . . the firm uprightness of your soul.

CLAY: You want a rod-like soul, a staff, a mast;
I have, I fear, a wand, much tenderer. . . .

LEMUEL (*impatiently*): The arm of God must have a bone
in it,
muscle firm as . . . as polished stone, a grip
rigorous, so it can control the slick
writhing of serpents—of error, flesh . . . of *man*.

CLAY: Man? Man? Oh, I confess I do not try
to close him in my grip. They come to hear me—
murmuring, gathering, collecting as the sea
rises around an inlet, feeling here,
perhaps, this opening, this easy way
will lead to some beyond: they stretch their arms
for consolation, praying this avenue
may mean escape from the sandy bowl they know,
where they toil away their lives of salt and cold. . .

LEMUEL: Nonsense!
Or, rather, they will, like that sea, extend
their waters to the pitiful, shallow reaches
of that inlet, only to find how sadly soon
sea swallows up itself. Oh, Clay, you cannot
smooth all over with a liquid simile!
I am concerned with life: with blasphemy,
voluptuary women—with Susannah!

CLAY (*blanching*): She is our sister in confusion. . . .

LEMUEL: She
is confusion's very amiable mother!

CLAY: I . . . I cannot take this anger from you, Lemuel.
It was you who first revealed to me the way
of light, the light within, the light that now
sputters, you say, so smokily. I try
to honor that light as it appears in others—
even Susannah. I cannot judge what God
moves her to do or say. . . .

LEMUEL (*apologetically*):   I did not charge
you, Clay. I agree, it is difficult to judge. . . .
(*with difficulty*) But you have become something
. . . I fear. It seems
puerile. More: dangerous. Even success,
the very way, these harvest days, that fields
of people sway like heavy-headed grain
and chant your name: Clay Harper, Harper,
    Harper—
that here is danger. I am stumbling for words—
as you will never do—but maybe we could
define it as the ancient rhetoricians
distinguished logic and eloquence. The fist
was logic—hard, unwelcome, strong—whereas
the open palm was eloquence, that makes
its way by friendliness. You have too much
in you of the open hand. . . .

CLAY (*desperately, closing Lemuel's fist in his palm*): Ally me
    to
your harder logic like a wife. . . .

LEMUEL (*jerking free*):   A curse
on your similes! Clay, truth and eloquence
conjoin like concubine and king, not man
and wife!

CLAY: I cannot slap down love. These people
see something in me that . . . They are sincere. . . .

LEMUEL: I am no novice, Clay.

CLAY: They adore you, too!

LEMUEL: And *would* adore me more—have done so. When
        I heard the call and spoke, to my surprise,
        I soon found that my message stirred the hearts
        of sinners, soldiers, sycophants, of ladies
        past usefulness who sought some new devotion
        to while away the hours of age, of girls
        infatuated with feeling anything,
        no matter what, just feeling, feeling. . . .

CLAY: I see no harm in feeling. . . .

LEMUEL: Mark me! I charmed the moralists who found
        my doctrine easier to twist and fit
        to their perverse rigidities than that
        of the Established Church. I drew the minds
        of lunatics who like the tides flowed after
        whatever moon was far and vague enough. . . .

CLAY: One can't distinguish. . . .

LEMUEL: One *must* distinguish! In those early days
        I first was flattered to have such response,
        and then despaired at finding seeds of truth
        flower in nonsense; next I doubted that
        the seeds *were* truth, that had such issue. Ah,
        I nearly gave up all!

CLAY (*sympathetically*):   That rotting doubt . . .

LEMUEL: Finally I came to understand, I think,
        our dearest, truest beliefs—because they put
        such emphasis upon the inner voice,
        such trust in men to find their way without
        ritual, law, authority, are for
        their very strength susceptible to all
        corruptions of democracy. . . .

CLAY: Corruptions!

LEMUEL: Aye, the variety that splinters us, fools us,
        so we become mere Bedlamites, trusting
        our private purple fancies. Then, like you,
        we forget if we are fathers, preachers, or lovers,
        stir public discontents, turn politics
        and passion all to religion, all confused. . . .

CLAY: All this you taught me!

LEMUEL: If you are on God's side,
        remember that Prometheus must be
        a traitor. God may have good reason to
        deny us certain kinds of light.

CLAY: Oh, Lemuel!
        Oh, love me, Lemuel! Love me as we
        loved God in one another in months gone by!
        Arms over shoulders were we, leaning down
        the backroads through the night, braving stones
        and constables in the name of truth—and laughing,
        even laughing. . . . When have we laughed since?

LEMUEL: The man in me, the *man* responds, dear Clay.
        But in me also there is God, who knows
        forgiveness is for his flock but not his shepherds.

CLAY: A shepherd learns. . . .

LEMUEL (*kindly*):   Too late for that. Too late.
                           (*Rises.*)
        To half of England you are seen, for bad
        or good, as standing for the Seekers. No.
        You must never preach again. I . . . must forbid it.

CLAY (*as they leave*): Your way is not to say that you forbid.

LEMUEL: It must become my way.

(*Clarence and Seth Cartwright are approaching the public square. Seth, a prosperous London merchant, father of Sarah Harper, is a squat, deep-chested man of sharp mind and, usually, jovial disposition. Not a religious man, he is nevertheless on amiable terms with those Seekers he knows through his daughter and through Clay.*)

CLARENCE: But such a journey, Mr. Cartwright! Crossing
        England pell-mell to stop a sermon! And on
        the heels of Lemuel, riding day and night
        to stop it too. . . .

SETH (*puffing*):   Aye, madness! A kind
        of highway tag, the black official coach
        of the Army, we in our fast calash, and bent
        to the mane, his coattails flapping, Lemuel. . . .
        Whenever I stopped for a pint we would see go by

one or the other, and Sarah, like a child,
would gasp, "Oh, Papa, there they go!" and drag
me belching out the tavern door.
CLARENCE: She did
not seem a child today, descending on
Susannah, striking sparks. . . .
SETH: Oh, yes, I know.
She seems bent on accosting everyone
like an avenging angel. I am to wait
here in the square.
CLARENCE: I left. I could not bear
to see the ladies brawl.
SETH: Her mood is one
of massacre. Poor Susannah! . . . But if
I know Susannah, I might well fear
for little Sarah, too. . . . Her way is not
my way! I brought her down from London thinking
we would take Clay by the ear and lead him home.
But Sarah wants to scourge your whole mad sect.
Her mind is set for root and branch. I told her—
there's nothing you can do about religion.

*(As they draw near the crowd the blind beggar, seated on a
market bench, strums his lute and sings:)*

BLIND MAN:

A farmer had a big fat sheep.
He fed him all the corn, oh my!
This sheep will win a prize and keep
me rich as a rich man born, oh my!
And three sheep starved in winter snow
and two went mad in the sun, oh my!
The farmer fed the fat one, though
till the wolf did come
and the skinny sheep fled,
but the fat one was
too fat to run,
and the wolf was rich as a rich man born, oh my!

This farmer had a little tree
with fruit like the sun at morn, oh my!
This apple will win a prize for me.
I'll be rich as a rich man born, oh my!
And his corn all parched and his cow went dry
and still he watered his tree, oh my!
And came the harvest by and by,
but at the fair
the judge did gulp
for the apple tasted
all of pulp
and the farmer was poor as a poor man born, oh my!

The sparrow on the hanging limb
is neither red nor blue, oh my!
His song will win no prize for him,
he appeals to very few, oh my!
And the hunters pass and hawks fly by
and little boys throw rocks, oh my!
for nightingales the lovers sigh,
but hunters, hawks,
and boys with rocks
and lovers let
the sparrow get
as much from life as a rich man born, oh my!

FIRST WOMAN: Foh! Even the blind have taken to moralizing these days.

BLIND MAN: Especially the blind, ma'am—for we would have *you* become as blind as we.

SECOND WOMAN: But do you think there are those who will follow the precepts of a blind man?

BLIND MAN: Lordy, ma'am, I think anyone who follows precepts follows a blind man. I'm blind only on one side.

THIRD WOMAN: Indeed? Which side is that?

BLIND MAN: The side my face is on. The other sides of me see as well as the same sides of you. And for every kind of blindness you have, I have a kind of sight.

THIRD WOMAN: How is that? You can see without your eyes?

BLIND MAN: Oh, lordy, ma'am, eyes let in too much light for some kinds of seeing. I have known men with eyes blind to charity, virtue, courage, fidelity, beauty and wit. I knew a tailor once so used to looking at fine work he failed to understand anything that would not fit in the eye of a needle. He recognized his wife by a blackhead in her chin—but a yard away he couldn't tell her from a gatepost. (*General laughter.*)

SECOND WOMAN: Is Mr. Harper going to preach today?

THIRD WOMAN: They *say* he will. . . .

SECOND WOMAN: And then I've heard some say he will not.

SECOND MAN: Aye, Lemuel Thomas has come to town, and I have heard there's been a falling out.

FIRST WOMAN: Susannah Potter says he stalked all glum about the house, arms folded, sour as an alderman, his face congested as ice on the northern sea—while Clay Harper studied him like a pup who can make no sense of his master's indignation.

THIRD WOMAN: Poor Clay . . . (*The other women giggle at her familiarity.*) (*protesting*) *Har*per. I was *go*ing to say Clay Harper.

SECOND WOMAN (*suggestively*): Wouldn't you *like* to know him well enough to call him Clay?

FIRST MAN (*piously*): Oh, this is sinful talk! The times are bad. A chill is in the air. God speaks in contrary voices.

SECOND WOMAN: Oh, I have seen Mr. Thomas preach in London. If I know *his* kind, he'll have God straightened out in short enough time. (*Women giggle.*)

FIRST MAN (*reprovingly*): Our leader, Mr. Thomas, deserves a more respectful tongue.

THIRD WOMAN (*sassily*): He's nothing to me. Mr. Harper is leader enough for me.

FIRST MAN (*piously*): This disrespect confirms me: It is a dim day, and not one of us finds an opening
in the grey cast of the sky. Our leaders give
conflicting inspirations and we choose

between them with no more than human prompt-
ings. . . .

THIRD WOMAN: Well, I can choose—between a man and an
ass. (*Shocked hush.*)

FIRST MAN: Your vile tongue soils the very name of Lemuel
Thomas!

THIRD WOMAN (*snippily*): Oh, I just said a man and an ass.
You pin the tail on which you please!

SECOND MAN: Both need our prayers. It is poor Mr. Harper's
time of trial.

THIRD WOMAN: Aye, with Lemuel Thomas figuring as one
Pontificus Pilate. (*General laughter.*)

FIRST MAN: Beware of blasphemy! These waggish jokes . . .

THIRD MAN: Aye, the mob disgusts me!

FIRST WOMAN: And who, pray tell, are you, Mr. Butcher, to
be complaining of the stink of flesh?

THIRD MAN: Not flesh, milady! I complain of straw
that blows along the street, lacking the dung
to keep it in its stalls! Such straw is a hazard.
A spark could touch it off and burn the town,
with stuff so light and so combustible.

BLIND MAN: Oh, you speak of people's hearts—and as a
beggar I must defend them for being so easily
touched. That very dark fire unseen that consumes
the breast is all I have to heat me by.

THIRD MAN: Spoken like a man without property! The fellow
would burn a barn to warm a backside.

FIRST WOMAN (*seeing Clarence and Seth on the edge of the
crowd*): Oh, here is Mr. Potter, Susannah's husband!

SECOND WOMAN: Oh, Mr. Potter! Can you tell us if Clay
Harper will preach today?

CLARENCE: The last I knew, he . . . he wouldn't be preaching,
ma'am.

SECOND WOMAN (*sighs*): I *did* hope Mr. Harper would preach.
My sister heard him once at a London meeting. She
said it was like a bath in the sea.

SETH: What if he tells you you are damned?

CLARENCE: This gentleman is Mr. Harper's father-in-law. . . .

SETH: And if his words roast you in Hell's fire. Is that a bath?

SECOND WOMAN (*shocked*): Why, I do hope he doesn't mention damnation!

SETH: It is the new way with preaching, I am told,
to skirt the subject. Natural philosophy
has lately replaced damnation with its notions
of how we ride the sky—other worlds whirling
in the night, and ours a drop of the sun's sweat,
and our blood running like liquor in a still,
and all our finest sentiments, like laws,
explicable. Oh, these philosophers
have quite monopolized the job of making
mankind feel worthless. And the preachers, ever
men to keep up with things, all go about
in leather breeches, telling us we are
as good as anybody else (which is
a way of saying just as bad). They pull
the velvet robes off of authority,
bless businessmen, damn monks. They're taking over
Parliament with guns and pikes—and prayers—
and all the while proclaiming human affairs
and individual consciences as the measure
of everything. They quite forget damnation!
Why, what I hear is—you hold meetings out
of churches so that boys and girls, inspired
by love of God, will have the grassy fields
available. Now, ask no more for preaching.
I've just delivered you a lay sermon.

SECOND WOMAN: Well, it did not make me feel at all purified.

(*Clay enters, seen from a distance, distractedly rubbing his
beard.*)

CLARENCE (*seeing him*): Here comes your purifier!

(*A hush falls over the crowd as they see him. Several run to
him, greeting him reverently—but he acknowledges them with
an absent, kind smile, walking among them toward the center
of the square like a shepherd ringed by frisking sheep.*)

SECOND WOMAN: Oh, Mr. Harper—will you preach today?
CLAY: No, friend. Today, nor any day.

(*There is a murmur of disappointment from the crowd.*)

My leader—and my dearest friend—has said
my service to our cause is at an end.
SETH (*shouting from edge of crowd*): A wise man, Lemuel!
CLAY (*sees Seth, works loose to cross through the crowd to him and take his hands fondly*): Oh, Seth, my long-
lost father! Here, in Bristol!
You have not changed, dear Seth, unless it be
in girth—a measure of prosperity. . . .
THIRD WOMAN (*pushing forward, interrupting*): Lemuel
Thomas is only jealous of you, Mr. Harper! You
must not listen to him!

(*Several murmur agreement.*)

FIRST WOMAN: Aye, you are our leader, Mr. Harper! You
are the breast of warmth we cling to in this night
windy with doubt and contradiction!
SECOND MAN: Aye!
God would not leave us here all stripped, exposed;
you are our comfort, your voice our consolation. . . .
THIRD WOMAN: All Lemuel Thomas means to us is a threat
of Hell. Is this the way to minister
to people lonely and afraid?
CLAY (*raising hands*):   Hush! Peace!
He is your leader, your leader, gentle people,
with a strength you must not damn because you
lack it!
Think what he saw, what moved him from the
church,
sustained him as he tramped a thousand roads
unarmed except with honesty! His vision,
when I heard it, brought me from the plow
summoned by angels singing. What have you?
Have I? What private vision draws our faith
as *his* still draws us?

A crank, they called

him in their kinder moments; oftener
they felt his danger (rightly! oh, rightly!), threw
him into jail or beat him out of town
with pitchforks. What was madness, what was truth
was long ambiguous—but now we know
his message rang so odd because he was
the first to publish God. That jaw severe,
those eyes like glowing rods, those hands of stone,
are urgent with compassion. Vision. If
we are not *good,* he tells us, we will die.

FIRST MAN: Amen!

CLAY: Now, if you love me, you will trust in him,
as . . . I must do. I . . . I do not . . .
I hardly understand him—but I trust
it is the Spirit telling him that I
must leave you. God, we know, speaks to his heart.

(*Clay turns from them, and the crowd moves disconsolately, uncomprehendingly away.*)

THIRD WOMAN (*to others, as they go*): Now we must save him
—as he has saved us.

BLIND MAN: Aye! Everybody should mind his brother's business. That is very Christian.

(*The crowd departs as though with a mission—leaving Clay futilely gesturing as though to restrain them—but he says nothing, his hands hanging helplessly, and in the ensuing quiet he clasps his face—as though in shame or prayer. Seth moves to comfort him, taking his shoulder firmly.*)

SETH: Mustered out, were you? Clay, you have served well
for four long years. Might you not think again
of home and Sarah—if Lemuel is ungrateful?

(*Clay does not respond, sinking to the bench, now hunched in prayer, oblivious.*)

CLARENCE (*diverting Seth*): I *knew* that Lemuel was suffering
from an indigestible idea when

he came: his face was like the bowels
of a ruptured rabbit. . . .

SETH (*laughing*): No, Clarence! No!
His face contorts all purply thus when God
is most upon him.

CLARENCE: I see.

SETH: They call it peace
of soul—and you can detect its consummate
divinity in its oppositeness to our
more worldly expressions of emotions.

CLARENCE (*contorting his face*):   Thus?
Like this the face goes? Do I have it right?

SETH (*studying him critically*): A more spiral texture in the
        cheek
muscles, suggesting how your mood aspires
upwards.

CLARENCE (*trying*): So. Thus you mean? . . . No, it's but
hypocrisy in me. A sickly earthiness
pervades my peace of soul.

SETH: It's your damnation,
Clarence, not to purple properly.

CLARENCE: Damnation!
Surely not damnation for a little
flabbiness in the cheeks!

SETH: Ah, it's a softness
you have, but not the divine softness, which
demands a certain brickishness of mien—
nor the divine gentleness, which slaps
about like a Parliament man, nor the divine
love, which in subtle tenderness dares never
touch for fear of pleasure or be kind
for fear such naturalness might be the death,
corrupt our exquisite and unnatural souls.
It takes some piety to tell when a man's
divine from when he's disagreeable.

CLARENCE: Ay me!
Salvation can change a man's whole way of life.

SETH: It changed my daughter into a very ramrod

of strong character—which, as you saw today,
she has maintained, though she has lost religion. . . .

CLAY (*rising in astonishment*): Sarah? Today? Is Sarah here?

SETH: We came
to save you from the Army, Clay. Sarah
and Lemuel have formed a new alliance—
a holy one, as you may see by the way
they so avoid cordiality. . .

CLAY: But where . . . ?

CLARENCE: She's home, negotiating with Susannah. . . .

(*Clay strikes off briskly, Seth and Clarence shrugging and following. We see Susannah and Sarah, inside the Potter house, Sarah at the table, Susannah spinning, her foot working with zest as she talks back over her shoulder.*)

SUSANNAH: Suppose Christ walked the earth again. What would
Parliament do with *him?* What accusations
would his neglected wife shriek at his converts?
Eh?

SARAH (*quietly*): Christ had no wife.

SUSANNAH (*imperviously*):   But if he had, he would
have left her. Right? A man's work comes first always!

SARAH: His work . . . *Clay's* work . . . I never fought. It's just
his madness—and the madness of you all. . . .
Susannah, there are people who believe,
who know the Word of God, but preach without
exciting screams and wild expostulation,
quaking of women, howling of converts, wails
of the blessed seized. . . .

SUSANNAH (*simply*):   Now there, Sarah, you see,
is your conformist streak. You are the kind
who likes to hear a royal bishop twanging
his nose from a pulpit, thinking enthusiasm
absurd, since he has lost the wherewithal. . . .

SARAH (*angrily*): Faith isn't physical fitness. . . .

SUSANNAH (*calmly, dreamily*):   Partly it is.
I want, when I hear preaching, to be whirled
and lifted high as a skirt at a country dance.

Without some throbbing of the blood I know
no way to recognize the spirit. Some
of you hope faith is a way to keep the flesh
in check. But flesh is *life*—and God *likes* life.
There are more ways to God than castration, Sarah.

SARAH: You sound like Father—though he would not call
it God you strive to please.

SUSANNAH (*laughs appreciatively*): Oh, Seth! He knows!

SARAH: He would say God and Clay are mixed up in
your mind. . . .

SUSANNAH (*frankly*): No doubt. His gift is love: he makes
men love themselves and one another. I,
perhaps in dreams, may sometimes sigh that his love
is wasted on the world at large. Is this
so bad?

SARAH: One does not want to sleep with saints.

SUSANNAH: Well, there are saints and saints. Some find their
thrills
in underwear studded with tacks; some feel
the best posture for honoring God is on
their knees, scrabbling for roots in a desert, or
hammering thus their bony chests with stones.
Another type prefers that their sweat serve
some good in the world. That serving, loving type
takes life for what it is and *makes it do*.
The hymn of such a saint is yea! The naying
type interests me not at all.

SARAH: I know
you are not one to be caught saying nay.

SUSANNAH: Ha! If you think that you can twit me out
of loving and serving Clay, dear Sarah, you
have lost some sense somewhere. What do you *want?*

SARAH: I want him home. Parliament has now
given orders to arrest such rebel preachers,
to obstruct such peace disturbance as he causes.
Oh, they see how religion is with you
merely a guise for license and subversion!
From what I know—I'll help them to that end.

SUSANNAH (*derisively*): From what you know! You haven't
      heard him preach!

SARAH: I've heard him preach. . . .

SUSANNAH: Four years ago, before
    his tongue was fired by God! Oh, Sarah! He
    no longer is a husband you can call
    in from the field at dinnertime! He belongs
    to all of us, to God! No Army can stop him—
    and, least of all, a selfish sniveling wife.

SARAH (*coolly*): The Army can stop him.

SUSANNAH: We have thrived on just
    such persecutions! *You* know this: you nursed
    the broken head of Lemuel in your lap,
    you blew the lamp and hid him from the mob,
    you watched the hurled stones bounce from your
      husband's back
    and saw him stand unarmed before the troops
    who thought truth was a weed to be uprooted.
    Oh, the seed scatters! Wind will bear it, earth
    will nurture any kernel that lives. You *know*
    that Clay is a force beyond all stopping!

SARAH: What
    if Lemuel decides he must be stopped?

SUSANNAH: Then Lemuel, poor dear, will be swept under.
    You know I love him, know what greatness was
    emergent in him in the days he stood
    like a prophet on the hill and called us forth.
    But, Sarah, he solidifies: the work
    of holding all the Seekers in his hand
    has tired the man. He grows afraid—and tired.

(*Noise of the arrival of the men outside the door. Sarah tightens
her fists tensely at the table, awaiting them, and Susannah falls
silent. The door opens tentatively and Clarence enters, followed
by Seth and Clay. Susannah resumes her spinning.*)

CLARENCE: Is all well here?

SUSANNAH (*without looking*): Are you afraid of women?

CLARENCE: Lovey, you know I am.

SUSANNAH: Well, these are tame.

(*Clay, inside the door, contemplates Sarah, afraid to approach, and she is looking at him, straight-backed, on the edge of tears.*)

CLAY (*finally*): Sarah, forgive me!

SARAH (*evenly but kindly*): God give me strength to love as
    you deserve.

CLAY (*crossing*): In these mists, who can judge desert? Oh,
    Sarah,
    love my intentions—not the things I do.

(*She stands and they embrace with relief. Clay then holds her shoulders.*)

CLAY: I am coming home—if you will have me there.

SARAH (*pulling him close*): I want you there, Clay. I . . . I
    came to fetch you home.

SUSANNAH (*rising*): I will not *hear* this! Clay, you can't desert
    your work, your friends, the cause. . . .

CLAY (*humbly*):   I can't desert
    my wife again, Susannah. I am used
    past using: all my work is done, and Lemuel
    has granted me reprieve. He let me go.

SUSANNAH: He has no right! He cannot stand between
    our people and their God. . . .

CLAY (*sharply*):   I am no God!

SUSANNAH: You are their access to Him! In your person
    you bear their spark of God. How can you let
    an envious and weak-toothed dog drive you . . . ?

SARAH: I think Clay loves that dog, Susannah, as
    I think he loves his wife and boys. You mean
    how can he let anything come between
    him and Susannah!

SUSANNAH: I am selfish, am I?
    Wanting to share this man with this whole needing,
    love-starved world?

SETH (*crosses and closes Susannah's mouth with a kiss*):
    Hush, squabbling women! I might tolerate

such wrestling if it were for me. At least
I am a man of means!

(*Goes to Clay, embraces him affectionately.*)

But *Clay!* A rag
like Clay will tear with so much tugging!

CLAY: Thank you, dear Seth—but their hot words express
the dialogue of my divided soul.
Why, as for tugging—I am pulled about
by you, by Lemuel, by each of the doubts
that shred my resolution like the ants
working discarded bread. Susannah, Sarah—
I've made no choice. I had no choice to make.

SUSANNAH: The time de*mands* you choose! The air is singing
with swarming of the bees that have no hive.
*Some*one must settle them: already you
are followed: they want *you*—not Lemuel!

CLAY (*weakly*): I've had no opening . . .
no inspiration comes to go or stay
and God has left me beached, mere man without
Him,
a straggling swimmer lost on an alien shore. . . .
I think I must go home.

SARAH: Plainly, you must, although, God knows, I'd rather
you came because of love. . . . But all is done
with the Seekers. Extravagances which you have,
my Clay, excited in your more erotic
converts have brought the law upon you. Bristol
seethes, now, with soldiers, prepared to seize
you straightway if you lift your voice again
or one more woman squirms with howling holi-
ness. . . .

CLAY (*shocked*): Cromwell is not so vicious. . . .

SARAH: I tell you, they are here!
A Parliamentary force, with General Friar
commanding their secret movements, aims to quell
the more extreme subversive sects and preachers.
You will be the principal arrest . . .

        unless you come away, never to preach
        again in any public meeting. . . .

CLAY: Sarah, how do you know all this. . . ?

SARAH: I promised them, I promised General Friar . . .
        I'd bring you home with me!

SUSANNAH: Oh, foul conspiracy!

CLAY: Sarah, you would not do this. . . .

SARAH: I would not have
        four years ago. You have had no way to know
        what loneliness did to me, nor have you seen
        how the Seekers, Clay, have worked upon your mind.

(*Clay sits as though stunned. Outside there is a noise of a gathering of people.*)

CROWD (*chanting outside*): Clay Harper, Harper, Harper!

THIRD WOMAN: Speak to us, Mr. Harper!

FIRST WOMAN: We know God only through your tongue!

CROWD: Clay Harper, Harper, Harper!

(*Clay clenches his hands, lowers his head, attempting to pray silently.*)

SUSANNAH (*lovingly*): Clay, listen how they need your pas-
        sion's tongue!

SETH: His tongue, his godly golden tongue, is that
        instrument of destruction I most fear!
        My own blunt flapper never charmed a mob
        to incantations nor stirred girls to fling
        themselves upon my bosom weeping—yet
        I hope it may have winning powers now. . . .
        A tongue, Clay, and I mean this as a friend,
        is just the meeting place of intellect
        and flesh: and there both sharply contend—like fires
        that would burn each other out. How sensitive
        the web of nerves that tastes and loves: how subtle
        the intricate muscle that dispels with words
        all tasting and all loving. . . . Your tongue, Clay,
        is coiled against itself. . . .

CLAY: Oh Seth! Please, Seth . . .

SETH: I've taken to you, Clay, since the day I learned
        that raw-wristed farm boy hanging around the store
        intended to cart off the merchant's daughter.
        Why, Clay, you were the sort of boy I would
        have backed in business—but even then you were
        more expert with your tongue than with your hands.
        Disaster comes of deep relying on
        so ambiguous an organ. . . .

CLAY (*gesturing toward the crowd outside*):
        How can I stop them? How can I stop myself?

SETH: I have no answers: you must think it out—
        what you call praying. You must decide—or, as
        your own terms go, must have an opening.
        The thrashing serpent in your mouth may strike
        and tear all hearts around you as it dies.
        Or maybe you can tame the fellow. We
        console you with our eyes and wring our hands—
        and keep our own tongues silent in their holes.

CROWD: Clay Harper, Harper, Harper!

SECOND WOMAN: Come take our outstretched hands!

FIRST MAN: No man but you has known our hearts!

SECOND MAN: No man but you can lead us to the bosom of
        God!

CROWD: Clay Harper, Harper, Harper!

(*Clay rises, deeply preoccupied, and moves apart, the others dimming in our view until they can barely be seen in tableau behind him. He looks up, arms spread.*)

CLAY: Am I ambitious?
        Have all these four dream years of dedication
        been martyrdom for Thee—or vanity?
        Is Lemuel, who seemed
        a prophet holding searing fire of Thine,
        but a blind man burned by jealousy?
        Come, God, and fill like the sea
        the mind that opens to Thee.

(*Drops to knees.*)

We trust, oh, God, to reception.
That this is the way, Lemuel himself
received from Thee—and with this vision opened
our thousand other hearts to him and Thee.
Oh, let us not be wrong, defenses down,
and open as to evil as to God!
What courage must inform us as we choose
not to resist—to hand our very wills,
our minds, our selves, to Thy great will! Inform
me now, my God.
My soul is open as a field of snow.
No. Not so treacherous!
As open as a sleeping child. No! Not
so animal. A sail, but not so pliant
to variations of the wind. A seed,
but not so nourished by the earth. . . .
Oh, I am helpless
as a soldier disoriented in the field:
the fires of soul those must be—ah, my friends!
But if they are the fires of mind, my enemy?
Oh, God, can one distinguish spirit from spirit,
spark from spark or fire from fire? Can one
do more than lie receptive in the night
to burn
in the first flame which finds him welcome fuel?

(*A protesting, disordered noise from the crowd distracts Clay,
who turns back to the others in the room.*)

LEMUEL (*outside, shouting angrily*):
          Disperse, you sad, misled and bleating sheep!
          This is the slaughter-wheel you've come upon!
          You are pressing Clay to ruin, yourselves to ruin!
          The world is waiting to consume you. Go!
THIRD WOMAN: Clay Harper is leader of the Seekers now!
          No longer can we hear you, Lemuel Thomas!

(*Lemuel bursts into the room as the crowd chants.*)

CROWD: Yea! Clay Harper, Harper, Harper!

(*Lemuel's face is contorted with fury as he crosses to Clay, but, suddenly, he half sobs, dropping his head on Clay's shoulder and embracing him.*)

CLAY: I did not want this, Lemuel!
LEMUEL: I know that, Clay. I ache for you, for them—
    who come in a herd, thoughtfully chewing grass,
    led by the bumping of bodies and unspoken
    confidence that somewhere someone is
    mindful of direction. I blame them not . . .
    I blame you not. . . .
                But, Clay, they must be
                stopped!
    We are observed. General Friar is here
    alert for blasphemy—and, Clay, that crowd
    is inflamed with personal adoration. You
    must hide yourself, must flee till this subsides!
CLAY: It is not like you, Lemuel, to run
    from armies, laws, and magistrates. Rather,
    we strengthen the movement in the face of
        force. . .
LEMUEL: Not this time, Clay! You know I do not fear
    the persecutors: *I* fear blasphemy!
    The mood of the mob, I tell you, Clay, is *wrong!*
CLAY (*pulling away from Lemuel, trance-like*):
    Then I must calm them. I must counsel them

    (*Going to door.*)

    to make a clear distinction. . . .
SARAH (*pleadingly*):   Clay!

(*But Clay hears nothing. He walks out, his face lifted to Heaven, and, after a moment, we see him crossing to the knoll, the people following in attitudes of reverence. Lemuel, Seth, Susannah, Clarence, and Sarah are anxiously among the crowd. Off to one side, calmly waiting, stand General Friar and two or three soldiers. When Clay is on the knoll he begins speaking very conversationally. His questions are answered by individuals in the crowd, and, as the sermon progresses, their*)

ejaculations—"Amen," "True," "Aye," *etc.*—*become more
impassioned, finally being reinforced by rhythmic body motions,
a physical pulsing to the beat of his language.*)

CLAY: You came, I trust, to hear the words of God.
            I am not God. I stand before you as
            a man.
                    Ask with me what that means. Was Christ
            a man? Are you? Or is that fellow standing
            near you a man?
                        What if he were a God?
            What if among you a savior stands, as Christ
            stood once among the ranks of men and waited,
            waited for wisdom, and when wisdom came
            published it in the world with human lips?
            Ah no. No miracles today. No one
            of us will multiply loaves or fishes. Times
            have changed. Divinity is subtler now,
            if, indeed, it exists at all. A modern man
            knows that he is a man, I warrant. He waits.
            Most of us, even, doubt that words will come
            from God.
                        You hear me as you watch a juggler,
            knowing there is a trick. Magic is done
            by pulling things from sleeves, and preachers learn
            their trade like any entertainer. Now
            we judge not what is said or done, but *how*—
            as though the world, once made, were disregarded
            and progress were refinement of method. Is
            this not the case?
                        Now let me tell a story,
            such as one tells to children who have not
            so firm a grasp of the facts of life as you.
            Suppose . . .
            there were a spirit in the world—like water
            in the soil, and each of you, like plants, were drinking
            constantly, each from the same source, never
            wondering where the moisture came from which

you use to make your body juices. Suppose
that plants could speak and once compared the green
of their leaves, the fragrance of their blooms, and then
questioned and found their roots, in darkness drink-
    ing.

"Why," one might say, "I thought I was a thistle,
a particular thistle, with defects and strengths
and an obligation to arrange things for
myself, to outgrow all the others and
contract for adequate supplies of sun.
But see, it is not so! Though I might seem
to add a cubit to my stature by
main strength, I never really will be so
distinguished: meadows will look level to
a passerby. But at my roots there works
this common sustenance, and now I know
the point of life is not emergence from
the field but drinking from the earth with all
my kind."
        Plants, I am sure you know, will never
formulate such an ethic: they blindly grow,
competitive. But did not Jesus use
the lily as a sign of what a man
should emulate? And even pesky thistles
drink at the springs with lilies. Such distinctions
as men are apt to make between flowers
and weeds appear to be unheeded by
water.
    By God.
        Then is God water?
               Churches,
you know, incline one to believe that God
wears ermine, speaks to certain noblemen,
receives the taxes of the poor and turns
them to affairs of state: perhaps the latest
war with the Spanish or with Lucifer.
One cannot imagine such a Royal God

seeping in soil, can one? In England we
accept the state and God and bad weather all
in a packet handed down like family papers:
dull reading, and like as not in Latin, anyway.

Suppose that God were as simple a thing as water,
available to one and all without a tithe!
Blasphemy?
            Hold!
                    Is it not blasphemy
to imagine otherwise?
                        Suppose that God
spoke English to common men. Suppose He were
your neighbor—or suppose that he were *you*.

The thistle, of course, is not water, but if you
were to squeeze one in a mill I think you'd find
it was three-quarters juice! the pulp would be
a tiny wad of waste.
                    Might not one say
the thistle *was* water, or so nearly so
it needn't brag about the difference?

Might you not say that you *are* God to all
intents and purposes—since who will claim
he drinks less from the earth than a thistle? Who needs
no more of God than plants require of rain?

Of dust we are made. But look at your fleshy arm!
Compare it with the dust upon your feet.
The difference is the spirit. God. That arm
you hold before your face all blue with veins,
pulsing with nerves, solid with flesh, is the arm
of *God*.
            Honor it! And honor your neighbor's, too—
and when you shake his hand or kiss his cheek,
remember that except for pulp the two
of you are a single spirit like the sea
with currents in itself commingling.

Love—
they tell you God is love—love *means* absorption
of individual selves in that single sea,
as grapes must lose their skins before they mix,
ferment, express their souls in wine.
                                        I said
I was not God, implied you would not hear
the words of God from these imperfect, mortal
lips. But I ask now, what *is* God but me?
What are His words but mine? What makes me speak
but spirit? I am no more than you—but as
I am a *man,* I am incarnate God!

You wish to marry God?
Then marry me—or marry any man!
You wish to embrace divinity?
Then take me in your arms, for as you lose
yourself in me you lose the dross that is
not wholly spirit!
                        If God is love, we worship
Him *as* we love, as we distill the essence
from our beings, as we discover soul within
our flesh!
                        Oh, the self is a great weight, a cross
we yearn to be delivered from. Consider
the agony of the waves as they make and make
and then, with such explosions of the heart,
cast off themselves!
                        Embrace the sea. It is
under you, around you, standing by your side!
Let all your individuality
dissolve in its embrace!
                        Listen! Silence!
Do you not hear God speaking as a spring
in a cave, darkly and cool and sweet? That sound
is in your several bosoms! What it prompts—
God bids.

> It trickles wordless till you give
> it tongue. Listen! It wills your growth, just as
> the water wills the thistle. And though it
> speak softly, it contains the strength of the spring
> to burst the stone! Its softest murmur can
> find no expression on receptive lips
> less than a ringing Hallelujah!

(*Shouts of* "Hallelujah!" *and* "Hosanna to the Son of David!" *and* "Hosanna in the highest!" *go up from the crowd. Several people are quaking in ecstasy. During the last part of the sermon there has been an increasing chant of* "Amen!" *and* "Praise God!" *punctuating the phrases, and now this rises to a crest. A knot of people have pushed forward and are on their knees around Clay, who looks down helplessly at them, moved by confusion, fear, and great pity. Women are kissing his clothing. They are pulling his arms, pulling him down into the crowd. Sarah, who has been standing severely apart, turns and leaves, breaking into tears; Seth sees her and leaves with her, comforting her.*)

FIRST MAN: Stop them! Stop them, Mr. Harper! Stop them, oh, the fools!

(*This man is hushed, attacked by others in the crowd.*)

SECOND MAN: Yes, Mr. Harper! Stop them short of blasphemy!

THIRD MAN (*pushing toward him*): You must leave here, sir! Leave!

FIRST MAN (*screams*): Say something to stop this madness!

CLAY (*helplessly, almost incoherently. Shouting dies as he speaks.*): It is . . . It is . . . the spirit . . . that moves them. Who am I to say Nay? God wells in them. . . . I have not the pride. . . . Oh, God, speak for me to their hearts!

FIRST WOMAN: God speaks to me! I feel the torrent swirling away my laggard senses! (*She embraces Clay's knees. Shouting comes up loudly again.*)

THIRD MAN (*by now has reached Clay, is leading him away, with women clinging*): Come, Mr. Harper. You do

not understand what they are saying. They will
harm you. They will damn you and themselves for-
ever!

(*Third Man disappears with Clay, still in the grips of two or
three women. The others hardly notice, at first, that Clay is
gone.*)

FIRST WOMAN: I hear the thunder of the Lord!

SECOND WOMAN: I hear the choir! I hear the music!

THIRD WOMAN: It tingles in my skin! It is a hot breath!

SECOND WOMAN: From the heavens comes a chord!

FIRST WOMAN: Lightning strikes within! Oh Angel of Death!

SECOND WOMAN: Oh feel it! Feel it! The hand of Jesus! Here!
Here!

THIRD WOMAN: My knees! My eyes! The flame that cannot
sear!

WOMEN TOGETHER: Hallelujah! Hosanna to the Son of David!

(*They see, now, that Clay has left and they run after him.*)

FIRST MAN (*shouting after them, running behind*): This is
riot! Get your senses! All of you!

SECOND MAN (*following*): You tread the edge! This spirit is
not true!

FIRST MAN: Silence! Silence, you frothing idiots! Hell has won
the day!

SECOND MAN: Repent! You go too far! Down to your knees!
Pray! Pray!

(*The crowd re-enters, writhing, stretching wild arms, some
rolling on the ground. The chant of "HOLY, HOLY, HOLY"
begins to develop among them and finally dominates all other
sounds: they develop into a fairly orderly column, chanting.
Susannah then emerges leading an ass upon which Clay is
seated, bewildered, defeated, his head on his breast, as women
throw branches, leaves, and clothing before him. They progress,
a seething, ragged column, to a point downstage—men occasionally trying to pull women away, but they, fiercely fighting, rejoin the procession, all to the swelling rhythms of a
chant:*)

HOLY! HOLY! HOLY! LORD GOD OF SABBAOTH!

(*In an eerie hush, when the ass has reached a central, forward position, Clay lifts his face and can be heard saying miserably:*)

CLAY: Lemuel! Oh, Lemuel!

(*Then the chant picks up again and the procession moves on. General Friar, who has watched all coolly from a removed position, nods, just before we lose sight, to his soldiers and they briskly follow the crowd.*

It is dark.)

ACT II

(*A prison cell casts long shadows of its bars. Two soldiers lead Clay with unnecessarily rough movements and hurl him into the cell, where he falls on the straw-littered floor. He gets to his knees and is praying, when the Blind Man enters and comes near, strumming his lute. Clay turns to listen to the Blind Man as he takes a bench outside the cell and sings.*)

BLIND MAN:

> I touched my finger to a honey bee,
>   such a little thing, such a little thing.
> Now I suck my finger, as you can see,
>   for she gave not honey, but a sting.
>
> I touched my finger to a maiden's knee,
>   such a little thing, such a little thing.
> First thing you know, she married me,
>   and she gave not honey, but a sting.
>
> I plucked a cherry from my neighbor's tree,
>   such a little thing, such a little thing.
> Now through the courts he is hounding me,
>   and he gives not honey, but a sting.

I lit a candle so that I could see,
   such a little thing, such a little thing.
Now all Hell's fires are consuming me—
   I reaped not honey, but a sting!

CLAY (*comes to bars*): In London, Blind Man?

BLIND MAN: The blind are everywhere.

CLAY: You sing mournfully, Blind Man. Have you no happier
   tunes?

BLIND MAN: Isn't that, now, the condition of singing! that a
   man in a dungeon would have me sing of feasts, and
   the man at the feast would have me sing of misery.
   It is the lady who sleeps late on a down bed and
   whiles away the day in a lace gown reading letters
   from lovers who would have me sing of deprivation.

CLAY: Ah, Heaven is what we have not!

BLIND MAN: Then I suppose it is the singer's trade to weave
   Heaven, like the emperor's clothes, out of imagination.

CLAY (*amused*): You have sense, Blind Man.

BLIND MAN: Enough sense to be on the street and not in a
   dungeon. What did you steal?

CLAY: I am charged with blasphemy.

BLIND MAN: Then you stole divinity, which is an impractical
   kind of thieving, like ransacking your own empty
   cupboard, as you cannot eat or wear what you steal.

CLAY: Wait! You leap ahead like a judge of the Star Chamber.
   I am charged; I am not convicted. I set off a crowd
   with a sermon. It seems to me they were the blas-
   phemers. My crime was not stopping what the spirit
   moved them to do.

BLIND MAN: A sad case. Like that of my friend who dropped
   a coal in his house. With his dying breath he held the
   rafters accountable for falling on him. (*Sings:*)

A candle in the straw, a candle in the straw,
   makes a pretty golden light.
A kitten in the yarn, a kitten in the yarn,
   makes a very funny sight.

A crevice in the dike, a crevice in the dike,
        makes a trickle all the night.

A little candle in the straw,
    a little crevice in the dike,
        a little kitten in the yarn,
            a little loving in the barn,
                a little trifling with the law,
these little things,
such little things,
alike . . .

a little sparring with a claw,
    a little leaning on a spike,
        a little tangling of the yarn,
            a little warming of the barn,
                a little picking at a flaw,
such little things
so terribly
strike!

A crevice in the dike, a crevice in the dike,
        makes a trickle all the night.
A kitten in the yarn, a kitten in the yarn,
        makes a very funny sight.
A candle in the straw, a candle in the straw,
        makes a fearful golden light!

(*Our vision of him fades as he sings and we see General Friar's official desk, Seth standing, slamming his hand on it for emphasis.*)

SETH: That matters not to me! I grant he may
        have behaved so like an ass one could not tell
        the rider from the ridden. But my point
        is that this Parliament is not fit judge.
        They have, since tasting blood in a regicide,
        been wild as dogs upon the moors. They will
        be barbarous to be consistent. All
        they bring to bear will be irrelevant.

FRIAR (*unruffled*): Speaking of dogs on moors . . .

SETH: I know. You think the Seekers are as wild. . . .

FRIAR: Exactly. I care less about Clay Harper
        than curing England of the whole disease. . . .

SETH: Cure it of Cromwell, too, then, General Friar. . . .

FRIAR: I'll not hear treason, Mr. Cartwright!

SETH: Treason or not—the principle is the same:
        no law or lawlessness should be allowed
        that stems from human traffic with the divine;
        once people claim to God's authority,
        then reason, justice, mercy, all are smothered—
        and such you get, combining church and state.

FRIAR (*figuring*): Suppose I granted Harper a parole—
        a day or two of freedom. What would he do?

SETH: I think he'd go to Lemuel, hoping
        for his forgiveness. . . .

FRIAR: Would he get it?

SETH: I
        am no oracle of Lemuel's mind! . . . Well,
        no. I believe he wouldn't. Lemuel
        is firm, once he's convinced. He was appalled
        at what occurred at Bristol. . . .

FRIAR: But he let
        Harper go on with it!

SETH: Oh, how he tried
        to stop him before he began!

FRIAR: But they are friends?

SETH: They are both men of trust and loyalty.

FRIAR (*to himself*): I think, perhaps, that this is worth the
        risk. . . .

SETH: You mean to trap them in a new alliance?

FRIAR: Oh . . . "trap them" . . . no. . . .

SETH: You needn't play your politics with me.
        I *couldn't* spoil your plot. Neither of them
        cares in the least for my advice. What's more—
        so you may make a proper estimate
        of whom you are confronting—neither would
        be swayed by the threat of danger, anyway.

If they ally, if Lemuel forgives,
his act will be on principle. I think
on principle he'll choose *not* to forgive.
FRIAR: Then simple honesty suggests I should
provide him with a choice. If he's inclined
to involve himself, the Seekers as a group,
in Harper's case . . . *I* should not bar the way.
SETH (*in disgust, leaving*): General, you can't trick such integrity!

(*We see the square, where a crowd of people swirl in like sparrows settling on a fence. First Woman, the center of attention, sits. The others crowd her, some ardently, some curiously.*)

SECOND WOMAN: She has a relic of him!
THIRD WOMAN: What is it? What is it?
FIRST WOMAN (*smugly*): A piece of his shirt.
THIRD WOMAN (*admiringly*): You tore it off his back?
FIRST MAN: What lunacy!
FIRST WOMAN: No. Susannah Potter sold it me.
SECOND MAN: Are you turned bloody Catholics?
FIRST WOMAN: Things have to start somehow. If he's a saint,
you'll all be envious.
THIRD MAN: And Susannah Potter, I daresay, will be rich!

(*Clarence approaches the square and is spotted by the people.*)

FIRST MAN: Mr. Potter!
CLARENCE: Yes?
FIRST MAN: Were you in London for the trial of Clay Harper?
CLARENCE: Yes.
THIRD WOMAN (*sentimentally*): Were they merciful?
CLARENCE: Indeed! Oh, I would say that mercy rose
like a dove in Parliament's collective breast.
They were most merciful. He has been sentenced—
but not to die. They were most merciful.
He is to sit in the pillory at Westminster
for two hours. But that is not death. They spared
him death. He is to be whipped through the streets

from Westminster to the Old Exchange and there
sit with his head in the pillory two hours more.
Death, however, is not for him. He will
be stigmatized upon the forehead with
a branding iron, a B for blasphemer,
and then be brought back to this city on
an ass, but this time riding backwards, wearing
a parchment listing all his crimes and in
our public square he will be whipped again,
and then they mercifully prescribe his tongue
be bored with a hot iron. They denied him death.
And then to Bridewell where by day he labors,
by night confined to solitary cell,
debarred the use of pen and paper, for,
I gather, Parliament would not be plagued
with his odes of gratitude for granting him
his life.

(*This speech has been punctuated with gasps and shudders.
Now the people fall silent; after a pause:*)

FIRST WOMAN: Where is he now?
CLARENCE: In a cell in the Palace Yard, where he entertains
such visitors and followers who still
remember their sometime savior.
SECOND WOMAN: We remember and pray for him, Mr. Potter.
CLARENCE: Oh, prayers, I'm sure, are very practical.
THIRD MAN: What can we do for him?
CLARENCE: Oh, nothing, nothing. You have done enough.

(*We return to the cell, where Susannah stands outside the bars,
Clay sitting on a bench inside.*)

SUSANNAH (*cheerfully*): You had them, several times. I nearly
laughed
to see their wigs ride up on their foreheads.
They pulled their chins and scratched their stomachs
thus.
"Kaf! Kaf! Do you regard yourself, Mr. Harper, as
the Son of God?"

> "I do," says you, "for all
> men are his sons. You are yourself the son
> of God."
>   He doubles back and pushes up
> his glasses, so. "But are you, well, the *spec*ial
> anointed Son?"
>   "Why, no," you say, as though
> shaming his ignorance. "Christ is that special
> Son."
>   "But," says he, "are you said Jesus Christ?"
> "Why, Christ is *in* men—and in you yourself!"
> I swear, I nearly died.

CLAY (*gently ironic*):   And so did I.

SUSANNAH (*sighing*): It *was* a mess, indeed. A fizzle, I
would say. But you were beautiful in court.

CLAY: Ah, you are sweet to say so!

SUSANNAH: Sweet?

CLAY: Indeed,
I love you for your honesty, your fist
of sense, your leather, loving heart. You are
my consolation. . . .

SUSANNAH: Clay . . . I would be more . . .
Clay, losing a tongue, you lose not everything. . . .

CLAY (*missing her point*): I will not lose my tongue. The jailer,
              who
savors such information, says the iron
they use to bore a tongue is just about
the thickness of a quill. The sore will heal,
and I will have my tongue.

SUSANNAH: Where will you go?
When healed, and finally free, where will you go?

CLAY: To Sarah. To my farm. Among the sins
religion led me to was that of leaving.
Heroic acts, you see, sometimes may be
the shining outcome of dark causes. I
must see if I am hero now enough
to resign myself to fatherhood. I will

                    not say I ran from regularity—
                    but stomachs that would not stay full and dear
                    faces that looked to me as the source of solace
                    were among the things I left—whatever I
                    was running to or from.
SUSANNAH: But, Clay—four years!
CLAY: Four years. Those babes are now in school, and Sarah—
                    I left a sturdy, brown, and plucky girl.
                    You've seen her now: a woman thin with care,
                    her round jaw set unnaturally in the square
                    hand of the fatherhood she assumed.
                    She said she understood. Most softly did
                    she go about the house arranging new
                    ideas in her head. She said she would
                    not interfere in my love affair with God. . . .
SUSANNAH: But now she would! Oh, she is not the same!
                    We leave the lives that we have lived, as spirits
                    depart from bodies flaking in decay.
                    Nothing can be again just what it was. . . .
CLAY (*hesitantly*): I have to follow what I know is right. . . .
SUSANNAH: Know? Know? How can you know up here in your
                    head
                    when your heart denies the wisdom of your skull?
                    I believe in what my under organs tell me.
                    Bellies have no imagination.
CLAY: I
                    have relied too long on unintellectual promptings!
SUSANNAH: You were not wrong! Please, Clay, you can't believe
                    the soldiers!
CLAY: Someone was wrong! The event was hid-
                                                            eous!
SUSANNAH: Are you Aladdin, fearful of the djinni
                    you conjured up yourself? The spirit raised
                    in those dear folk was real: now ride its crest—
                    or you'll be tumbled under, Clay. . . .
CLAY (*standing, taking bars in his hands*):   Oh, how?
SUSANNAH (*taking his hands*): In love.

You named it many times. Now speak to it—
and take up its warm hands: this is the love
you named. Is love a word in the Bible, only?

(*She draws his hands to her and puts them on her breasts; Clay
stands frozen in confusion.*)

Feel it as real as my flesh! Ah, do not jump
away! Here is a balm to heal the scourging. . . .
CLAY: Is this the djinni I have raised?
SUSANNAH (*pulling herself closer, lifting her lips through the
bars*):
Such giants can do wonders once released. . . .
Oh, hold me, Clay, with that firm arm that holds
my soul. Are souls and flesh not rolled together
in our brief incarnation?
CLAY (*embracing her through the bars, kisses her—then rests
his head on the bars in despair*): The thought
. . . of branding, boring . . .
the hiss of moisture on my tongue . . .
I twinge and cry for easing. . . .
SUSANNAH: None of us has resources all alone
to bear our body's pain without its love. . . .
CLAY (*drops his arms and turns from her, reproving himself*):
Foh! Foh! What *are* we, to be clinging here
like guilty youngsters stealing a hug in hiding?
SUSANNAH (*reaching through, holding his arms*):
What are we, if on this whirling earth we may
not steal a human hug or two for comfort?
CLAY (*turns again, taking her hands in his, but holding them
gently away*):
Susannah, no.
I do it for fear—I do it whimpering!
My love for you is sullied by our kiss. . . .
SUSANNAH: Living is but brief kissing—then we go. . . .
CLAY: Oh, no: I see, now, clearly—how I failed—
my deadly confusion in the fervid days
that brought me to this cell, this covert moment.

       I see a thousand blunted inclinations
       which asked for love—of me, myself, of Clay. . . .
SUSANNAH: We all want love. . . .
CLAY: I grant, there's nothing wrong
       with wanting love—but I have wanted, wanted
       and yet deceived myself. . . .
SUSANNAH: Oh, don't we all?
CLAY: The sin is not the self-deception . . . but . . .
       Susannah, I hated that mob—I think I must have—
       except as I might bring them to loving Clay.
SUSANNAH: Such love is their redemption. . . .
CLAY: But I used God to get their love, as a rapist
       might use a knife. And that is blasphemy!
       I spoiled the innocents, each soul divine,
       for a brute lust; and that is blasphemy!
       I sought to dominate by the worst of tricks:
       renunciation of power; I cloaked myself
       in inspiration. And that is blasphemy!
       In short—and dear Susannah, you must know
       that I mean not to hurt you—when I find
       you here as a fruit, wantonly, absently plucked,
       and I have no appetite, I see that I
       have all unknowing been luxurious
       with fruits too precious for these profane hands—
       and that is blasphemy!
SUSANNAH: Oh, Clay—the sins
       we commit in sleep must be forgiven us!
       Perhaps such moral thoughts will help you bear
       that sizzling B that Parliament imprints
       upon a forehead. If so, accept such guilt—
       but, in self-castigation, do not lie. . . .
CLAY (*dropping her hands, sitting*): I'm only learning to speak
         truth. . . .
SUSANNAH: The truth of Lemuel—that rips the heart!
       You cannot deny me, Clay! Abandon all,
       but do not deny the only one who loves you!
       Lemuel rejects you; Sarah has not been seen.

Clay, I will take up London lodgings, wait
out your term, haunt Bridewell as a beggar. . . .
Oh, make my nest your world, dear Clay! The last
Christ never found that love which makes the flesh
tolerable to spirit. . . .

CLAY: Quiet, Susannah.
You have not listened, and now grow desperate. . . .
You must, dear, understand. Go home to Bristol.
Live out the arid days in thought and learn
that single kiss we shared is a kind of sore.
Regain your calm. . . .

SUSANNAH: Sore? Oh, I have sores
streaming for want of your care. Blood on the moon!
and the day dark! and this austere God would die!

CLAY: Peace, Susannah. Home. You must be cared for.
Susannah, look to Heaven—there our marriage
will be with the soul of the world and one another.

SUSANNAH: Die, then, divinity, lesser thing than man!
I may not love? I will teach myself to fear. . . .
But you are mine! They keep you here for me!

(*A look of grim distraction has come over her, and she gropes
backwards from the cell staring at Clay with growing horror.
He reaches for her in concern and calls her name, but she turns
and runs off with a kind of guttural scream. After a moment of
darkness we see the interior of the Potter home in Bristol. Seth
is seated, waiting. Clarence comes in quietly from the back
room, closing the door after him.*)

CLARENCE: She is sleeping.

SETH: Good. Three days she has not slept.
Those great eyes staring as the horses ran,
the carriage swaying, and she swaying as though
with babe in arms, murmuring hymns and phrases
as one possessed. . . .

CLARENCE: She *is* possessed. Or, rather,
dispossessed, I think, of Clay. You found
her on the street, you say?

SETH: On London Bridge.
    Hair snarled, cloak filthy—I thought that she was
        drunk.
    It took main strength to get her home, where Sarah
        cleaned her and fed her. Who would think Susan-
        nah . . . ?

CLARENCE: Ah, love is harder on her than religion.
    But she'll come round. She's had such fits before,
    and comes to hug me to her like a doll
    until her sense returns. She wants a child.

SETH: You are tolerant, Clarence.

CLARENCE: I am small. Had we
    but children. . . . Well, no matter. Her lusty gift
    for life sometimes exceeds life's boundaries—
    but I would not have her other. What news
    is there of Clay?

SETH: He's free—two days parole.

CLARENCE: The guile of General Friar?

SETH: Exactly. He
    was heading straight for Sussex where Lemuel
    is preaching, the General's spies close following
    to see if Lemuel will take him in.

CLARENCE: Our people there might hide him, might they not?

SETH: Of course! He has friends all over England, but
    he will return. He promised to return.

CLARENCE: On principle! At that point Clay and I
    part company. I never trust a man
    who acts on principle.

SETH: It's not good business.

CLARENCE: Cowardice, anger, lust, hate, fear, disgust—
    or any motivation I understand
    I will learn to get along with. But principle!
    A man might turn his mother over to lawyers
    on principle! There's no predicting what
    abstractions might incline a man to do.

SETH: No gypsy takes advice from her tea leaves.

CLARENCE: Just so! Beware the man who takes his notions
    seriously. Sarah is here in Bristol with you?

SETH: Sarah has gone to Sussex, too. She hopes
            to persuade Lemuel to take Clay's part with Crom-
                well. . . .
CLARENCE: Just what the General wants!
SETH: No danger. Those
            three are the most bull-headed in this land
            of stubbornness.
CLARENCE: Just so! Principles, you see.
            Let's have a pint and toast their principles.

(*A meeting hall is discovered, a clapboard building with rows
of benches and a raised platform at one end. Lemuel and Sarah
are alone on the platform, a lamp burning on a speaker's table.
Lemuel is defending himself.*)

LEMUEL: I heard the sermon. Yes. He spoke of releasing
            a spirit working in the earth. I saw
            what I had never seen before: that spirit
            works. Aye, it works! But Sarah, sometimes it is
            the surge of darkness pulsing from the earth,
            demonic spirit of the heart unleashed!
SARAH (*cautiously, as though agreeing*):
            He was a witch, then, stirring Satanic powers?
LEMUEL: A witch solicits Satan with conscious skill.
            Clay is no witch. I doubt that anyone
            with a brew of balderdash can summon Satan.
            Ah, no! He comes to those like Clay, inspired,
            they think, with good—and so aroused, with people
            so aroused, evil becomes its own crusade.
            Tyrants—that is, the worst of them—believe
            they slay for God; their armies chant their names
            as names of saviors. Sarah, we were in
            the fearful presence of incarnate Evil.
SARAH: So may be grateful Parliament has put
            him safely sealed into an iron tomb?
LEMUEL: There's accusation in your voice. Am I
            the stone upon the tomb wherein he lies?
SARAH: Have you the power to roll that stone away?

LEMUEL: You want that, do you? Want him out again
and all his rabid women clamoring after?
SARAH: I find it odd that you should side with Parliament.
LEMUEL: They are against fanatics. So am I.
They are against subversion. So am I.
They are against the seizure of power by
ambitious individuals, and so
am I!
SARAH: Oh, you and Cromwell *do* see eye to eye.
LEMUEL: On some things, yes. I've talked with him about
perversions leaders are sometimes subject to.
I implored him *not* to take upon himself
the crown he might easily have—and this is why:
a person dies, but principles endure.
A nation, or a small dissenting sect,
must have a firm authority to last:
but if that rule depends upon a man,
all dies with him. The people left behind
are like a rich man's children raised without
a trade, dependent, liable to dissolve.
I want my flock to be so trained that they
will never miss their shepherd. Clay confused
himself with leadership—and so was jailed.
SARAH: But you *could* get him off, since you have
access to Cromwell, and his confidence . . . ?
LEMUEL: I have more friends than Clay. . . .
Now think! You know how practical it is
(leave ethics out) to have your word, your yea
or nay, dependable. So I have Cromwell's
good faith: in these times that is like a license.
Thousands of Seekers suffer if I strain
his trust in me.
SARAH: A strain—to plead for Clay?
LEMUEL: Of course it is! He is a blasphemer!
For all I know, he'd do it straight again!
And innocence would rot because I would
have wasted, then, the means to set it free!

SARAH: And you cannot forgive a blasphemer?

LEMUEL: As a man of God, I must defend God's name.

SARAH (*pretending relief*): I came, Lemuel, thinking that I might
      console you for the loss of a dear friend,
      misunderstood. I see that you, like I,
      could grieve but in hypocrisy. . . .

LEMUEL: I grieve, Sarah,
      I grieve.

SARAH: Oh, so do I! And yet I must
      confess to a kind of pride. He would have God,
      would he? He has Him now—and may his soul
      (in his cell) be comforted!

LEMUEL: A kind of pride?

SARAH: That such rewards come to those blessed and called.
      That I, so cast aside for finer things,
      should have, at least, the freedom of the streets. . . .

LEMUEL: Insipid woman! His cell is far beyond
      such comforts as you find in winning out!

SARAH: But blasphemy!

LEMUEL: Indifference is blasphemy!
      Your housewife calm is unholier than Hell!

SARAH: Ah, then! You think his jailing unjust, but for
      sheer jealousy would keep him there?

LEMUEL: For jealousy?

SARAH: I must confess a strain of jealousy
      induces *me* to sufferance of his loss.

LEMUEL: His kingdom is not of this earth.

SARAH: Ah, you,
      like I do, think him, then, divine—and fear
      his rod! In fact, I am quite happy to
      have judgment fall on him from hands I hate.
      I feel myself absolved, and so must you.

LEMUEL: What do you *make* of me, woman?

SARAH (*suddenly facing him squarely*):   To be plain,
      until I heard that sermon I resented
      the call that took him from me. But there, Clay
      was radiant with a spirit so sublime

I felt my pettiness, my womanish sniveling,
fall from me like a husk—and I was clean!
LEMUEL (*seeing how she has played upon him*): Ah!
SARAH: I came to ask you for forgiveness for
my schemes, my accusations, smallness of heart—
but here I find an adamantine soul
so blind with justice that it cannot love
a man whose crime is his excess of virtue.
You refuse to dress the wound where spirit burst
the skin because it could not stay confined!

(*People are filing into the hall, taking benches for a meeting. They are not, of course, the crowd we know from Bristol. Sarah sees them and, with a hard stare at Lemuel, turns to leave, stepping off the platform. Lemuel stops her with his voice.*)

LEMUEL: The times, not I, have put the Bible and
the law in public hands—and sacred things
must suffer public uses.
SARAH: I thought you were
his friend, that you might help—because you loved
him.

(*She starts to go. The hall is now nearly full, but Lemuel seems oblivious to the others, even of Sarah. As he speaks she stops, and the people listen attentively.*)

LEMUEL: God! God! Must thus all the ideals which man
has wrought so painfully lose their enforcement—
when jaws must close on personality?
Ah, each particular is an exception,
and in a moment laws of a century's making
are disassembled to accommodate
the fellow everybody loves. The few
ideals that man has shaped extend like a pier,
a pitiful, wobbling pier, into the black
wide sea of ignorance, and even that pier
is dismantled in a trice when someone needs
a slat for opportunity! Christ taught
forgiveness: I forgive the thief for thieving—

but I lock him up! I do not blame the mad
for idiocy—but I approve of Bedlam!
Oh, you cry, "Consider circumstances,
consider who he is, consider love . . .
consider *anything*, but do not make
the law apply to Clay!" Ah, but it must!
like the wind that knows no cases—or law itself—
and, Sarah, *man* himself—will wither away!

(*Sarah turns silently and works her way through the gathering.
As she goes, there are shouts from the crowd, and individuals
gesture scornfully at Sarah, making way for her with contempt.*)

FIRST MAN: Aye, Mr. Thomas! We must uphold the law!

SECOND MAN: Accept the fact! You're married to a madman,
lady!

FIRST WOMAN: And didn't he look pretty in the pillory!

SECOND WOMAN (*laughing*): With half a melon squashed upon
his head!

THIRD MAN: Now, that was cruel.

FIRST MAN: They were wrong to revile him so—but let him
have

the proper punishment of law.

(*Sarah leaves, suddenly weeping. Lemuel, on the platform, is
disturbed.*)

LEMUEL: What's this you say? The crowd was torturing him?

(*But Clay himself enters at the far end of the hall. Lemuel falls
silent, and the crowd, hushing, follows his gaze to Clay. He
walks humbly among them to stand below Lemuel, who glares
down at him from the platform.*)

CLAY: Lemuel . . .

LEMUEL: This is no place, Clay. . . .

CLAY: I do not come begging, Lemuel.

LEMUEL: Oh no?
Perhaps, then, with terms? What must I do to be
anointed as a disciple?

CLAY: Oh, Lemuel!
What turn has brought you down to peevishness?

LEMUEL: Peevishness! This man says "peevishness!"
He corrupts the word of God, divides the movement,
elects himself a Christ, makes all the Seekers
the butt of public indignation—and then finds
placidity to turn and call me *peevish!*

SECOND WOMAN: Who sprung you from the jail, Mr. Harper?

THIRD MAN: He walks on water, don't you know? He trotted
right across the Palace moat!

LEMUEL: Silence those foul tongues!

CLAY: Lemuel, I would kiss your hand. . . . I want
you *not* to intercede for me: I know
I must endure the dismal consequence
of extravagance. I would not taint the cause
of the Seekers by attaching my bad name
to your good work. And, Lemuel, I know
I have offended you in speaking, that day,
against your wise advice. But let me kiss
your hand to symbolize how I did all
in pure misguided love, to symbolize
that you can understand me and forgive. . . .

(Clay reaches for his hand, but Lemuel jerks it away and stares in rage down at Clay. Finally, while Clay stands there questioningly, Lemuel deliberately extends his foot for Clay to kiss. Clay drops to his knees in shock, dismay, and prayer. Lemuel steps down from the platform and stalks off, passing through the crowd, people making way for him in awe. After a moment of silence:)

SECOND WOMAN: Aye! Kiss *that!* Kiss his foot!

FIRST MAN *(sanctimoniously)*: Ah, Mr. Harper, blasphemy
even God will not forgive.

(We move to General Friar in the Bristol public square with Seth and Clarence following him in pleading attitudes.)

SETH: At least you must protect him from the mob!

FRIAR: Ah, the angry investors in a failing enterprise!

CLARENCE: Your soldiers, come from London with you, say
        they were not needed there to force him back
        to his cell after his parole: his own
        dear converts drove him there. . . .
SETH: And stormed the bars with stones! with clubs!
FRIAR: Are you surprised? They have democracy
        in their religion. This means that a man
        has no more history than that of his last act.
CLARENCE: I would not think they had such passion in them!
FRIAR: You saw them love him, did you not?
CLARENCE: Of course,
        all this was London. The soldiers say that when
        he was branded with that smoking B the crowd
        cheered on the executioner as though
        he were an expert juggler in a show.
        But tomorrow, here in Bristol. . . . Clay is loved
        in Bristol. . . .
FRIAR (*calmly*):   It will be much worse in Bristol.
SETH: You *know* this! Then you can restrain them here!
FRIAR: I will restrain them just as he restrained
        insanity that might consume us all!

(*Back in London, we are inside Clay's cell. Sarah is being admitted by a soldier for a visit. She stands just inside the door, which the soldier locks behind her. The soldier leaves. Clay, who has been sitting on a bench, rises and looks at her tensely, questioningly. His forehead is scarred with the still fresh brand of a B.*)

CLAY: I . . . I didn't expect you to visit. . . .
        Sarah, I've failed you so. . . .
SARAH: No, Clay, wait. I want to say this first . . .
        there is so much that you don't know. You see . . .
        I am the one to make apology.
        At your sermon at Bristol, I . . .
        Clay, I was moved. You spoke . . .
CLAY: You cried and left!

SARAH: I know. You spoke so simply
              to my heart I felt . . . nude in the crowd. I ran
              because I couldn't stand myself—laid bare. . . .

CLAY (*puzzled*): There were no accusations in my sermon.

SARAH: No, no! I don't mean that! But, Clay, I was
              ashamed to think that I had hoped to stop you!

CLAY: Oh, that *some*one had stopped me. . . .

SARAH: No, Clay! No! Don't believe that. Clay, your voice
              ran limpid as a mountain brook just sprung
              from the granite groin of truth itself. Oh, Clay,
              how I was humbled, realizing I
              was married not to Clay, a man who snorts
              in his sleep unless he's on his side, a man
              who wears his elbows out too soon, a man
              who wants his meat boiled till it's like a rag—
              but married to the splendid tongue of God!
              You are a great man, darling. This I saw.

CLAY (*in gratitude goes to her, kisses her*):
              Oh, Sarah, you are probably wrong—but how
              welcome, these days, is any such illusion!

(*They walk lovingly to the bench and sit. Sarah gently caresses
his branded forehead.*)

SARAH: Be sure to wash this new wound often, sweet.

CLAY: It will not ever, from my washing, wash away.
              Sarah, how are the boys? How big they must
              have grown to be!

SARAH: They're with me, here in London,
              and you can guess how glad they are to miss
              their school. James is a little man. . . .

CLAY: At nine!
              I guess he's had to be. And William is
              in school now, too. Why, he was just a baby,
              a jabbering child of three when I left home.

SARAH: He has a pet crow he calls Papa Clay—
              I guess because it squawks so eloquently!

CLAY: You've told them, then . . . about me?

SARAH: Jamey remembers
the games you played: he has that bird nest, still,
you brought him from the field—with three blue eggs.
And he tells William how their father went
to work for God. I haven't talked about you. . . .

CLAY: No need, of course, to make them miss me more. . . .

SARAH (*gently critical*): I haven't *known* about you, Clay, until . . .

CLAY: How cruel I was!

SARAH: It was a cruel, great gesture—
to leave, so blinded by the light, to be
compelled, as carried by a wave so tall
as to tumble over all the good and bad
of ordinary lives. Cruel—like a saint!

CLAY: Or like a coward? Vain for notice, selfish . . .

SARAH: Oh, Clay, dear, don't lie here in jail bedeviled
by some eternal mouse of shame in the walls,
tracing nobility to dirty roots.
What does it matter where things start? On this
earth all good things begin in soil. Why must
you smutch the blossom with the dirt it left?
Don't all of us have things we run from, and
isn't what matters where and how we run?
If cowardice was in you, so was courage.
It is not easy, so to fling yourself,
sustained by nothing but some sense of truth. . . .

CLAY: What if . . . Sarah . . .

SARAH: Yes?

CLAY: How can I say it? Oh, that mouse of shame
worries about the walls convincingly!
But we must name our weakness to ourselves
to learn to live with what we are. Sarah,
suppose I, ignorantly, in my preaching . . .
were reaching for a love . . . a carnal love
I did not know I wanted, that these people . . .
women, I mean . . . responded not to God. . . .
Oh, this is dreadful . . . and I had not seen it. . . .

SARAH: I tried to tell you this. . . .

CLAY: I think you did—but I was in a trance,
obviously dreaming—until they put me here.

SARAH: Father and I have talked about it. You know
he has a way of cutting into things. . . .

CLAY: Oh, yes, Seth cuts—but cuts with truest steel!

SARAH: He said these women have a sentiment
below the waist they take to be divine.
He can't approve of muddling up our terms—
our language is, with all our honest effort,
a flimsy enough way of labeling the world,
and feelings wrongly named can turn perverse
and double back upon themselves in anger.

CLAY: Yes, yes! This is what I fear!

SARAH: Well, I was jealous, too. To sacrifice
a home to God is not the same as suffering
a husband gone to sing the ladies love songs!

CLAY: I know, Sarah, I know! I see this now. . . .

SARAH: But Father has a sense of humor, too.
You know, he says, the feeling *is* divine—
and God knows how God operates. He'd rather
see people writhing with an honest instinct
than think the spooks had got them on the ground.
Some notions, maybe, need disguising if
they walk upon the public thoroughfare.
And since I heard that sermon, Clay, I've been
more tolerant of love songs—and of you.
Whatever it was you gave that crowd was good!
The issue, the issue, is what we must judge:
the makings are in all good work transformed.

CLAY (*bitterly*): The issue was this branding with a B!

SARAH: Oh, Clay—we don't judge goodness by success;
or, rather, never know when we've succeeded.
The heart responds in the doing—does it not?
Our pulse informs us—and we think we're right.

CLAY (*puts his head on her lap*): Our pulses contradict themselves, my sweet—

but I believe you, since I need you now,
your hand in my hair, on my cheek, to close my eyes
and dream of days before I heard a sermon.

SARAH (*caresses him, sings*) :

The house is dark, the cattle still,
the wind now sleeps behind the hill.
Does Father tread upon the sill?
No, Father treads not, never will—
　　Oh lee elai oh lullaby.

The sheep are restless in their pen.
Hush, child, and count from one to ten.
Will Father ever come again?
No, he has duties fit for men.
　　Oh lee elai oh lullaby.

The fire is low, the window black.
The moon hangs skull-like in the tree.
The wind can find a tiny crack,
but close your eyes, you will not see.
Why, what means he for you and me?
That we forgive—and let him be.
　　Oh lee elai oh lullaby.

I had a dog, now I have none.
And thus you grow to manhood, son.
What shall I do when growing's done?
Why, kiss and grieve and leave someone.
　　Oh lee elai oh lullaby.

I hear a call outside the door.
Oh, sleep and you will hear no more.
I must go see; I must explore.
I will return. . . .
　　　　　　So Father swore.
　　Oh lee elai oh lullaby.

(*They disappear gradually as she finishes the song. In total
darkness we hear angry noises of the crowd, with individual
shouts of such things as:*)

BLASPHEMER!
HA! BEHOLD THE SON OF DAVID NOW!
WILL GOD NOT HELP THE KING OF ZION?
HE RIDES THE ASS LIKE A STRAW-STUFFED
 DUMMY!

(*As these shouts diminish, we see the interior of the Potter home. Clarence is looking fearfully out the window. Susannah stands aside in abstracted serenity. There is a desperate banging on the door. Clarence seizes a fire-poker for protection and goes to the door, putting his hand on the bar.*)

CLARENCE: Who is it?
LEMUEL: Lemuel Thomas, Clarence! Let me in!

(*Clarence cautiously unbars the door. Lemuel bursts in and Clarence replaces the bar.*)

LEMUEL: We must stop them! They are mad wolves!
CLARENCE: Dear me! I don't know how one stops mad wolves!
LEMUEL (*crosses to Susannah and embraces her, his head falling on her shoulder*):
      Oh, what have I done, Susannah? Whom have I condemned?
SUSANNAH (*not returning embrace, distantly*):
      If God walked here, He would be struck to earth.
      Who can behold the face of fire and live?
      It is ordained that God must walk—and fall!
LEMUEL (*turning away, going to bench*):
      Not God! Not God, you poor impassioned woman!
      My anguish is, I have condemned my friend!
      To see the faces of those people! I feel
      a crumbling in me of cliffs eaten under
      as grimacing they go, eyes round, tense grinning,
      the grin of hate, of pleasure in the hurting,
      skipping, with poles, like children hurrying to bonfires!
SUSANNAH: You fear the spirit, Lemuel!
LEMUEL: And do you not?
      Are you here gloating in your hut, your senses lost?

SUSANNAH: I do not fear the spirit. The spirit is good.

LEMUEL: Spirit? Tormenting madness! Susannah, you
pretend great love for Clay. This blaze burns hot
to destroy him totally—and you, you say
you do not fear the spirit! Oh, I've been heartless—
but this grim aspect of yours makes me seem kind!

CLARENCE: Indeed, Lemuel, she has been strange this past
week.

SUSANNAH (*sweeps her arm imperiously, a hard, distant gaze in
her eyes*):
Blood dims the moon; the day is dark by day.
Who has an ear, why, let him hear: the air
shouts with the orchestras of angels—we
will be shattered like the vessels of the potters,
earth quakes, hail falls, the sun is black as sackcloth!
The spirit moves that God must die by the sword!
Lemuel, be serene—and prepare your heart!

CLARENCE: You see, she seems to wobble with a sickness. . . .

SUSANNAH: He shall ascend! No stone can seal his tomb!
The clouds explode with glory, and night shall close
warm as death about us: Jerusalem is prepared
like a bride for the bridegroom. The holocaust
streams golden in the sky like a marriage bed!
I feel death closing, closing, and shall sink
my head upon the breast of God; his arms
shall fold me to him and his kiss shall close
my lips in that last night's fast embracing!

(*She begins shaking with a soft tremor that soon convulses her,
causing her to collapse to the floor, still trembling. Clarence
runs to hold her. Lemuel goes to the door, horror-struck. He
opens it and looks out.*)

LEMUEL: You must keep her here. . . .

SUSANNAH: Do not oppose the spirit! God must be slain!

LEMUEL: I will try to turn their blows from Clay.

(*He is going out as the scene fades. We see a hill. A man runs
up it, stops at the top, and looks beyond. Another man runs on,*

stops further back. Another. Another. The shouting of the crowd can be heard in the distance.)

SECOND MAN: Can you see him?

FIRST MAN: He bleeds! He bleeds most grievously!

THIRD MAN: Are they whipping him still?

FIRST MAN: The executioner appears to spare his blows, to strike
the ground as often as his back. But the people!
Oh! Oh!

SECOND MAN: Like apes! Like very apes! What do they do?

FIRST MAN: They stone him! They prod him with sticks! Oh!
Oh! A boy who has not got his growth, all gangly
like a skeleton, is making after him with a pitchfork,
a very devil!

SECOND MAN (*runs to top of hill*): I cannot bear to see or not
to see!

THIRD MAN: The women? Do the women stone him?

FIRST MAN: The women are the cruelest of the crowd. They
press near, with great needles!

(Suddenly the crowd offstage is silenced.)

THIRD MAN: What is it? What do they do?

SECOND MAN: Someone, a man, opposes them. He stands before them, arms outstretched.

(Crowd noise up again.)

FIRST MAN: They strike him! They bear him down!

SECOND MAN: It is Mr. Thomas! It is Lemuel Thomas they
strike!

FIRST MAN: He stands again! Oh, they are coming round!

*(After a moment a silent procession comes around the side of
the hill, people with sticks and pitchforks, but now subdued, an
executioner in a black mask, soldiers, an ass, with Lemuel, in
a bloody shirt, leading it. Clay is riding, his back bare, scored,
and bleeding. He is facing backwards. Around his neck is a
piece of parchment with his crimes listed on it. The people*

following are now hushed and reverent. Seth and Sarah, she on his arm, are part of the crowd. As Clay lifts his head slightly he sees Sarah.)

CLAY: Stop a moment, Lemuel.

(*Lemuel stops, and Seth breaks a way through the crowd, leading Sarah. Clay's hands are tied, so he cannot get off, but he bends to kiss Sarah and she embraces him tearfully. The executioner indicates that Lemuel should proceed, so he does, and the procession moves ahead, leaving Seth and Sarah standing still among them. They reach the square, where a platform is raised and, on it, a brazier of smoking coals standing ready with a rod sticking out of it. Soldiers help Clay from the ass and lead it off. He lifts his chin for attention and a hush surrounds him.*)

CLAY: While I have tongue, I would give tongue once more
        to certain notions wincing with the pain
        behind this branded brow. A holiday,
        a holy day, is this—that brings the butchers
        from stalls, the blacksmiths from their forges, to see
        such curious application of their art.
        I must confess you put me out of temper
        by some gratuitous blows administered
        spontaneously in the spirit of the day.
        Those blows, I mean, on Lemuel Thomas, who
        shares nothing of my guilt—and need not share
        this wild reward, your angry vindication.
        I do not hate you for your blows on me:
        you taught me much. There is much good in you,
        and you, as I, make errors born of good.
        The times have put new life in us and new
        responsibility: we have to learn
        to harness such spurts of power. And if we
        put out our tongues to taste new things, we may
        be burned . . . (*Murmur of uncomfortable laughter.*)
        but that is not to say we should not taste.

Moreover, I know you are not beating me—
nor Lemuel. The men residing in
our skins are part of your crowd—and we are beating
as viciously as you the things we stand for.
We beat ourselves: and you are beating *your*selves.
And Parliament is beating all of us—
and we are Parliament. Oh, bloody confusion!
How can we learn, who whip the self in us
which would, if let alone, be our schoolmaster?

That self is a gentle pedant—full of all
the world has learned, but will not listen to.
He prophesies to a sleepy class. Once out
of school we swarm back to the cruelties,
perverse impulses, travesties of reason,
we keep like old diseases, from the past.
You cannot spear my tongue to silence, nor,
when it speaks, can you nor I quite hear its words.

I leave the paradox with you: that you
must feel and also think, have heart and mind,
must sometimes spank the child you love because
you love him, must extend God's open hand
of love and wield his fist of terrible justice.
How can we learn, who hate so much our wisdom?

(*Clay drops to his knees and the executioner starts for the iron, but there is a murmur in the crowd. The Blind Man has entered and is tapping forward.*)

BLIND MAN: I sniff a gathering, a still one. It is a bad day for begging.

CLAY: Come forward, Blind Man. In a moment you may lead me down.

BLIND MAN: Are you losing your eyes?

CLAY: Ah, no. They spear my tongue—which I have tried too long to see by.

BLIND MAN: I recommend incapacity. It has made me what I am.

CLAY: You may instruct me.

BLIND MAN: You will not need me. You will be more eloquent
        with a still tongue.
CLAY: Then to it. Stab, executioner, for I
        have words to be released from. Some dazzlement
        begins to swirl its stars about my head,
        like an unfixed heaven. I would not drop too soon.
        Forgiving hearts urge warm about to fill
        the gap your rod makes. I would have it so.
        I have some little boys I want to be
        a hero for. I need silence for mending.

(*The executioner, steadying Clay's head with one hand, lifts the
quill-like rod with the other. As he does so, the crowd rises
around curiously so that he is hidden as the rod is driven, and
then the crowd falls back, struck to silence. Sarah and Lemuel
move forward to support Clay as, in the company of the soldier, they move slowly off, the crowd following, leaving only
the Blind Man, who casually takes a seat on the edge of the
platform and strums. In dimming light he sings softly:*)

BLIND MAN:
        A crevice in the dike, a crevice in the dike,
                makes a trickle all the night.
        A kitten in the yarn, a kitten in the yarn,
                makes a pretty funny sight.
        A candle in the straw, a candle in the straw,
                makes a fearful golden light!

(*It is dark.*)

I am indebted to Bernard A. Backman for permission to use these songs, for which he composed the music.

SONGS FOR *Candle in the Straw*

"The House Is Dark"

The house is dark, the cat-tle still. The moon now sleeps be—

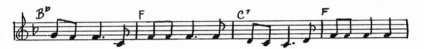

hind the hill. Does fa-ther tread up—on the sill? No, fa-ther treads not

ne-ver will. Oh lee o— Lai oh lul-la—by.

"A Frog and a Cricket"

A frog and a crick-et I tell you once sat on a li-ly pad

one and two, on a sum-mer night 'neath an i- v'ry moon and

each sang out his own sweet tune.

"A Farmer Had a Big Fat Sheep"

The farm-er had a big fat sheep. He fed him all the

Corn, oh my! This sheep will — win a prize and keep me —

rich as a rich man born, oh my! The three did starve in the

win-ter snow and two went mad in the sun, oh my! The

farm-er fed the fat one though till the wolf did come and the

skin-ny sheep fled, but the fat one was too fat to run. And the

wolf was as rich as a rich man born, Oh my!

"I Touched My Finger"

I— touched my fin-ger to a hon-ey bee, such a

lit-tle thing, such a lit-tle thing. Now I suck my fin—ger

as —you can see, for she gave not hon-ey/ but a sting.

"A Candle in the Straw"

IV

Edenitis:

Notes on *Winter in Eden*

According to reports the United Nations has plans to reopen Eden as an International Park. Oil derricks are being cleared. There will be a Scenic Drive along the West Range, with a special dirt detour for early-day motoring enthusiasts; an area of picnic shelters and barbeque pits and tables, with play apparatus and wading pool, landscaped right into a hillside, all native stone and stained cedar, Lebanese; a restaurant and souvenir concession of the same material (no alcoholic beverages, but try the soft nectar); a hiking trail along which inconspicuous bronze plaques will identify geological formations and biological specimens; a formal garden centered around the Tree of Knowledge of Good and Evil (*Malus sylvestris prohibitus, sui generis*), tastefully enclosed by a high clear plastic partition (satisfying the terms of an agreement made between the Mesopotamian Delegation and Higher Authorities); boating facilities on the delta at the juncture of the Tigris and Euphrates; a fig grove maintained by the Agricultural Extension Service; a serpentorium; and, protected by the gentle curve of Rib Hill, Four Rivers Campsite, with individual marked parking places and tent-floors, concrete fireplaces, stacks of wood, and central toilet, shower, and laundry facilities with hot and cold running water, plus electric outlets for trailers.

Those inclined to rough it (I would be one) should drive

around to the bleak East Gate (do not feed the cherubim), where just beyond the granite monument to Abel, within the wall, the road ends and marked trails fan out into several thousand acres of wilderness surveyed only by lonely Rangers in isolated fire-towers, where there is no sign of civilization except a First Aid Kit in the Halfway House, battered by the East wind on the scarred bluff a few thousand feet below Purification Peak. A First Aid Kit and a Gideon Bible.

One of these days I'll be there. Again and again. I can't take Eden or leave it alone. Like a mirage Eden seems always to lie shimmeringly ahead until one discovers that it lies shimmeringly behind. One of my favorite Edens is Rocky Mountain National Park. I had a fine week's camping there recently, the first in nearly twenty years. I tried to summarize my syndrome this way:

EDEN REVISITED

Here is all humidity and committees,
    drunk to bed and solace of the groin.
I think of that thin air, free around old granite,
    detest myself—and often think of going . . .

        Stepping out of the car into dry pine needles
        I breathed it all back with the scent of sage:

            . . . boys with canvas packs and bare knees
            climbing, with the long breathing of prophets,
            sleeping slim and brown in celibate bedrolls,
            dreaming vines of flowering hypotheses
            by incense flickering in the spatial night.

            I remembered purity of fright,
            of shivering, of laughter in the rain
            of afternoon, the mystery of morning
            before the sun, the gladness of light,
            the tooth-breaking chill of mountain water,

            coffee too harsh for the budding tongue. Later,
            returning, "fat and scant of breath," among
            peaks breaking clouds on their shoulders,
            sun-cured faces of granite, faces of leather
            emitting aspen in year after year of weather.

One may easily be readmitted, wearing
   his glands like sores, thoughts like snakes,
and climb and have a smoke upon the summit,
   descend, and camp with whiskey by the lakes.

But are those moral mountains not all fakes,
   a nursery of stuffed animals? Wishing
is indulgence, my evening Eve: would you want
   more than an hour's hike, a week-end's fishing?

Oh I too feel the thickening of white flesh
   and panic of the brink, and sliding, sliding—
but for all our tears for innocence, would we change
   the guilt of doing for the guilt of hiding?

My first book, written when I was sixteen, now mercifully lost, was entitled *Birds in the Wilderness* and concerned the adventures of the Trailblazers Patrol of Troop 50 (which met Friday nights in an upstairs room of the Riverside Baptist Church). We went camping on every occasion. Camping, for boys living in Houston, meant striking out on foot or bicycle as far as one could go in a day in a straight line, along shipworker-infested highways, until, say, a tree, or on lucky days a stagnant bayou, served as an example of nature—perhaps out of earshot of the highway. There one could open cans and bat mosquitoes till morning.

Shipworkers were our symbol of evil. They went roaring past in endless streams, first one direction and then the other as their innumerable shifts replaced one another, in steel helmets, honking at our little file to get off the damned road, banging their fists on the car doors and shouting obscenities as they screeched and swerved to avoid us. We were sure they made not only ships in those acres of off-limits factories, but schools, diseases, bosses, landlords, breakable bicycle chains, mosquitoes, lawnmowers, girls, newspaper routes, and Latin assignments.

Water was our symbol of good. We always dreamt of finding the source of a stream, and spent days climbing through blackberry vines and canebrakes following the sluggish course of water in the direction it seemed to be coming from—a bayou, or, better, a small tributary (since the smaller the stream, the more likely we were to find its source). A "source" would be, we knew, if we ever found one, a limpid spring of potable, icy water pulsing eternally out of the Texas soil. We forgave water for being corrupt as we found it, for we knew it began clean, around some bend and beyond some drainage ditch.

I don't believe I have ever found a source quite in that classical mold: just a hole in the ground with a stream trailing down from its lips. Streams actually begin—whether on the Continental Divide or in the Kiamichi Mountains (a degenerate spur of the Ozarks extending into Oklahoma) or Okinawa or the plains of East Texas—in swamps. Suddenly the ground goes muggy underfoot as you are following the stream, and you find yourself desperately trying to trace the current in a field of weeds and muck. We tried to believe that this was just a phase the water was going through and would forgive it. The true stream, the real water, came from beyond. After sloshing around awhile we would give it up. Perhaps that pure source, that hole in the ground, was out there in the middle of the swamp somewhere, overwhelmed by its own abundance. Or perhaps the stream entered the swamp at some point on the periphery which we hadn't discovered. But our failure was owing to our own frailty and in no way discredited the water, which worked in a way that passed our understanding.

Our faith was most nearly shaken in a large, wild park near Houston where a certain irregularity and rare rockiness of landscape seemed to us about like Colorado ought to look, and therefore any mystery was possible. We found a little runlet splashing down the bank into the central bayou. It was clear and cool—and we scrambled up the bank like bloodhounds, literally chasing it upstream as it twisted and spilled, running brightly over rocks, standing clear in tiny pools, and we began laughing in spiritual delight as we raced along, paddling in it, stopping to dash our faces, even wash our mouths (afraid, still, to swallow it, though the temptation was maddening). For its size, it was incredibly long and persistent. Finally, of course, our hearts sank as we realized that it had led us out of woods onto a headland, and though it still babbled on clearly through the meadow, we felt the hot sun, the mosquitoes in mid-day, caught the heavy, muddy Houston odor and knew that a swamp was inevitable. We could see houses across the fields, a road, cars. We were approaching a long ditch, and there we found the source clearly marked with a series of little, weathered signs: "Old Latrine, 93rd Infantry, October, 1940."

We were not really nature-lovers. Oh, we could identify rabbits and squirrels and birds and trees (that is, we could tell birds from trees and either of these from rabbits or squirrels). We were reverential about growth and naturalness, absolutely anal about burying campfires and waste, never cutting green unnecessarily. We had an engineering bent, loving to make stepping stone bridges in difficult crossings, a lean-to, a fireplace, stairs down the creek bank. We hadn't the least interest in hunting or fishing. We liked hiking to get places, but not for itself, certainly not for exercise. Basically (like literary scholars) we were source-hunters: it was always up, up, up, always following water, always searching for what the English call "the unspoiled," the heart of darkness. We would break through the brush and come upon a vista (this was in central Texas, near New Braunfels) in which there was not a single visible evidence of human life. No houses through the trees, no cleared fields, no barbed wire, no Kleenex or condoms underfoot. We stood there gasping, afraid to move or gaze an inch to right or left—until (literally) a beer bottle came bobbing down the limpid creek.

Progress. We ourselves wanted to *use* that virginal land, and though we had no beer bottles and would be tidy with our bean cans, our urge must have been partly to defile. We wanted to go out there in nature and live in it. We wanted to be the first. Nature, for us, as it must be for everyone, was something ultimately to overcome.

Of course we also wanted to cleanse ourselves—with fright, labor, exposure, weathering. To cleanse oneself and to conquer, with nature as antagonist and material to be worked: how far it all is from any sentimental nature-loving!

Let me dwell a moment on fright. "Oh let's go up the hill and scare ourselves," Frost begins "The Bonfire." Fright is one of the most stimulating and purifying emotions available, and the desire for it must motivate a lot of religion and camping trips: pushing into the Mystery, the spooky and inexplicable. As you go plunging through the woods the experience of back-crawling dread is most conveniently provided by snakes. I am scared to death of snakes and so is everyone else. (How wise was God to know that an alliance with a snake was the definitive betrayal of man's essence!) Actually I have encountered very few in the woods, but I travel continually alert, stepping onto logs rather than over them, avoiding sunny patches of leaves or pine needles, splashing the bank before stepping out of the river. I worry about their being in my bedroll when I wake up in the morning. I sometimes think the desire to go camping is a desire to go out and be scared by snakes, to go deep into the woods and survive the night and come home again without being bitten.

I have never seen a snakebite, either, though I am vigilant and prepared to make X marks with my penknife and suck. Once upon a path alongside a bayou a sleepy moccasin dived across the path for the water and encountered, mid-air, the boot of the fellow in front of me. For a minute or so the boy hopped round and round on one leg, swinging the other, from which flopped about three fat feet of snake, whose teeth had gotten embedded in his rubber heel. The boy was thereafter changed. He had a kind of distance, a distracted, spiritual dignity which set him off from us, and we no longer included him in our adventures. There is a close link between fright, especially by a snake, and salvation.

Fright and pain. Deliberate exposure to discomfort is only on the face of it a curious way of having fun. Look how far the Pilgrims traveled to camp out and find fulfillment. One summer I dragged my wife and first daughter (who was then eighteen months old) clear up the Maine coast, up New Brunswick, up to the northernmost tip of Nova Scotia, pointed out into the bleak North Atlantic, and purified the hell out of all of us. Windbeaten walks by the noisy sea, spray flying under a

sky of grey wool stretched off to the dark northern rim of darkness . . . a strange way to get kicks!

GULL AT PLAY

From the dune-crest I saw an idiot gull
bucking a squall on the fringe of a fretful sea,
awkward and suicidal, flapping for no good end,
fat, overcivilized, no windhover he,

but my heart stirred, for in my flapping jacket
I, too, had hurled myself for fun headlong
into a wind too big and had begun
to feel the cleansing chill. Who knows what fun

is any more? I remember pilgrims streaming
out of Boston to the sea, their autos heavy
with sacramental freight (their Kleenex boxes,
innertubes and cameras), gazing, dreaming

of some salty absolution, bringing their young
to be blessed in the ceremony of the out-
of-doors. This Sunday morning sand-in-the-teeth
set has few libertines; they are devout,

wear hair shirt (blazing tropic fires), submit
themselves like penitents to the salt and sun:
not to the exquisite, artful agonies, but
to discomfort, crude and pure. Since I am one

of such a holy breed I can explain
somewhat what moves the gull and me: suppose
in your pale condition, ignorant of the soil,
your hands no longer agents of your brain,

you woke on a desert island in a jock-strap
and pocket-knife—and somehow you devised
a gimcrack the city makes in plastic, sells
for a dime back home. Just think how you would clap

your rediscovered hands in celebration!
Similarly, if in the granite State of Maine
by the clear cold sea you wrest some campfire comfort
from driftwood, scrubby spruce and rocks, or rain

cutting around a stretched tarp does not
quite penetrate, or if at Fundy, where
the headlands loom all shaggy in the fog,
the coffee perks, and in the duffle a pair

of dry socks waits your weakening, you know
my recluse ecstasies. Even the beach crowd
enjoys a form of flagellation, not
to feel the pain but to feel after each blow

some measure of relief. Of course no pleasure
is more phony, more a sign of civilization
past the crest, when we feel pressed brutally
to sensitize our faculties, to treasure

our crude things—a rusty nail in a grimy hand—
but the need lies deep: life lives a self-willed test,
or else that gull fighting the wind out there
over the curling breakers would welcome rest.

Fright and pain are, of course, but necessary conditions for
the ultimate object, an encounter with the unknown. Like
Ahab, we would give our lives to know for certain whether
nature really gives a damn. We expose ourselves until numb,
awed, silenced as Job, we stare into the fathomless universe
and try to imagine (or not to imagine) that it was all inten-
tional:

A STORM TIME

Last night here on Cape Breton winds
bearing a buckshot rain descended
off the highlands, flattening ten tents

on a bluff across the brook. They rocked
us in the car: the windows spat,
the surf outside rolled pebbles, boulders

in its bony jaws. All you could see
was whirling spew of the wet wind,
tossing grass and the light-splashed

instants of waves charging low
into the wind with shoulders bent
and faces full of froth, bellowing

as they laid into the rocks and breathing
hard. (I thought of desperate, tight-
lunged men at a shot dropping to knees

and scattering white arms of spray.)
All night this elemental curse,
this faceless sky; today is grey,

clouds in a chilly boil. The waves
on the beach, ten in a minute, heave
themselves like fragments of a half-

forgotten dream. We stopped by the shelter
where the evicted tenters stood,
all unfamiliar, shielding a hot

wood stove. Out front one sawed at a pump
handle, his jacket flying, a stream
whipping in wind from the pump spout,

the rest, in damp clothes, waiting for
a sign of clearing weather, door-
leaners, eaters by ritual, chiders

of children, sodden, sociable hermits
far from their cities, each one piecing
together scraps of last night's squalling

horror, the banging of canvas, tangle
of rope, the drenching black, fingers
numb fumbling with property and long

night and now longer day by these massive
things: the round brown hills, wind, sea,
not friendly, hostile (or derisive),

rolling their regular rhythm, cold,
oblivious, but (how dreams hang on!)
at storm times seeming to take hold.

Unfortunately the weather in Eden is rarely that exciting.
When I think of camping the first image that comes to mind
is of Edwin squatting on a bayou bank, his long knees in the
air, monotonously hacking the dirt with his hatchet, whistling
mindlessly through his teeth. Okay so we're here and the tent's
up so what do we do? Or of Mike gaping by the breakfast fire
at ten in the morning, in the hot sun, when we had camped too
long, had let ourselves become too indolent and dirty and
stupid, and in hysterical revolt I struck off down the mountain
for the city, yearning to find purification *there:*

DESCENT OF MAN

After a month in the Rockies Mike's arms hung,
his jaw hung, beard was matted black around

his stagnant mouth, his eyes, lumpish in membranes,
hung in their pods as he sat beside the fire.
Our burros, hobbled on the meadow, grazed like a pair

of Greeks relieved of animality—
but we had let centuries take us, sank
in the lunar ebb, the slime of the past. These blue
peaks had not brought the grandeur boys require
just at the age they sniff themselves in fear.

We had reverted: the fish we mostly fed
upon were fried, now, trailing intestines, pasted
with scales, and soon we would, with beak or paw,
lift them out wriggling, eat them raw. I broke.
A look at Mike at breakfast made me choke.

I shook my skinny arms and screamed (while silent
mountains averted their faces like polite
neighbors). I kicked my dew-damp bedroll. I
was going home. Home in my mind was sheets,
radio music, sanitary streets.

Bride-like, I had found exudation in
the exercise of life. I sought my dream,
where things were starched and done for one in kitchens.
Mike, huge in his blundering haste, packed up, agreed—
like one who had exposed what he should hide.

We rolled our stuff in tarps and scuffed the fire.
An hour later we were filing down
a cliff lip overlooking the glinting river,
Mike goading our two burros, their great packs
rocking their rhythm, winding past the rocks

with aspen epaulets—just like the books
said outdoors ought to be. Civility
regained, we watched the leaves—grace in their gold
going—and how the woods decayed with pride,
and nodding burros took their waste in stride.

But camping can be done at home. There is a virginal waste-
land right inside my skull, complete with dramatic vistas, pre-
cipitous drops, thick woods, pure air, gurgling innocence, and
snakes and streams whose sources can never be discovered.
Eden, ignorance, innocence, is a place to start out from, cring-
ing under the lightning, to till the soil. Eden must be like the
Communists say Communism would get to be—or as those

who yearn for Heaven think of Heaven. I have always felt I could wait, that (like Wordsworth) I had a vague sense of having been there before and that I left because of the absence of theaters.

When I read discussions of literary sources (those holes whence pulse the first water), I am amused by how tangential these are, at least in my own experience, to the events in an author's life which no one can ever know and which are the real springs of inspiration. The source of *Winter in Eden* is obviously *Paradise Lost,* whose source is obviously the Old Testament. *Winter in Eden* is, in a way, an interpretation of *Paradise Lost,* as it says what I think Milton meant—that pure goodness is at best meaningless and at worst intolerable, that life without evil is one-dimensional and bad theater, and that though Satan is not a hero in the sense of one to be admired or emulated, we owe the negative pole as great a debt as we owe the positive for the juice which runs us. Milton helped me see the meaning of earlier experience. The image which comes to my mind as the real source of *Winter in Eden* is of Edwin squatting on the bayou bank.

The play got started in my head, however, when we were returning from that three-month camping trip in Maine and Nova Scotia. Incorrigible feminist, I have always had great compassion for Eve. Sailing along in a miniature and ancient touring car we had purchased on a whim in Maine (my own Eve following with the baby in a station-wagon), I began singing Eve's song: "I pick and hoe and cook and sew, am considered automatic . . ." to an improvised tune. I wrote most of the present song in my head as we traveled. And the idea of doing the Eden story as a musical comedy is somehow associated with our return from the discomfort, hard work, and enforced innocence of a season in the woods.

I was decidedly of Satan's party when I began. I gave him sandals and beard and wine bottle, a thin volume of poetry under his arm and lechery in his eye. He was a left-wing angel, "evil" as imagined by my enemies. In an early version he actually seduced Eve—which was the noblest gesture his variety of feminism could conceive of. But I have aged with the play. By the time it was produced as a musical comedy, I hoped that the audience would be left with a sense of balance —and I must confess that by now I find myself at times inclined to God's side. It seems to me that Michael's speech at the end of the second act is irrefutable, much as I hate it. Since it favors peace above justice, perhaps it is more leftish than was that hippie Satan I originally had in mind (some years before hippies had that name). He has been barbered and properly dressed. Of course my sympathy, as that of any human being with a spark of uncooperativeness within him, tends naturally to Satan—but in reflective moments I have to recognize that Satan and I are wrong. It's a good thing we're around, but it is also good that we are inevitably defeated by what Michael calls "the mass mind."

When you produce this in your imagination, do not do as was done in its single actual incarnation. The play then had no choruses, only the four central characters; costuming appeared to be simple, and so it was a very low-budget amateur production. The necessity for economy worked a subtle and deleterious effect upon reason. In this modern world of art, if you lack funds or skill, be abstract. Each decision seemed to make sense (or be necessary) at the time, and I consented step by step. But the cumulative effect was pretty hideous as I look back on it now.

For example, the director, a very wise man about theater and other things, and a dear friend, had taught me that no playwright had adequately exploited the technical facilities of the modern theater. I had this in mind when writing, for example, the sunset song, imagining a scarlet fantasy of lighting which would burn off the back wall. But it turned out that all the necessary lights had blown, or the gels or whatever they use were missing. So we got an abstract sun, like a Japanese flag on a dirty sheet, as a background for Eve to belt out her song. I imagined an Eden of fertility and abundance, dappled green rolling away to a mile-high wall, like the landscape of the film of *The Wizard of Oz*. We actually got a giant chessboard ramp, with red and white squares (inspired by the song beginning, "In life's great game of chess"). This tilted toward the audience. Beside it stood the Tree of Knowledge of Good and Evil—not the gnarled grandfatherly tree I imagined but a missile penetrating a mushroom cloud (more doughnut-shaped) decorated with mathematical formulae, looking (perhaps appropriately) like a Shipworker's Phallus penetrating a grey nest. (The cylinder was a pillar left over from a production of *Caesar and Cleopatra*.) In fact, the whole production took on a kind of shipworkerly character. There was no time, when we finally got some music written, for orchestration, so we used a jazz combo who could improvise their harmonies. The show was noisy, pink (there was an excess of pink paint left from another production), angular, open, and sterile—whereas I had thought of something curvy, cozy, luscious, and gentle.

I learned a great deal about theater by this whole gruelling experience—chiefly the superiority (for my purpose) of the theater of the imagination. Do you want your four characters to go winding around the apple tree like the couple in *The Fourposter* around that eternal bed—or do you want visual variety, with lots of places for small scenes? One way you get intensity and monotony, the other you get four lonely actors on an acre of stage (which is what we settled for). It is all so much different sitting and seeing it than it is in the study or in the imagination. The lines are different. The script used for that production was altogether too collegiate and vulgar, and the horse laughs (which it was very successful in eliciting) drowned my point. The songs were too many and too long. I was contemptuous of the idea of choruses (especially in Eden), but I began to see why they were used, for the play is not only its plot, its poetry and meaning, but a succession of experiences, and a tense duet almost demands a chorus coming in with cartwheels and capers to follow it, whether it makes any sense or not. I had hoped to make the music integral—a necessary part of the action and dialogue. But songs are a very poor means of communication. I found that I couldn't follow the sense of them myself as I sat in the audience—and this was not only because of the nerve-wracking jazz (it was good jazz, but I don't like jazz) and the singers, who did nobly. And I learned how details can defeat you—like ping-pong balls.

The ping-pong balls obsessed us the last twenty-four hours. The script calls for a fire which springs up instantaneously at a snap of the fingers. (Never underestimate the technical facilities of the modern theater.) Now, to have a fire glowing in a hearth is one thing, but to have one noticeably spring to life is another. Lights aren't enough. I suppose someone could crackle paper in front of a microphone backstage as we did in radio days, but that seemed inadequate too. And I suppose in more opulent theaters something like smoke bombs could be released by remote control—but we didn't have those, either. Someone, possibly I, had the bright idea (in keeping with the abstraction of the set) of putting ping-pong balls in a plastic cone, illuminating them with red and activating them with an air-jet. There happened to be a line of compressed air in the theater, so we did this. The jet made a whoosh like a departing missile and the balls rattled like a machine-gun, all this drowning about five minutes of dialogue—not at all the floating ball effect one might have hoped for. Sometimes the balls got stuck and we just had the whoosh.

It is with relief that I return to the imaginary theater. I am grateful for the production experience I had with *Winter in Eden,* but I don't know whether I could take it twice. It was a raucous success with every audience (but I kept seeing my friends slink home in embarrassment). I sat in the back of the theater blushing deeply to hear those things said out loud in front of all those strangers, and I was gratified at the good nature of the audience for laughing. I tried to correct the defects I saw in rewriting, added choruses, toned down the sex, and—perversely, for I seem to have a suicidal urge about plays, to guarantee that they will not be produced—put it mostly in rhyme. I delight in rhyme—a pleasure in language which in our puritanical and self-consciously artily artless century is much scorned. I hope the rhymes don't jangle your ear in reading.

Actually, what I would most like to see—and what I invite you to imagine—is production in a marionette theater, the sound taped so that the words are very clear above the music. It seems to me that the artificiality of the rhymes, the form, the nudity and naivety of the whole conception, could best be realized in a miniature setting with wooden performers. It would lend poignancy to the discussion of free will, and the angels could fly more easily.

V

Winter in Eden

A Musical Play in Two Acts and Epilogue

ACT I

An overture dissolves into music of the spheres. Two figures can just be seen engaged in a pantomime of laborious combat, banging swords on shields. Music more dramatically underscores their fighting as we begin to see them more clearly: Satan, dressed in red, and Michael, the archangel, dressed in white, with medieval helmets and shields, wielding broad-

swords, grunting and clanging. The music fades. In the succeed-
ing silence there is suddenly the sound of a gong. The fighters
stop, startled.

SATAN: What was that?
MICHAEL: That means eternity is half over.
SATAN: Time for a break?
MICHAEL: Just for the sake
                  of doing better in the second half.
SATAN: Ha! That's a laugh!

(*They lean on their swords, panting heavily, a grey light diffus-*
ing over them, revealing them still more clearly. They are both
sensible-looking angels of middle age. Satan wears a Vandyke
beard, cape, and traditional horns and tail. Michael is more
portly, dressed in togalike angelic robes, with small wings and
a halo. During the following lines, Satan takes out a pack of
cigarets, offering to Michael, who refuses, and lighting one him-
self. Michael takes out a pocket flask of nectar and collapsible
cups. With a glance over his shoulder at Heaven, he pours a
shot for Satan and one for himself.)

MICHAEL: What's this? You don't believe in progress?
SATAN: No. Only in change.
                  What do you say
                  that we arrange
                  to battle out
                  the rest of time
                  in some more cultivated way?
MICHAEL: Oh, I'm
                  for that, without a doubt.
                  You mean a more
                  civilized war . . .
                  like advertising?
SATAN: Oh, all the Arts and Sciences, you know—
                  psychology and salesmanship,
                  the expense account, the business trip,
                  and poetry and priestliness
                  and educated beastliness

like manners and duplicity,
diplomacy, hypocrisy,
and ritual and management
and courts, and courte*san*agement,
and marriage and legality
and sexual equality
and weekends on a yacht—
and all that rot.

(Michael sets aside his sword and shield, takes off his helmet. Satan follows suit. Michael stoops to fix a sandal.)

MICHAEL: That's to my taste—
    although it's understood. . . .
SATAN: Oh, yes, I know—the same old waste,
    clanging and banging,
    red against white.
    Sometimes I feel like being good—
    just for *spite*.

(Michael glances above dubiously: this has not been covered by instructions.)

MICHAEL: Now, Satan! We have to go
    according to our proper pursuits!
SATAN: Yes, Michael, I know:
    whoever dreamed us dreamed in absolutes.
MICHAEL *(encouragingly)*: But the Management has a plan
    which may mean some relief
    from these vacant monotonies of space and time.
    We have invented Man
    and a Garden—beyond belief—
    a green and tender life in a sunny clime . . .
    and there we may continue
    our flexing of sinew
    in this new dimension—
    manipulating this invention
    upon the green sward.
SATAN: Ah! Like a chess board!
MICHAEL: Except these creatures are self-willed.

SATAN (*jealously*): Self-willed!

MICHAEL (*sharing bafflement*): Yes. We can move them only
                    by eloquence!

SATAN (*sensing an advantage*): Ah! That makes sense!

MICHAEL: To start with, there are two. . . .

SATAN: One for each of us?

MICHAEL: Oh no, that would not do!
                    Their charm, you see,
                    is in their ambiguity.
                    They are neither white nor red—
                    but a shade of pink, instead—
                    and though of clay,
                    the best clay.
                    Our side, for having made them, goes
                    first—
                    but, then, who knows?

SATAN (*incredulously*): You don't mean . . .

MICHAEL (*somewhat grumpily*): Well, yes. . . .
                    I suppose He knows—
                    but He won't say.

SATAN (*in disgust*): Oh fine! Such play
                    will be like trying to outguess
                    an electronic computer!

MICHAEL (*drawing Satan to one side, confidentially*):
                    But they are beguiling,
                    all pink in their skins,
                    their eyes sweetly glazed,
                    blind to ideas and sins—
                    like angels newly plucked,
                    like apes without fur,
                    she leaning on him,
                    he bending to her,
                    their reason all sullied
                    by seeping of glands,
                    unaware, in their Garden,
                    they walk holding hands.
                    Trees shade them, grass rests them,
                    and ripe fruits entice. . . .

Oh, Satan, just wait
till you see Paradise!

(*As Michael finishes, they disappear. Lights come up suddenly on a luxurious pastoral landscape around the mouth of a cave bathed in the rosiness of late afternoon sun—an unreal, hazy atmosphere. A sturdy apple tree bends over the mouth of the cave. The terrain is rolling, giving us a view far into the distance, with trees, shrubs, oversize fruit, rocks, logs, dotting the well-trimmed grass. A hammock swings between two trees with Adam reclining in it. Eve is working with a crude implement in a neat little garden patch. They are formlessly, unprovocatively nude. Adam's characteristic manner is slumping, gracelessly masculine, innocently direct. Eve, a lovely blonde, is rather borne down by her domestic duties: she is not one to find fulfillment in gardening. She meets life with a flat-footed blank stare, but there are signs about her of the sensitivity and intelligence which will make her, with education, a richly mature and interesting girl. The air is full of Angels wheeling piously over this colorful scene.*)

ADAM, EVE, ANGELS (*to an insipid tune*): They (We) have it
    nice
    in Paradise,
    back here in the beginning,
    with everything
    that they (we) might want
    except, of course, for sinning!

ADAM (*sits, stretches*): My health is good
    in Paradise.
    You see, my cheeks are ruddy.
    The only things
    I have to do
    are Art and Nature Study.

EVE (*leaning on hoe*): I have it good in Eden.
    For nothing am I yearning.
    Right now, of course, I'm innocent . . .

    (*over her shoulder, as she hoes viciously*)
    but gradually I'm learning.

SATAN (*appearing majestically on one side of stage*):
        Why don't I just
        leave Paradise
        all free from moral warring?
        I would, except
        except for me
        life would be rather boring.

MICHAEL (*appearing on opposite side of stage—pontifically*):
        Oh, life is good
        in Paradise.
        Consider what it features:
        hills and dales
        and fields and streams
        and dumb and docile creatures!

COMPANY: There is no vice
        in Paradise—
        at least in the beginning.
        The air is full
        of angel songs—

(*Angels pull violins from their robes, put them to their cheeks to play.*)

        and their sweet violining!

(*A chorus of Devils pops up from behind rocks and shrubs. No one sees them but the audience, to whom they sing sardonically:*)

DEVILS: The fertile earth
        is planted with
        tomorrow's seeds of sinning!

(*Devils, Michael, and Satan disappear. Angels flit about Adam, in his hammock, and Eve, hoeing, presumably trying to make them comfortable. Adam is reading a book and is bothered by the flitting of an Angel. He slaps and waves his hand around his face as at a gnat.*)

ADAM: Drat this gnat!
EVE: That is only an Angel, darling!

ADAM: I say it's a gnat—
        and it's *not* so nice
        to have these bugs in Paradise.

(*Angels, insulted, flutter off to Heaven.*)

EVE: They're just creatures, dear.
        They must live *some*where!
ADAM: Well, not here!
        Talk like that, and you'll have all
        the riff-raff of the insect world
        inside the Wall.
        They'll be the death of the human race!
        You have to draw a line some place!
        Besides, I'm cold!
EVE: How could you be?
        We have a permanent guarantee
        of perfect good weather.
ADAM: You're warm because you've been working!
        I don't care whether
        it's guaranteed or not—
        the thermostat's stuck—or else they're shirking.
        They ought to send more heat around
        this hour before the sun goes down.
EVE (*crosses to him and embraces him, rubbing his arms to
        warm them*):
        Adam, you shouldn't scold
        the elements. You think too much, dear.

        (*Rubbing forehead.*)

        You get all hot up here;
        the rest of you gets cold.
ADAM (*surprised*): How did you find out about that?
EVE: About what, dear?
ADAM: About circulation of the blood.
EVE: Nowhere, silly. I just thought of it. You
        needn't think I'd be poking into your books.
        I pick and hoe and cook and sew,
        am considered automatic.
        Just plug me in and I will go;

I have never dared be erratic.
I am muscle-bound and barefoot,
as any woman ought to be;
I am ignorant and blonde and cute
and give my services for free.

ADAM AND EVE: A woman's work, a woman's work
outlasts the sun.
A woman's work, a woman's work
is ne-e-ever done!

ADAM: Athough strong and sweet and barefoot,
your Will is dangerously free.
Free Will in ladies is uncouth.
It was meant for men—like me.

EVE: Why, Adam, could you doubt me?

ADAM: Indeed, I think I could.

EVE: You know I never think of things
except the things I should.

ADAM: But just because you're female
I think you'll be untrue.

EVE: But there's no one here in Paradise
to be untrue with . . . to? . . . but you.
(*reassuringly*)
There is no beast in Paradise
who interests me but you.

ADAM: But how can I be positive
you will not use your brain?

EVE: Why, busy me
and dizzy me
and cuddle me
and muddle me
and work me to the bone.
Then I will be your own.
My mind will weaken with the strain:
I'll never cause you pain.

ADAM AND EVE: Just pick and hoe and cook and sew
You (I) needn't bother to be human.
The only thing you (I) need to know
is it's enough to be a woman!

EVE: What have you been reading about today, dear?

ADAM: Science.

EVE: What is science, Adam?

ADAM: All the Latin names for things, dear. I have a
      responsibility for them.

EVE: Tell me some of them, Adam.

ADAM: Please don't bother me about them, Eve. They are
      very technical, and you'll get me confused.
      Just look at the sunset, how the air, suffused
      with the yellowing of fire
      glows like a flaming pyre
      or what we've heard of Hell.
      I think it shows off Heaven quite well.
      I wonder how they do it.

EVE: I'll bet they never knew it
      made such a pretty show.

ADAM: Don't be naive
      and sacrilegious, Eve.
      Though you don't know—
      you can be sure it's all a part of the Plan,
      to the last orange glimmer.
      Refraction, mostly.

EVE: What's *that*?

ADAM: You see that ghostly shimmer
      on the horizon? That is light
      that bounces on the clouds
      from out of sight. . . .
      Daylight, you see, is directly proportional to the
      length of time the sun is above the horizon and
      inversely proportional to the cloud coverage, except
      when the angle of incidence . . .

EVE: Oh, I'm sure they planned all *that*!
      But the sunset surpasses such pat
      laws that define
      its shine.

      No mind could conceive of a sunset.
      It is too grand a thing for design.

Its scarlet fires roll
beyond all control
and swirl plans away like red wine.

Oh, just look at the blue of the evening!
It is deeper than depth should appear—
and no rational view
can endure a hue
which makes infinite sky seem so near!

Oh, just look at the gold of the sunset!
How it saturates clouds, how it flows—
the blood of the sky
swells up like a sigh
and unfolds like a gold-spangled rose!

I'm sure that Michael, for example, simply has no
color sense.

ADAM (*whispers*): Hush, dear! Someone will hear you!

EVE: Hear me, indeed!

No landlord should listen;
his eyes should not glisten
to hear what we say alone!
There is no need!

ADAM: How do we know what they need?

EVE: Well, must it be snooping, tormenting,

behind every shrub, as though looking for tips,
observing our every act?
In fact,
I have the creepy feeling they're inventing
every word as it comes from my lips!

ADAM (*whispers*): Hush, dear, please! He's coming now!

(*Right out of the gold and purple splendor of the sunset comes
Michael on tremulous wings, accompanied by properly magnifi-
cent orchestration. Landing gracefully, he folds his wings and
crosses to Adam and Eve. Michael is a gentleman of the old
school, quite accustomed to lying politically for the general
weal, quite able to dogmatize, but he has a witty side too, and*

a susceptibility to Eve's charms. He represents the rationale of civilization: he just wants no trouble. Meanwhile, one can live in genteel comfort.)

MICHAEL: Yes, Eve, dear. I overheard you.
>But Heaven is not liable for the words of women.
>Where they come from, we really aren't quite sure.
>They're made of sugar, with a squeeze of lemon,
>and something else that must remain obscure. . . .

(*Takes out bottle of nectar, hands it to Eve.*)

>But let's have no philosophy tonight.
>Here is some nectar. Let's have one around,
>an extra stiff one for me.
EVE (*going to cave, anxiously to Adam*):
>Do you think he's already tight?
ADAM (*reprovingly*): He has to drink it, dear, to be profound.
>Besides, it gives him immortality.
EVE (*whispering*): Well, you don't have to match him, shot
>for shot!
ADAM (*whispering*): A little immortality never hurt anybody.

(*Eve goes into cave with bottle.*)

MICHAEL: Ah, nectar warms a soul on a chilly evening. . . .
ADAM: I meant to mention this chill. . . .
MICHAEL: I know. You think that Heaven
>is somehow failing to fulfill
>the terms prescribed for your tenancy—
>but, quite otherwise, as you will see.
>It's all your education. We

>(*Gestures to Heaven, summoning a horde of helpful Angels.*)

>will have some sticks and logs piled here . . .

(*Angels gather wood, humming a sweet melody, over which Michael continues.*)

> (although I'm not quite sure I should
> use heavenly hosts for gathering wood)

(*They pile the wood for a fire.*)

> and make a lesson of it—never fear.

(*Angels curtsy and fly off. Eve enters with three stone cups and the bottle on a wood-slab tray. Devils secretly pop out of their hiding places with long roasting forks, each with a wiener speared on it. They form a military column, forks on their shoulders, behind Michael while he fusses with final arrangements of the wood, Adam and Eve watching. No one seems to hear the Devils.*)

DEVILS: Hurray for the building of fire!
> Any flame that you make will attract us.
> We haven't the meat we desire—
> but we gladly roast wieners for practice.
>> Hup, two, three, four.

> Three cheers for the heavenly host
> that so pleasantly tries to defeat us
> with Eden and this wiener roast:
> it seems more like they're trying to treat us!
>> Hup, two, three, four.

(*Michael now pushes Adam and Eve back to a safe distance, making a great show of getting everything exactly right. Then he backs off and snaps his fingers at the pile of wood. It bursts rosily into flame, making Adam and Eve jump in astonishment, the eyes of the Devils shining in the dark behind Michael.*)

MICHAEL (*proudly*): That is called "fire"!
> Perfection, as, perhaps, you've seen,
> is from time to time inclined to be dull.
> Selection of experiences
> varies the routine
> and provides a little lift in the lull.
> So when the air is chilly
> to complain is rather silly.
> It is all a part of our benign Plan.

> A campfire, as it blazes,
> makes warmth for colder phases.
> All hail for Heaven's gifts to man!

(*Angels appear suddenly with long trumpets and blow a peal of congratulation.*)

ANGELS: Hallelujah! Hallelujah!
> For the plan in which all pleasure
> just compensates some misery
> doled out in equal measure!
> Hal-le-lu-jah!

(*Meanwhile, the Devils, still unnoticed, have sneaked forward and are dancing around the fire. At the end of the Angels' song, the Angels leave, the Devils stop around the fire and roast their wieners. Michael sees them and shoos them away in annoyance. Devils skip off into the dark, leaving Michael, Adam, and Eve standing around the fire, their faces lighted cheerily.*)

ADAM (*delightedly*): Hey! Just feel how it titillates the skin!

> (*He warms his hands, turns and warms his rear.*)

> You sure that enjoying this is not a sin?
MICHAEL (*uncomfortably*): Well, just don't burn things you
> don't want burned!
> Let's have that nectar, now.
> Your lesson for today has been adequately learned.

(*Michael and Adam sit on rocks near the fire while Eve unenthusiastically serves them. Michael watches her as she goes to a rock herself and downs her cupful in a single slug.*)

MICHAEL (*fatherly*): Something, Eve, is depressing you.
> Tell Michael all about it.
EVE: Oh, Michael, did the Powers plan carefully
> what women in this world are meant to do?
> I doubt it.
> I am restless, useless, mentally sick. . . .
MICHAEL (*thoughtfully*): This problem must be faced.
EVE: . . . and I know I will be totally replaced
> if, as you say, things all become electric.

MICHAEL: I wish your part in the scheme of things
        could frankly be expressed—
        but the fine line between predetermination and fore-
           knowledge
        must not be transgressed.
EVE: What? I don't follow you.
MICHAEL: Well, although
        we *know*
        what is going to happen, we
        are not allowed to say, you see,
        for that would make it so—
        or since it *will* be so
        will *seem* to make it so. . . .
EVE (*uncomprehendingly*): Oh.
MICHAEL: It's a problem in morale.
        People must be made
        to want to do
        what they have to do
        for fear, without such aid,
        they would not want to
        because they had to. . . .
EVE: Oh.
MICHAEL (*with long breath*): So,
        if you knew what you *had* to do
        you probably wouldn't *want* to. You
        are built that way.
        But just because your wanting to
        is the point of doing what you do,
        anyway . . .
EVE: Never mind, Michael. I'm not confused any more.
MICHAEL: Nevertheless, I'll try to create for you a vision
        of woman's part in Creation.

(*Gestures to Heaven. Angels enter on high.*)

        Someday you'll have a cottage
        with roses by the door,
        the happy cry of children—you'll have this
        and so much more. . . .

ANGELS: That's what life has for you.
        Here's something you can do:
        keep warm the fires of home!
MICHAEL: You'll cook a Christmas dinner
        and season it with sweat
        and look on radiant faces—while there's this
        your life is set.
ANGELS: Someday you'll make a sampler
        with a motto to inspire.
        Put it high above your fireplace—who could wish

        (*Each brings out a sampler reading "Home Sweet Home."*)

        to put it higher?
MICHAEL: Let Adam be the horse, dear,
        and you can be the cart;
        for God gave woman do-mes-ti-ci-ty,
        the noblest art.
ANGELS AND MICHAEL: That's what life has for you.
        Here's something you can do:
        keep warm the fires of home.
ADAM (*jumps up angrily*): The horse, eh? Domesticity, eh?
        Well, Michael, I know Eve better than you do, and
        I'll tell you she makes *me* mentally sick, too!
        A woman can't be trusted.
        With this my mind is crusted.
        She can corrupt a saint,
        make things seem what they ain't.
        She has a tireless tongue
        hooked to a bottomless lung.
        I also wouldn't trust
        her apparent lack of lust.
        When once she gets a mirror
        must men begin to fear her;
        for if she *learns* what she looks like
        and how to use her hooks right
        and how to give her rear end
        the best shape to appear in,

> the ravage will be ruinous
> with women always doing us
> in!
> Oh, men must, must, must—
> oh, they absolutely must
> protect themselves from women
> armed with sin!

ANGELS (*marching across the air*):
> Oh, a girl has nothing but her morals!
> Without her virtue, she is nothing at all!

ADAM (*looking up, agreeing*): Only work, work, work
> can ever straighten out the quirk
> which inclines her to lead man to his fall!

ANGELS AND ADAM: Oh, a girl has nothing but her morals!
> Give her an inch and she will take a mile.
> Only watching, watching, watching,
> will keep a girl from botching
> all Creation—and smiling all the while!

(*Angels fly off self-righteously.*)

ADAM (*to Michael*): In fact, I think it might be better if Eve,
> here,
> were dressed.

MICHAEL: Absolutely not. Nudity is the best protection of
> virtue!

EVE: Why is it we go this way—and you go covered so?

MICHAEL (*embarrassed laugh*): Why, rank has its privileges,
> you know.

EVE (*fingering his robe*): Could I wear clothes?

MICHAEL (*firmly*): Not so long as you live in Eden.

(*Eve lifts a loose section of his robe and drapes it longingly
across her leg.*)

EVE: Not decorate myself in any way?

MICHAEL: Why should you want to?

EVE: It would give me something to think about.
> I have nothing else, goodness knows.
> If I ever were to leave Eden, it
> would be so I could wear clothes!

MICHAEL (*indignantly*): You may leave anytime you wish, you know.

EVE (*teasingly*): I couldn't, Michael. I haven't a thing to wear!

(*There is a thunder clap and flash of lightning, revealing Satan perched ominously in the Tree of Knowledge.*)

EVE (*frightened*): What was that?

MICHAEL (*with a forced casual air*): They must be working on the wiring.

(*Another flash of lightning. Satan is rocking the tree with suppressed laughter.*)

MICHAEL (*nervously*): Looks as though they're having trouble up there.

Perhaps I had better get back.

ADAM: What do you suppose is causing it?

MICHAEL (*looking around*): I'm afraid there may be resistance in the air.

I think you may expect a visitor.

ADAM: Oh?

MICHAEL: Yes, probably in the form of a man.

EVE (*with interest*): Oh?

MICHAEL: He might take any form—
a bird, a toad, a snake,
mosquitoes in a swarm,
a catfish in a lake—
no telling what shape he will take!
But since this world began
I believe he thinks it most proper
for him to appear as a man.

EVE: Well, I, for one,
will think it fun
to have another someone around.
The silence here is getting me down!

MICHAEL: NO!

(*Adam and Eve look at him, startled.*)

Do not traffic with him!

ADAM AND EVE: But, Michael, why can't we be friendly?

MICHAEL: I would say that he is evil . . .

> but that word means nothing to you.
> Let it suffice . . .
> he . . . isn't very nice. . . .
> In fact, I would say he's taboo.

ADAM: How are we to know him?

MICHAEL: By his curious intuition.

> Something there is about his past
> that makes him understand
> the human condition.
>
> I really must be going. I can be of no help to you
> in what happens next. Cheer up, Eve. We have plans
> for you, simply divine plans. Be sweet, Eve. (*Leaving.*) Be stolid, Adam. And both of you, dream no
> dreams. (*Floats off.*)

ADAM: I think we'd better go into the cave. It's early in history
for rain—but, nevertheless, this looks like bad
weather. I'll bring this thing inside. (*Goes to fire as
though to lift it. Burns himself and jumps back.*) Ow!
Angels and their practical jokes!

EVE: What do you suppose he will be like?

ADAM: Who?

EVE: The visitor.

ADAM: Probably the scholarly type—if he understands the
human condition.

EVE: Just think how complicated our lives will be

> with someone in the Garden—besides you and me.

ADAM (*smiles happily*): Yes! Like a triangle!

EVE: What's a triangle?

ADAM (*making a diagram in the air*):

> Well, you have three points, and you join them
> all . . .

EVE (*suddenly shocked*): Oh no!

ADAM (*obliviously*): with straight lines. . . .

EVE: But we must have nothing to do

> with that other corner! Oh, we
> will have someone we don't speak *to!*
> Think how much closer we'll be!

ADAM (*lighting up*): Someone we're better than!

EVE: Feel sorry for!

ADAM: But never deal with, man to man!

EVE: Oh, listen! Oh, listen!
	The wind is growing stronger.

ADAM: Oh, listen! Oh, listen!
	We can't stay out much longer.

ADAM AND EVE: Oh, listen! Oh, listen!
	I think that I hear thunder.

EVE: Come in, dear. Come in, dear!

ADAM: A cave is to get under!

EVE (*approaching cave*): How cozy our home is—far from
	the busy street!
	I'll crochet little doilies, and life will be so sweet—
	with only you and me, dear, and someone else out-
	side.

SATAN (*in a flash of lightning, from the tree*):
	With horns and cloven feet!

		(*He laughs a sinister laugh.*)

ADAM (*as he and Eve huddle more fearfully together*):
	I see a little bungalow which ivy adorns.
	And I will be the king there. . . .

SATAN: Your crown shall be thorns!

EVE: With carpets, and a fire-place . . .

ADAM (*hastily*): *You* can tend the fire. . . .

EVE: How cozy—except for someone
	whose absence no one mourns. . . .

SATAN (*in lightning*): With cloven feet and horns. (*Laughs.*)

ADAM: We'll cultivate our little patch of space and time. . . .

EVE: With love in our hearts, how can we fail?

ADAM: Except, of course, we hate the one outside. . . .

SATAN (*laughing*): And thereby hangs a tale!

EVE (*as she and Adam enter cave*): I wonder if I can do some-
	thing different with my hair.

(*It is quiet for a moment, the air surging with jungle sounds of
singing insects, the fire looking very red and lonely as it sinks*

to coals. Satan drops out of the tree and comes into the dim circle of firelight. He stirs it skillfully and the flames make an ominous light on his face. He swaggers around surveying.)

SATAN: Damned if there shouldn't be a white fence around here with roses. If these aren't the most beans-for-supper, lace-curtains, Sunday-picnic and God-bless-our-happy-home stick-in-the-muds I have met since I fell from Heaven! But Heaven likes the type! Milk-toast shall inherit the earth—unless I do something about it. Ha! Isn't it just like that Prince of Light and Navel-Gazing to people this planet in his own image! Or tried to, anyway. It looks as though someone stirred some monkey-blood into the chowder!

But why do you suppose old Pokerface
risked everything by giving them Free Will?
And started their life off in such a place
that Progress could only be downhill?

Of course, with his controlling the means of production, their Free Will can only make them want what they can't have—so everyone will be miserable and solemn and quite ready for Heaven!

But this world! There is hope for it!
These human creatures have more hope than I.
Since Heaven they will find in one another's love
once they become aware that they must die . . .
How they can learn to live
if they learn how to spin
their trembling web of life
from Death and Sin!
(*with sudden burst of bitter gaiety*)
There's never a joy in the world, la, la,
        that is not compounded in sin.
You can always learn not to cheat, la, la,
        if you learn not to care if you win!

(*The earth takes on a red glow, and Devils appear at various distances across the landscape in silhouette. They move in a*

*macabre ballet ironically in contrast with the rather gay air
they sing.)*

DEVILS: The whirl of the wheel at the fair, la, la,
        is purchased at frightful expense.
          You're up, but you must swing back down, la, la,
            joy leaves, and you never know whence.
SATAN: And never a wine that was sweet, la, la,
        but was born of the death of a grape;
       if you lift up the skirts of a saint, la, la,
         you find there the legs of an ape.
DEVILS: And never a maiden was loved, la, la,
        but she lied, before she was laid.
SATAN: The heart has no songs of its own, la, la,
        and its singers are praised, never paid.
DEVILS AND SATAN: Oh, the flower that grows from the swamp,
          la, la,
       cares little how flowers begin.
There is not a joy in the world, la, la,
      that is not compounded,
        that is not compounded,
          that is not compounded in sin!

(Dancing continues as light fades to darkness.)

ACT II

*(It is dawn in Paradise. Satan is asleep in the bushes, out of
sight except for his head, which we do not notice at first. Eve
comes out of the cave, stretching, and Angels appear hurriedly,
wiping sleep out of their eyes. They begin glad undulations in
the air as Eve, hands on hips, surveys the morning.)*

ANGELS: The morning is like butter,
        another perfect day. . . .
EVE *(stretching)*: Ho-hum! Ho-hum!
ANGELS: The birds begin to flutter,
        the sun comes out to stay. . . .

EVE: Ho-hum! Ho-hum!

> I can't endure this simple life much longer.
> The days are just too gauzy soft for me.
> And day by day my virtue's growing stronger.
> I wonder just how virtuous
> a girl has got to be!

ANGELS (*optimistically*): This rustic . . .

EVE (*sourly*):   . . . stuff is highly over-
> rated.

ANGELS: A field and stream . . .

EVE: . . . amuse me just so much!

ANGELS (*puzzled, to each other*): What do you do when appe-
> tite is sated?

EVE: Go back and try your best to give
> the cave a homey touch!

ANGELS (*enthusiastically*): Oh, milk and eggs and spinach
> . . .

EVE: . . . give me gas pains!
> A little health with me goes a long way.

ANGELS (*crossly*): We hope that you're around when it at last
> rains!

EVE: And then I hope I never see
> another perfect day!
> (*Satirically*)
> The birds begin to flutter,
> the sun comes out to stay.
> Ho-hum! Ho-hum!

ANGELS (*reaffirming*): The morning is like butter,
> another perfect day!

EVE (*bored*): Ho-hum!

ANGELS (*shrugging shoulders*): Ho-hum!

(*Eve scuffs disconsolately toward the bush where Satan lies as
the Angels, discouraged, sail away. Eve accidentally kicks
Satan, waking him. She jumps back and screams as he sits up.*)

SATAN (*calmly*): Good morning.

EVE: Oh! For a moment I thought you were a snake!

SATAN (*rising, brushing himself*): Women see snakes every-
　　　　　where!

EVE: But there are no snakes in Paradise.

SATAN: Oh, *now* there are—because you are aware
　　　　　of snakiness. Thought and creation are all one!
　　　　　Snakes slipped into reality—whoosh!
　　　　　You can't retract a scale or fang.
　　　　　One may be coiled behind this very bush!
　　　　　Ideas, just like acts, once done are *done.*

EVE: Why, what a dirty, slimy thing for me to have created!
　　　　　But I didn't think of *you.*

SATAN: No, I was created by another mind than yours, long ago.
　　　　　I was a thought that pained the thinker.

EVE: Are you the visitor
　　　　　to whom we must not speak?

SATAN (*making light of it*): Must not? But you have—since
　　　　　your first shriek!
　　　　　The Powers would protect you from evil,
　　　　　don't you suppose?

EVE: I know! You must be an angel—
　　　　　you're wearing clothes!

SATAN: Well, more or less
　　　　　an angel—yes.
　　　　　Where is Adam?

EVE: He sleeps late.

SATAN: Oh? Does he work hard?

EVE: No, but his days are spent
　　　　　in such an inactive state,
　　　　　just reading in the yard,
　　　　　that he drops right
　　　　　to sleep again, unless he's had
　　　　　sufficient rest at night.

SATAN: Oh, I see.
　　　　　Then work has not yet been made a virtue?

EVE: Only for me.
　　　　　Michael says that work
　　　　　will help me keep my mind off things.

SATAN: I guess he fears the jerk
      of life that thinking brings. . . .

EVE: You mean that I've
      been less alive
      because my mind
      has been confined?

SATAN: Eve, thinking is nine-tenths of living!
      Now take the finest cheeses.
      Actually, they're stinking.
      They simply are not fit to eat—
      but you can make them so, by thinking.

EVE (*catching on*): Or take the stars in heaven.
      The poets say they're winking.
      In truth, their light's continuous—
      but you can make them blink by thinking!

SATAN: Regard the *bon vivant*
      who gets his wit by drinking.

EVE: His manner is ridiculous. . . .

SATAN: But his wit is in his thinking!
      Illusion is the leaven
      that keeps our lives from shrinking.

EVE: Reality is quite a bore.

SATAN: But what a joy in thinking!
      Oh, Eve, you have a body like
      a sack of canteloupe.
      You have two eyes that bulge out like
      two bubbles of soap.
      Your flaxen hair is stringy, and
      it hangs down in your eyes.
      Your lips look like two liver strips—
      like meat before it fries.
      But leave it to the mind of man
      to rectify all this.
      Let his imagination work
      when he decides to kiss.
      Your hunk of misbegotten flesh
      is bound in time to be

the undisputed archetype
of femininity!

You will make men addled fools—like this:
(*sentimentally, taking a lover's posture*)
Love has transformed me, and given me eyes
that see only magic—and tell only lies.
I see a beauty where once I saw you.
Surely my vision cannot be true!
My judgment is stricken whenever you smile.
If only this fragrance would linger awhile
I'd know if it's roses—or you, dear. . . .

SATAN AND EVE (*she, as though hypnotized*): Illusion is the leaven
   that keeps our lives from shrinking.
   Reality is quite a bore—
   but what a joy in thinking!

(*Adam backs out of the cave, pulling a rope. The rope, it develops, is attached to a crude, wooden, wheeled dolly on which there is a large, uncompleted marble statue of a flat-footed, awkwardly posing woman, looking something like Eve, but, clearly, not idealized. He looks up at Satan sleepily.*)

ADAM: Who are you?

SATAN: A . . . an itinerant philosopher.

ADAM: From Heaven?

SATAN: Distinctly.

ADAM (*suspicious, but softening*): Well, we are supposed to be on the look-out for a dangerous visitor.

SATAN: I know.

ADAM: You know about that, eh? Were you sent down to protect us? We're rather innocent, you know.

SATAN: Yes, I will protect you, you might say—
   in my itinerantly philosophical way.

ADAM: Well, I'm new at philosophy—but I am very earnest.

   (*Sees remains of fire.*)

   Hey, look! This thing died!

SATAN: Here, I'll fix it.

(*Satan snaps his fingers to summon Devils, but, in response, Angels wheel in and hover above him.*)

ANGELS (*sweetly*): Did you call?
SATAN (*annoyed*): Sorry. Wrong hand.

(*He snaps the fingers of the other hand. Devils come marching in with their wiener-forks and wieners.*)

DEVILS: Hurray for the building of fire—
SATAN (*interrupting them*): Never mind. Just get it going.

(*Devils start assembling fire, piling wood, blowing, fanning coals.*)

ADAM: Do you know anything about science?
SATAN (*wearily*): What did you have in mind?
ADAM: Well, last night I touched this thing—and burned myself!
SATAN: Most good things are better
      the moment before you touch.
      They improve as you get closer—
      and then: you've had too much!
SATAN AND DEVILS: Oh, we are acquainted with fire.
      We believe in the art of good cooking . . .
ANGELS: Oh, rely on the heavenly choir.
      We can't cook, but are much better looking.
SATAN AND DEVILS: The best blades are hardened by flame.
      The best souls are strengthened by burning.
      So to singe all the world is our aim.
      You can chalk all the pain up to learning!
ADAM: Oh no! You won't catch *me* getting burned again!
SATAN: What harm do you find in a burn?
      There is time to recoil after that.
      Unless the fat gets in the fire
      you eat, you know, raw fat.
      Monotony rewards those who refrain—
      and all you suffer for excess is pain. . . .
ADAM: Pain, now. I don't like pain! And Michael tells me it
      is quite unnecessary.
      Michael says that

        happiness
        is a matter of refraining.
        No one needs
        to suffer pain
        if he keeps himself in training.
ANGELS (*sanctimoniously*): That's what Michael says,
        and Michael seems to know.
ADAM: He says that food is
        harmless if
        it's consumed in proper measure.
ANGELS: People die of
        indigestion
        if they simply eat for pleasure.
ANGELS AND ADAM: That's what Michael says,
        and Michael seems to know.
ADAM: Moderate drinking,
        Michael says,
        helps increase a man's endurance. . . .
EVE: Just be certain
        that you have
        paid for adequate insurance.
ADAM AND EVE: Sex, he says, is
        dangerous
        once you've started to enjoy it.
        It has its proper
        uses if
        people carefully employ it.
ANGELS: Michael says
        you can dull
        any thrill you set your mind to—
        that you may
        do anything,
        just so long as you don't want to!
ADAM, EVE, ANGELS: That's what Michael says—
        and Michael seems to know!

(*Angels depart in ecstasy, Devils in disgust. Satan, bored with the whole performance, has gone to study Adam's sculpture.*)

SATAN (*to Adam*): I see you're the creative type.

ADAM (*frankly*): Yes. And I'm also a great one for reading.

SATAN: And what does Eve do?

ADAM: Well, I learn things, and she's
        the one who puts them into practice.
        Lately, I've studied care of trees—
        and Eve, on my advice,
        is pruning all the trees in Paradise.

SATAN: Oh, good! It clearly would not please
        the Powers that be for man to wed
        practice and knowledge in a single head.

ADAM (*pointing to apple tree*): Of course, we can't prune that
        one.

SATAN: No? Why not?

ADAM (*indignantly*): Why, it's against the law!

SATAN: You don't say! Why?

ADAM (*puzzled*): Why, I never thought to ask.

SATAN (*going to it*): What is it?

ADAM: It has a long Latin name. In the vernacular, it's
        called the Tree of Knowledge of Good and Evil.

(*Satan walks to it, casually picks an apple. Adam and Eve put their hands over their ears as though expecting an immediate explosion.*)

SATAN: And you're not allowed to prune it?

(*He starts to take a bite. Adam runs toward him—then away from him in panic.*)

ADAM (*huddling*): Stop! Look out there! We're not allowed to
        touch it—let alone eat its fruit! And . . . and if you
        . . . if you *eat* it, I'll not answer for the conse-
        quences!

SATAN: We higher beings have a natural immunity to Good
        and Evil.

(*Takes a bite, comes back to them chewing, while Adam and Eve stand agog. He talks with his mouth full.*)

Best fruit, I daresay, in the Garden. I can't imagine
anyone would mind much if you tasted it.

(*Offers the apple. They recoil in horror.*)

Come now! It is a God-like fruit, and it is God-like
to eat it!

(*Chomping heartily.*)

Didn't they give you Free Will?

EVE (*starting forward*): Yes. They did give us Free Will.

ADAM (*restraining her*): As a matter of fact they did—but
there's a flaw
somewhere in your interpretation. Michael says
freedom is a matter of staying within the law.

SATAN (*laughing*): Well, you can have Michael's freedom. I'll
have mine.
What do we do today? I have till noon.

ADAM: Well, you can go with Eve and prune—
or stick around with me and chat.

(*Indicates statue.*)

I plan to do some work on that.

SATAN: Art in Eden! How can you have an urge to art—
unless you expect to die?
Why should you wish to shape your thought in stone
unless a sense of death eats at your heart?

ADAM (*scratching head*): Well, Michael says that art is entertainment—
a harmless way of helping us endure. . . .

SATAN: Ah ha!
You think you can remain
a perpetual amateur!
But don't deceive
yourself. You can't maintain
such innocence in art; it will achieve
meaning beneath your hand. Already you
have made a comment here—on Eve.

EVE (*looking at statue in alarm*): Oh dear! I think he has!
ADAM: I'll have to think this out.

>   (*Suddenly irked.*)

>   Now, look, you! It isn't polite to come along
>   and make a guy uneasy with a doubt!

(*Adam goes to statue, picks up his hammer and chisel and looks puzzled.*)

EVE (*concerned about statue*): It looks so naked, standing there!
>   Why aren't we allowed to wear clothes?
SATAN: Goodness knows!
EVE: Why do *you* wear clothes? Is it for sitting down?
SATAN (*startled, laughs*): Is it for *what?*
EVE: Well, Michael says that angels have
>   a kind of sensitivity back here . . .
>   and that, besides, clothes keep them warm
>   when traveling through the stratosphere . . .
SATAN (*doubles with laughter*): Oh no! Oh no! That old sinner!
EVE: I don't see what's so funny.
SATAN: It's just that Michael tried to dodge the issue.
>   He knows that life becomes more interesting
>   when bodies are draped—even in the filmiest tissue.

>   (*Takes off his cape.*)

>   Come, let me show you with what beauty you're en-
>   dowed.
EVE (*looking dubiously at cape*): I'm not sure I am allowed.
SATAN (*starts to put it back on*): Oh, well. You might not feel
>   much different in it.
EVE (*hastily reaching for it*):
>   Maybe if I put it on my shoulders for a minute . . .
SATAN: Yes. Much better. Drape it loosely around you, now.

(*Gives it to her and she puts it on.*)

>   Yes. And stand like this.

(*He shows her a model pose which she imitates awkwardly.*)

No, lift your eyebrow like this. Straighten your back, so that your chest swells amply. That's better. Now put a leg forward and point your toe—like this. Exactly! Now have a look at yourself. . . . Damn! We must create a mirror!

(*Adam has been watching all this curiously and now comes closer, looking at Eve with fascination. Satan snaps his fingers, and Devils dance in with a mirror, a prancing satire of vanity —one holding the mirror, others cavorting vainly before it. They set it up, and Satan waves his hand, dismissing them. They leave.*)

SATAN: Now stand just as you were over here.

(*Eve is engrossed in study of her reflection.*)

Now take it off and compare.

(*Eve takes the cape off and then hurriedly puts it back on, lifting her chin in a majestic pose.*)

EVE: Why, why . . . I have dignity.
ADAM: Dignity, hell. You're desirable!
SATAN: This hand, a moment ago,
was a gadget for pruning trees—
but now it is a tease,
an invitation to probe,
making us wonder what there is
beneath that robe. . . .
EVE: But you already know.
SATAN: That doesn't, for some reason, make the slightest difference. Open the collar; let the cape break at the thigh. Why, if you were fully clothed you might incline a man to violence!
EVE: I might?
ADAM (*somewhat aroused*): You might anyway. You'd better take it off.

(*Eve does.*)

Hey, let me see that thing a minute.

(*She hands it to him. He takes it to the statue and drapes it over.*)

> Much better, eh?
>
> (*Reclines in hammock to study the statue.*)
>
> Indecent. But indecency seems more appropriate in art.

(*Eve, distracted by her recent experience, walks to cave and picks up a crude pair of pruning shears. Satan watches her in amusement.*)

SATAN: Ah, yes! The pruning!

ADAM (*settling comfortably in his hammock*): Well, take frequent rest periods. I've read that working in too concentrated a fashion cuts down on your efficiency. This is especially true in my work, which is more intellectual. I sometimes notice that after I finish a paragraph I hardly have energy to close my eyes. Fine day. Looked like a storm last night—but nothing came of it.

SATAN: Don't worry. No rain for generations.

ADAM (*lazily*): The morning is like butter,
> another perfect day.
> Ho-hum! Ho-hum!
> The birds begin to flutter,
> the sun comes out to stay.
> Ho-hum! Ho-hum!

(*Adam falls asleep. Eve returns to where Satan is waiting, carrying the shears. She has a worried look.*)

EVE: I have let this day get off to a terrible start!

SATAN: Why do you say that?

EVE: That cape caused a tingling of blood,
> a strange, wicked pounding of my heart.

SATAN: Wasn't it pleasant? And must you call
> it wicked? A simple rise in temperature . . .

EVE: If wickedness is anything like that,
> it is more than a body can endure.

SATAN: But, Eve, it was for wickedness
        that bodies were intended!
        The bulk of you all pulls one way,
        but in your head some ounces of grey
        convolutions haul you back
        against yourself; between
        these forces there you hang, suspended!
        The machine is jammed, its gears involved
        in inner contradiction. If you lean
        all one way, that's wickedness—
        or saintliness: depending
        on how the forces are resolved.
        For you, I'll bet on wickedness.

EVE: But I am *not* wicked?

SATAN: No—you are unaware.
        Your consciousness sits in your head
        like a mirror in an empty room,
        reflecting nothing in its glassy stare.
        Sin, goodness, pleasure, tragedy, can bloom
        only in the mind that knows,
        the heart exposed to care.

EVE: The pendulum that ticks the clock
        is very very much like me.
        My heart knows its own rhythm but
        the hour it cannot see.

        Oh tick tock tick! My heart is sick
        of clicking its eternal song. . . .

SATAN: Oh tock tick tock! Let's stop the clock—
        or, better yet, let it be wrong!

        Come here for a moment, Eve.

(*Taking her chin in his hand, he kisses her.*)

        What did you feel?

EVE (*disturbed*): That tingling again.

SATAN: You would get the same tingle if you were unexpectedly
        licked by a dog.

EVE: I don't think so.

SATAN: Then you are farther along than I imagined.

EVE: Let me try on that cape again. (*She goes to the statue, removes cape, and puts it around her.*) That's better. I feel more conscious now.

SATAN: Oh, you *like* feeling conscious?

EVE (*discovering her own feelings*): It's not so much that I *like* it—but that I can't retract it. I can't even wish I were any less aware.

SATAN: Exactly. (*Turns away disgusted.*) And that's why it is all nonsense about that Tree.

EVE: The Tree of Knowledge?

SATAN: Absurd, beyond dispute,
           that you cannot, *will* not taste that fruit!

EVE: But we were told not to.

SATAN: I know—but Heaven's thunder
           stirs my rebellious heart, demands some answering voice.
           You, too, if you ate the apple, would sense the meaning
           of emerging here, unfettered, under
           the distant sky, the high clouds screening. . . .
           You would have values, choice. . . .

EVE: Do you mean it would make me like kissing more?

SATAN: Perhaps. Not kissing *me:*
           you would hate me instantly.
           All gifts that touch the heart inspire such hate.
           But, yes. You are a woman to the core
           and once you knew what life can stimulate,
           you would like kissing more.

EVE: Then why is this forbidden me?

SATAN: It is a Heavenly trick. You have Free Will . . . ?

EVE: So we were told. . . .

SATAN: But you are free as a stream is free
           that freely runs on a mountain-side, fast, cold,
           with only one direction. You may see
           only the banks along the way, your rate
           of movement fixed, your ripples and currents set

         by what you pass: a rock on the bottom, a branch
         projecting from the shore. Like an avalanche
         you roar in celebration of your fate.
EVE: Why, that doesn't sound free at all!
SATAN: No. But what would it be to flow *up hill?*
EVE (*shocked*): That would be against Nature!
SATAN: Of course! The only freedom is discord,
            disobedience, revolution, sin!
            Assertion of the will,
            dignity of the proud.
            Unlike that stream you *can* flow up the hill!
EVE: I can't if I'm not allowed.
SATAN: Ah, but you can!
            Look here, I'll show you how!

(*Plucks an apple from the tree and holds it toward her. She shrinks.*)

         Touch it! Your hand can rub its skin!

(*Timidly she does so.*)

         Your lips can touch it. Now,

(*She allows him to touch it to her lips.*)

         come tingle with *this* kiss!
         Your teeth. Your tongue. You *taste* it. This
         is not so far from eating, is it, Eve?
EVE (*who has been cooperating to this point, now jumps back,
            frightened*):
         But I'm afraid!
SATAN: Ah! Fear!
         Not that you want, really, to obey—
         but are afraid of life—and jump away!
         Only with courage can you achieve
         true greatness and fulfillment, Eve.
EVE: Your words send my soul fluttering
         like a fledgling from the nest,
         a desperate journey in indifferent air. . . .

SATAN: A necessary journey, for the best . . .
EVE: Oh wild bird, oh wild bird,
> the night is dark and long.
> Come down, bird. Come down, bird.
> Descend and hear my song.
>
> There is an end to wandering,
> to loneliness and pain.
> I'll give you my heart, bird—
> my heart . . . upon a chain!

SATAN: Take wing yourself and follow.
EVE: I want to eat the apple.
SATAN (*holding it back from her*): But wait! Before you do,
> I want to say
> I am that visitor of whom you were warned!

(*Eve is shocked, but stands up to it.*)

> I am an outcast from Heaven. I flung away
> in proud rebellion comfort that I scorned.
> Nor will I hide from you just what it means
> if you should eat the apple: your life will be
> rounded with death, infused with new intensity.
> Wax fruit will last forever, true fruit will not—
> the juices of its flavor make it rot.
> You will be dispossessed of this bright Garden.
> You will bear the curse of God and travel under
> His clouded visage and his angry thunder.

(*As he says this, clouds come over the sun and the wind stirs, rippling their hair, blowing leaves across the ground. Eve is chilly; she pulls the cape tight around her body.*)

> But worse than these punishments shall be
> your new awareness of uncertainty.
> Right now you *know* what is right, what wrong.
> The apple blurs your view:
> things good will seem not quite so good,
> things bad not quite so bad.
> Gone, with a single taste,

are perfect black and white, clear laughter and clear
    song!
Evil, you will see, sometimes has benefits,
and virtue is the source of tragedy.
The world out there springs verdant, dies in waste;
its blossoms are intense for a moment only,
in the dew, in the sunlight, and wither. Truth
which here is so clear, is shadowy out there,
perceived as in a sea which screams its hurricanes,
shatters on the coast its salty spray, mist in the air,
or rolls its warm, soft shoulders, greenly mute,
and hiding in its still, deep dark, down, down,
some silent Absolute.

EVE: I want it.

(*She takes it and bites. There is a terrific crack of thunder and flash of lightning. Adam, startled awake, rolls out of the hammock and falls on his knees, looking up mournfully at the sky.*)

ADAM: It's getting so you can't even trust perfection any more. Last night, and today again; it must be an expression of God's fury.

SATAN: That doesn't sound like you, Adam.

ADAM: What do you mean?

SATAN: Well, look there to the East, at that long low line of boiling clouds. Now, are you sure that signifies God's fury?

ADAM: Well, actually, it looks like a low pressure front.

SATAN: Exactly.

ADAM: It's hard on a man's nerves, nevertheless.

(*He sees Eve huddled in the cape, the apple half-eaten. She looks guiltily at him.*)

Eve! Eve! What have you *done?*

EVE (*slowly*): Adam, Adam, I am ashamed.

ADAM (*taking apple from her*): Ashamed? You have damned us!

EVE: I've damned only myself.

ADAM: You've eaten the Forbidden Fruit!

EVE: I flowed just a little bit upstream.

ADAM: Upstream! Look at what you've done! Michael *trusted* us, and now he will be in all kinds of trouble with Headquarters. He will—*we* will! Why, when they see this bitten apple, its bright skin broken by human teeth, its pulpy meat crumbled in lustful lips. . . . Oh, Eve! Just *look* at what you have done! Look at that apple, bitten to the core! (*Suddenly preoccupied in a different way.*) Look at that seed structure! What . . . what did it taste like, Eve?

EVE: Oh, Adam, you must never know!

ADAM: But can't you describe it somehow? Simply in the interests of science?

EVE: I don't know, Adam, how I can describe a taste. . . .

ADAM: Well, it's hard, I know. I suppose I will have to taste it myself to find out.

SATAN: Careful, Adam! You know to eat it means you will be driven from the gates of Eden!

ADAM (*thinking this over*): Eve. What will happen to Eve?

SATAN: I am sure that she will have to leave.

ADAM (*with decision*): Then I guess I'll have to go, too. (*Pauses for a moment, looking around him, then lovingly at Eve. He winks at Satan.*) I can't spare another rib, you know!

(*Eve reaches to stop him, but Adam takes a healthy bite of the apple.*)

ADAM (*with his mouth full*): Oh! Good. Sort of sweet and tart all at the same time. You couldn't have the sweetness without the tartness or the tartness without the sweetness and get the same effect. We'll have to serve these to Michael when he comes tonight. Oh, that's cruel of me! Poor Michael. How disappointed he will be. No doubt he has heard of this already and is on his way right now. Unless I get something on he'll catch me naked as a jaybird. Eve, what can I wear? . . . Never mind, I'll find something in the woods. But I'd better hurry. The way news travels around this universe, you know . . .

EVE (*confused by his burst of spirits*): Adam, you're not angry, frightened?

ADAM: Never felt so good in my life!

> Sin becomes me!
> I am a criminal at large!
> I can see transgression as my new obsession:
> it hits me like a hormone charge!
>
> Sin becomes me!
> Why should I mope and be morose?
> I feel an alteration and a new elation
> that hits me like a vitamin dose!
>
> I'm a new man
> on a new plan!
> I have new zest
> after long rest!
> I'm an ex-clunk!
> I have more spunk!
> Life is ready to begin!
> I owe everything to sin!
>
> Sin becomes me!
> I'm like a birdie in the breeze!
> I'm like a fish in the ocean, like a wheel in motion!
> I'm ready to burn calories!

(*Breaks off singing, but music continues as he speaks excitedly to Satan and Eve.*)

> Nothing is as refreshing as a new discovery! Besides, I had the feeling we were getting into a rut. This ought to do great things for our marriage! Let me have another one of those! (*Picks another apple.*) See you in a few minutes. I want to get something on before all Hell breaks loose! (*Runs off, eating apple.*)

SATAN: Do you want another kiss, now, Eve, for comparison?

EVE: I don't even know your name.

SATAN: My name is Satan.

EVE: A bachelor, I suppose.

SATAN: You might put it that way.

EVE: Well, no, I don't think I should kiss you. And I want to find something else to wear—I feel very improper using your personal cape.

SATAN: That apple made you very moral. But you are quite right not to kiss a fly-by-night fallen angel. And although I find myself much attracted by the human female—I think, in the long run, I'd rather not be any more deeply involved.

> In life's great game of chess
> you must be wary of the queen;
> don't let some bishop sail across
> and trap you in between.
> In the battle of the sexes
> the odds are always weighted.
> Be wary of the queen and keep
> yourself from being mated . . .
>> or you'll march double-file
>> down an endless one-way a-ai-aisle!

(*Devils and Angels enter, Angels this time on the ground. They spread themselves like pieces of chessmen and in a hopping ballet, one piece moving at a time, the Devils on the offensive until they get into tight places and then fleeing.*)

SATAN AND DEVILS: Oh, life's great game of chess
> is tiresome for the little pawn.
> He plods his straight-and-narrow path
> the way the squares are drawn.
> Just as he sees his goal
> and feels himself elated
> elsewhere upon the board his king
> has gotten himself mated!

ANGELS (*as they watch a Devil knight approaching*):
> In life's great game of chess,
> you must have pity for the knight,
> who hops a crooked hop because

such crookedness is right.
He can pounce on the queen—
a chance for which he's waited—
but suddenly he hears his king
has gone and gotten mated.

(*Satan and Eve step into the game, she on the side of the Angels. Satan plays the part of the king.*)

COMPANY: In life's great game of chess
the king is said to have his way
since he is monarch of the eight
small squares his eyes survey.
The notion that he rules
is quaint and antiquated.
His strutting comes abruptly to an end
the moment he is mated.

ANGELS AND DEVILS (*as Satan and Eve engage in a courtship dance by themselves*):
In life's great game of chess
the bachelor is the only king.
No piece can get too close to him.
He only fears one thing:
the freedom of the board
to be loved and to be hated
is his until the game is up . . .
at last he is checkmated!
    and they walk double file
    down an endless one-way a-ai-aisle!

(*After the song, Satan and the Devils laugh uproariously in a comradely way. The Angels are shocked by this behavior and run off gossiping. The Devils and Satan slap one another on the back and the Devils go off in a gang. Satan, giddy with his victory, seems to have forgotten the presence of Eve.*)

SATAN (*to Devils, as they are leaving*): Well, fellows, it was no
trick at all for the old master!
EVE (*disturbed, calls after him*): Satan!

(*He turns, questioningly. Eve doesn't know what to say—then reminds him:*)

> Your . . . cape.

SATAN (*conscious of his masculine audience*): Oh . . . ah.
Well, when you get on something else, just hang it
on the Tree, here—or some place that won't be too
compromising.

(*Devils break out in insensitive laughter. Satan looks at Eve
with a shade of embarrassment, and then joins his boys, laughing. They leave. Eve stands forlornly by the mouth of the cave,
clutching the cape around her. After a moment she bursts into
tears and runs into the cave. There is a still, deserted moment.
Michael then flies blithely in, humming to himself. As he lands
and comes forward he sings happily.*)

MICHAEL: Oh, women are all gentle,
> and men are all he-men,
> their children are all angels and
> their infants cherubin.
> Well,
> it isn't what it is, but is what ought to be!

> And friends are always loyal
> and enemies forgiving
> and neighbors always loving and
> life always is worth living.
> Well,
> it isn't what is, but is what ought to be!

> Oh, pigeons are all homing,
> and dogs all lick your hand,
> and horses bear your burdens and
> fish jump into the pan.
> Well,
> it isn't what is, but is what ought to be.

> (*changing tone*)
> The world of is is dreadful.
> Reality is cruel.

Life is a slow starvation on
a bland and watery gruel,
so
don't think of what is, but of what ought to be!

(*He goes to the mouth of the cave, calls in:*) Adam! Eve!
Adam! Eve! (*He walks around looking, calling into the woods:*)
Adam! Eve! (*But just then he kicks an apple core which is
lying on the ground. He looks down, picks it up and sadly
shrugs his shoulders.*)

God will be disappointed.
In spite of his foreknowledge,
he always expects the best.
A sloppy way this was
to fail a test!
And what is more:
they didn't even pick up the core!
No ceremony, no invocation, no poetry!
Beyond all measure, what makes God rage and
storm
is infidelity
in Bad Form.

(*As music continues under*) Well, my pair of doves has let
themselves out into the winter. Maybe they'll find
pleasure in that world—although pleasure in general
is something I'm rather skeptical of. It is staying
clear of pain that means happiness to me. It takes
all my wits to remain dull. Keeping up the payments,
keeping a family healthy, keeping out of trouble with
the law, and keeping a decent reputation in the eyes
of neighbors—that's life enough, indeed. The best
thing we can achieve is equilibrium.

Deep down, you know, I don't think Right and
Wrong are very important: that's all arbitrary, anyway. But I do believe in *Peace*—with others, with
myself, with the natural world around me. Now
Peace, when you find it, is always tentative and un-

dramatic. No one gives you a medal for washing
the ring out of the bathtub or just driving on your
side of the road or patching your umbrella in a dry
season. But in my mind, that's Virtue. Satan, now,
is against Peace and Virtue. He upset all of Heaven
—and we had to throw him out. And this world, too,
will learn to damn those who disturb it. Society can
never tolerate unpredictability, irresponsibility, and
society knows God's will. He may lose out in the
individual case, but He always lives in the mass
mind!

(*Angels join Michael for a haunting, poignant rendition of the
music that ended Act I.*)

ANGELS: There is not a joy in the world, la, la,
     that is not compounded in pain,
   and never a moon that is full, la, la,
     but is just beginning to wane.
ANGELS AND MICHAEL: The touch of your lips on my cheek, la,
     la,
     reminds me that lips must decay.
   No flower that blooms in the morn, la, la,
     will last through the heat of the day.
MICHAEL: Whatever is easy to have, la, la,
     is easier lost than a dream.
   Things never are, after they start, la, la,
     as good or as bad as they seemed.
ANGELS AND MICHAEL: Our homes are the bargains we make,
     la, la,
     to stay out of the sun and the rain.
   There is not a joy in the world, la, la,
     that is not compounded,
      that is not compounded,
       that is not compounded in pain!

(*Darkness.*)

EPILOGUE

(*In semidarkness we see silhouetted on high crags Satan and Michael sitting thoughtfully, staring down at a greenly glowing ball far below them. Satan, standing as music fades, nods in a self-satisfied way at Michael.*)

SATAN: Okay. Your move.

MICHAEL (*shakes head in sad resignation*):

    No. Our side will abstain.

    From this time on, they're on their own—

    and physical laws shall reign. . . .

SATAN (*indignantly*): I object!

    This has no meaning!

    Machines of blood and bones,

    like any apparatus, must be used,

    be pointed somewhere, be maintained. . . .

MICHAEL: We must not be accused

    of meddling with their freedom:

    our reputation for fair play would then be stained.

SATAN: Oh listen, oh listen, to the fable of the fly!

    With face of soot

    and gluey foot

    the fly is vain of power:

    he grows his height

    and learns to fight

    and takes a mate

    and meets his fate—

    all this within an hour.

    He soars perhaps

    ten feet and snaps

    a gnat out of the air.

    With sweaty brow,

    I don't know how,

    he lugs the giant

    home defiant—

    and dumps it in his lair.

His home is full
of larvae (you'll
agree they breed like flies).
With buzz dramatic,
defeats traumatic,
he climbs and sinks
and, old, he thinks
his life was long and wise.

A pinch of time,
he's past his prime.
Who, then, are you or I
to find design
or truth define,
say right or wrong
or short or long
to the suffering of a fly?

MICHAEL: Unlike the fly, these creatures can *create* meaning
—if they discover law and order.

Law and Order!
I stand for Law and Order,
for standards and for decency, thus:
for separate booths for ladies
and regular shots for rabies.
These are bigger things than both of us!

Law and Order!
I stand for Law and Order,
for neckties and propriety, thus:
for rubbers and umbrellas,
and roses on a trellis,
These are bigger things than both of us.

Law and Order!
I stand for Law and Order,
for doilies and legality, thus:
for regular lawn-mowing
and milk for children growing.
These are bigger than both of us!

(*They disappear into darkness, and Eden is revealed—a chilliness in the air. The ground is covered with apples and cores. The Tree and shrubbery are stripped of their leaves, the grass is brown, grey clouds boil overhead. A curl of smoke comes twisting from the mouth of the cave. The statue stands on a pedestal of stones near the Tree. With a musical background, Adam comes from the cave, dressed in skins. He is carrying a crude sign, on which irregular printing reads:* EVE. SHE FELL, AND WARMED THE WINTER EARTH WITH HELL. *He places it lovingly at the base of the statue and stands beating his hands on his arms for warmth, admiring it. Then he is dissatisfied. He goes to the hammock and takes it down, then uses it as a garment for the statue, draping it over her shoulder and across her hip. Again he stands back and admires, again finds something missing. He hunts around on the ground for an apple and sticks it in the hand of the statue. Again he stands back, again is not satisfied. He takes the apple and bites a big hunk out of it. He doesn't like the taste, so spits the bite on the ground. Then he puts the bitten apple back into the hand of the statue. Now, admiring it, he is satisfied. He goes up, stands on tiptoes, and kisses the statue on the lips. Eve comes out of the cave, also dressed in skins. She goes up behind Adam and rests her hands on his shoulders, both of them looking at the statue.*)

EVE: Your first poem, dear.

ADAM: Michael says another man named Milton will one day
        revise that poem extensively.

(*Eve squeezes Adam and turns from him enthusiastically looking around her at the transformed landscape.*)

EVE: It's a good day for a journey!
        I love the sound of the earth creaking
        and groaning like an aged man. It makes
        the blood pulse in my cheeks, eyes run with tears,
        with springs that never freeze: to sense life leaking
        beneath the crust; it cheers
        to feel such clean economy, such cold aches
        of the bare boughs, the congealed sun, the brown

> chattering fields, the just perceptible breath
> of life enduring ravage. It will not down,
> and though it gives an inch, the skin crying
> with pain, the soul endures like a rock on a cliff,
> meeting the wind, the wind defying.

ADAM: Yeah! Spring is for the birds!

EVE: Oh, Adam!

> Forgive me, forgive me!
> This day of darkness, wind, and ice!
> Forgive me, forgive me!
> Gone, gone is Paradise.
> And Winter in Eden
> has stripped our lonely apple tree.
> But Winter in Eden
> brings love and warmth to me.

ADAM AND EVE: The winds of the Winter

> force life into the seed.
> Oh, Winter in Eden
> shows me my deepest need. . . .

EVE: And bearing the curse of

> a knowledge God cannot forgive
> I turn now to Adam:
> his love will let me live.

ADAM AND EVE: Oh, Winter in Eden

> is Heaven's gift to man below.
> Oh, Winter in Eden
> makes human lovers grow,

EVE: drives deer to their shelter,   ADAM: The winds of the Winter
    shrieks down from angry   force life into the seed.
    clouds above.   Oh, Winter in Eden
    Oh, Winter in Eden   shows me my deepest
    drives me to seek my love.   need.

ADAM AND EVE: Oh, Winter in Eden

> drives me to seek my love!

(Michael flies in wearing a space suit. On earth, he removes the plastic helmet and comes forward, carrying his helmet under his arm. He wipes his forehead.)

MICHAEL: Whew! This Universe is getting bigger every day!

ADAM: You going with us?

MICHAEL: No. I just came to lock up afterwards.

(*Satan comes out of cave, carrying a couple of bundles on sticks, tied up in skins.*)

SATAN (*to Adam*): Everything's packed.

MICHAEL: You seem to have made yourself quite at home around here.

SATAN: I thought perhaps I should help them get used to the facts of life.

MICHAEL (*sarcastically*): And perhaps create a few new facts of life in the bargain?

SATAN: Oh, don't despair. You operate better on the mass. Adam and Eve together are more angelic than either of them alone. And when they get out there . . . (*sweeps arm over audience*) righteousness will inherit the earth. Morals will multiply like rabbits. . . .

MICHAEL (*angrily*): Well, goodness may be a bore—but no one has been able to think of anything better!

SATAN (*ironically*): Oh, I have faith in God, you see. Men will always float in an ethical sea which overcomes their individuality. My business, I suppose, is just to see that they don't submerge.

ADAM: Let's be on our way! Let's have more action and less philosophy!

SATAN: Right you are. Fall *in!*

(*Devils leap out from behind the rocks and bushes and fall into an orderly column at attention. Michael looks on in alarm, as Adam and Eve, shouldering their bundles, take places at the head of this column.*)

MICHAEL (*shouts*): Oh no! It is too uneven! I can't bear to imagine such a future—without law and order, without gentility, the graces of art, music, poetry, without decency at the toilet and the table—the life of man will be solitary, poor, nasty, brutish, and short! Fall *in!*

(*Angels enter on high, filing in military rank, their angelic faces faces set sternly, large swords awkwardly on their shoulders.*)

SATAN, ADAM, AND EVE (*as they begin to march*):
        We're on our way! We're on our way!
        The world outside is wonderful, we think.
        We're drunk on apple cider.
        We need a world that's wider.

ADAM AND EVE (*to each other*): Oh, let's go out and make a
        missing link!

SATAN AND DEVILS: They're on their way! They're on their way!
        The world outside can be no worse than this.
        And we have made them able
        to keep the world unstable
        and leave behind their ignorance and bliss.

ADAM: We're on our way! We're on our way!
        For growing chickens always break their eggs.
        We leave the shell in shambles,
        but we prefer the brambles. . . .

ADAM AND EVE (*to each other*): Oh, let's go out and drink life
        to the dregs!

MICHAEL (*sonorously*): They're on their way! They're on their
        way!
        And they leave here with all my blessing.
        They have my pity since
        in my experience
        reality is quite depressing!

(*Music continues under as Angels descend and engage Devils in silent combat. Adam and Eve, meanwhile, come forward and begin looking curiously at the audience.*)

ADAM (*extending arms*): All my sons! Think of it! All my genes,
        perpetuated!

SATAN: What an enormous memorial to your primitive virtues!

EVE (*pointing at crowd*): Look what they wear! The jewels!
        The furs!
        How they sprinkle their faces with flour!

MICHAEL: You see a glimpse of what occurs . . .
　　　　　but not the baby strollers, grocery lines,
　　　　　the weariness at five, the lonely hour. . . .
EVE (*rapturously*): To be feeling I care not what . . .
　　　　　To have freedom, I care not why . . .
ADAM: To take a bus for nowhere in particular . . .
MICHAEL: With a vacant stare, a hanging jaw . . .
EVE: What rapture, after Eden!
SATAN: Exactly! Damnation is the only worthwhile way of life.
ADAM: It's so *hu*man!

(*Behind them the battle between the Angels and Devils has
become flirtation. Now they are standing in couples.*)

COMPANY: We're (They're) on our (their) way!
　　　　　We're (They're) on our (their) way!
ANGELS AND DEVILS (*coming forward in a long line, alternating
　　　　　Devils and Angels, arm in arm*):
　　　　　With sin and virtue marching side by side!
ADAM AND EVE: We managed to take Paradise in stride!
ADAM: And move into Nature's laboratory!
COMPANY: What we (they) will discover . . .
　　　　　What we (they) will uncover . . .
MICHAEL (*sadly*): Well, that is quite another story!

(*A clap of thunder. Michael glances upward, then hastily replaces his helmet and, while the column of Angels, Devils, Satan,
Adam, and Eve marches off through the audience, Michael sails
prayerfully back to the blue.*)

VI

Go East, Young Man:
Notes on *Drums*

LOVE, THE FIRST DECADE

(1958)

Ten years ago our courtship had become
serious, as they say. That holiday,
a New Year's Eve, when I proposed was gay
as a Steig cartoon: a joke of love, ink-drawn,
moderne, all psychological. We stole
upstairs in the frat house, there said those droll
and ceremonial words of tender troth,
then called your parents, who were shocked. Oh youth,

they cried: we had not had a period
of trial. We said we'd tried. In this we lied,
and spent the midnight wondering whether it
were more sophisticated to resist,
comply or lie. We lay all night, quite dressed,
before a mock-wood fire and made commit-
ments, listened to Sibelius, were distressed
by Henry James. Our hearts were full of wit.

Season of love! Remember Christmas, when
your mother, free-expressing, danced to de Falla,
swung her behind too low across a candle
on the coffee-table, spilled her punch. Oh, then
our wassail was mature, our gifts were graced
with dirty rhymes; deep feelings were expressed
in black and white abstractions on long cards.
Liberal '48! Gone. With regards.

The World has aged. Republicans have won.
Gramma can dance, still, but cares less for funny rhymes and gin. Grampa plays with babies,
rarely reciting Catullus, Rabelais,
or making drunken confetti of Aquinas.
We pop walnuts and grin all Christmas day.
The fire is bright behind our knobby stockings
and the twinkling green is looped with ruddy strings

of cranberries. Romance, like a party, passed;
the hangover passed. This year sobriety
is heavy-bottomed as a bourgeois tree.
Back then a Wallacite told us in the night,
his finger wagging, and he, too, being tight,
how liberals tend to fall away in the fight,
how stodginess conquers love. Love, love me fast
and witlessly: the serious years fall fast.

On a recent birthday I looked into the mirror with horror.
Perhaps somewhere a portrait (as of Dorian Gray) was aging,
but I looked younger than I had the day before: the wavy hair
and dimple and smooth cheeks and happy, insipid little eyes
denied that I had ever lived at all. Of what use is experience if
you can't have a badge for it in the form of a grey streak or
rough, square jaw or lizard creases, announcing to the world
that you have seen and done and are qualified to speak?

At some point in the last ten years bartenders have stopped
asking for identification: my image must be that I am of voting
age. But I am making little progress toward the shore of maturity—if that is where I should be going. It recedes like the hair-
lines of my friends, while with upturned nose and innocent
amiability I slip back toward the quicksand of adolescence like
a film run backwards.

Ponce de León, according to the old legend, came to our
shores in search of eternal youth. Whether or not he found such
a fountain, perhaps it bubbles in the interior of our continent
and now, like fluoridation, is leaking into all our water taps,
keeping our grins ingratiating. For regardless of how individuals
may age, the nation seems to share my plight: the world sees
us as the young man in white shorts who is always bouncing on

stage to ask, "Anyone for tennis?" And the nation seems to search, as I do, endlessly eastward for some Fountain of Age to release us from our enchantment.

Up until about twenty years ago our innocence (my country's and my own) was charming. Until I was drafted (remember those old posters of the young man with goggles up looking challengingly at the skies?) I was cute, neuter, admitted to confidence of girls, cuddled, and thought precocious. I was Peter Pan in high school, cocky in college. But the Army made me feel fierce pangs of missing manhood. I looked like a stray Boy Scout among the soldiers. On weekend passes the girls only giggled. I was not served in bars. This, particularly, seemed an indignity, as I wandered the misty streets of Seattle the night before shipping out, old enough, I reasoned, to commit myself to treacherous seas and oriental soil, my head reeling from a flu shot, the burlesque theater closed, an hour until bus time, and all the other soldiers—my age but looking older—in the bars. This face I wore was a mask, I told myself, covering my real maturity and wisdom. But the mask was hideously stuck, like a rubber casing, and I was suffocating.

As our half-empty Liberty ship crashed and groaned through stormy northern seas, I moved, with the help of Thomas Wolfe, into tragic acceptance of myself. His problem was that he was too big and old for his age—and I knew just how he felt, I told his grizzly spirit, only my problem was the opposite. As that rusty drum of a ship reared and dove headlong westward to the East and the seas flooded through the scuppers, I clung to the cable up on the bow, near the anchor, looking for a stone, a leaf, an unfound door, exhilarated by my suffering, drenched, and the only one of the passengers or crew not to be sick (experience took no toll on *me*).

Some have manhood thrust upon them. Because I could type and had a couple of years of college, and all the real soldiers had been sent home by the winter of 1945–46, I was soon Acting First Sergeant of a small photo-technical unit—running the orderly room, bouncing coins on taut blankets in the tents during morning inspection, lining up my thirty or forty men, smoking a long cigar (though the troops were not allowed to smoke in

ranks), my burred hair standing ragged in the sun, making
moral speeches about dress and saluting and proper procedures
for signing out vehicles, all in the voice of an adolescent Harry
Truman, or Skeezix, or overgrown escapee from Our Gang. I
was a wheel, with control over the jeeps and trucks, supplies to
expropriate, passes to grant, records to examine (classifying my
men mentally by AGCT and MOS), drinking beer at the NCO
club, bargaining with the brass for liquor and airplane rides.
They called me Pee Wee.

Luckily there were no girls. Nothing brings out a fellow's
lack of manliness like girls. Of course there were nurses and
Red Cross girls for the officers, and I accompanied them on
dates (according to orders) with a .45 pistol (referred to as a
"persuader") strapped like a cannon to my narrow chest; while
they made love I sat in the dark jeep and sneered. But women
(in their compounds, surrounded by high barbed wire) and officers were of another world, mysterious and irrelevant to those
of us acting out our cowboy and Indian game in enlisted uni-
forms. Our roles, our responsibilities, our decisions, our function as Occupation Forces, all seemed made up as play.

In Shanghai, where I was sent for what the Army called Rest
and Recreation, actually a long, weary drunk, I encountered
girls again. By that time I had pretty well developed a bitter,
sensitive pose: I bought a copy of *Man's Fate* in a bookstore
on Bubbling Well Road, traveled the clamorous streets in a
rickshaw, contemplated the human condition, cultivated a
heavy-lidded, urbane mien, with cigaret bobbing in my lips,
eyebrow arching. But it could all be belied in a moment by, say,
a laugh, which would make my eyes pop and my cheeks crack
into a boy's glad grin. I sold purloined film on the blackmarket.
I delivered a message to a buxom White Russian who received
me in her negligee, a lady who entertained various high-ranking
American officers and who turned out to be a Communist spy.
But let me tell you I came out *clean*. I took a pretty shop girl to
nightclubs, where I couldn't dance because my boots hurt and I
didn't know how, bought her drinks and left her at the door
without a kiss, for fear she might giggle—and I would have had
to stand on tiptoe. I was a pathetic world conquerer.

That sort of thing was perhaps climaxed in San Francisco, on the Barbary Coast, where I had a one-night pass before discharge. Separated from my buddies for a moment, I caught a *hsst* from an incredibly striking woman—a six-foot mulatto, gorgeous, with, literally, a turban and a large gold ring in one ear. "Want to have some fun, soldier?" she asked huskily. I looked around for a soldier and discovered that she could mean no one but me. "No, ma'am," I gasped (home from the War, top sergeant, big roué)—and dashed for the safety of the pack.

Yet I wore my pride like a boil. In civvies, with a ruptured duck worn even on my T-shirt to distinguish me from the other little boys, I nurtured my *Weltschmerz,* reciting "Prufrock" at the drop of an aunt's lower jaw, endeavoring to be dissolute. When bartenders accused me of youth (as when, earlier, bus drivers had accused me of age and refused, finally, to let me ride for a nickel), I was bleakly haughty and stalked out in indignation, flinging myself upon the night. I would cut them off without a penny.

I thought of myself as seasoned and savvy at nineteen, a couple of years of college and the Army behind me, and it was with some condescension that I began dating the high school girl I had left behind me—until she folded me in her motherly arms and told me about the abortion she had recently undergone. That was in Houston. I fled Houston, went to Oklahoma City, where I had been living before being drafted. There I found seven people, including my alcoholic father and a cat, sharing a three-room apartment (civilians were having a housing shortage), and so I went on to Norman and the university. I think I may have been smoking a pipe. The students all looked scrubbed, well-dressed, conventionally collegiate and rah-rah. They looked, I thought, very young. Ah, no. Not for a man with my past. I decided to go East.

East was, to a Southwestern boy, the land of the pale and the literate, the sophisticated and sinful, the Mandarins who, thin and yellow, were familiar with evil and ruled the nation with elegant cynicism and culture. They probably all knew "Prufrock" by heart. They were not only served in bars, but knew what to order there that would make bartenders respect them. They were above Tchaikovsky and Aldous Huxley and Thomas Wolfe, and I was trying very hard to get above Tchaikovsky, Aldous Huxley, and Thomas Wolfe. Hell, I was trying to get above Gershwin and Kenneth Roberts. I was trying to advance from Will Rogers to Thurber. I didn't know whether they would let me in the East, but I wanted to go there and be damned, to answer the Call of the Tame shouting in my heart, "Go East, young man!" I went to the Oklahoma City depot and bought the longest ticket I could afford, which got me as far East as Chicago.

Well, actually, that was Yankee enough for me. I arrived on a vicious February midnight, shortly before my twentieth birthday, in my thin Southwestern clothes, and encountered sleet, darkness, smoke-darkened faces, and strange accents: everybody spoke too fast. I had to take a cab—and I don't believe I had ever ridden in a cab before, unless it were with an aunt. I had one magic phrase memorized, learned from some traveler who had been to the City and returned alive; as I climbed into the cab I tried to say it casually: "Lawson Y." Off into the dark streets—probably to be hijacked of my remaining $20.

Before long I was accustomed to it all: a job as a typist, a room with a cancerous landlady on the near North Side, subway rides, Steinway breakfasts, Pixley lunches, evenings of wandering jealously by the noisy bars and writing, writing into the the night and through long Sundays because that was the one activity which seemed to give me a vague definition. I practiced the poses and postures of sophistication. I considered suicide continually: I had no suitable tragedy, but it seemed supremely sophisticated to threaten myself with it. Someone had left a fedora in the closet of the room I rented, and though I never wore it in public, I dreamed of having a portrait made of myself wearing it. I would take it in a paper sack to the photographic studio. There, as props, I would have a steaming coffee cup and cigaret. I would loosen my tie, have the hat shoved back, lower my lids—and, snap—I would be Clark Gable. I went so far as to describe this plan to a lady in a studio on Michigan Avenue, one which specialized in men of character. She listened soberly, set a date, and told me that it would be $40 for the first print, and so, of course, I agreed with a casual nod, left, and never returned. But the day would come when I could legally go into a bar, be indignant when asked for identification, whip out my selective service card, and order with such aplomb that the bartender would think I was surely from New York (which, I had discovered, was a good deal farther East). When my twenty-first birthday actually arrived I had spoiled the card in a crude attempt to alter the date, so was unable to pull this off.

Meanwhile I had been admitted to the University of Chicago and had begun dating the niece of my landlady. This little girl (now my wife) was only sixteen, but she was enormously sophisticated. She was not only above Grieg and Chopin and Maugham and Cummings, but was rather blasé about Beethoven, Eliot, Joyce. And her parents had gone on to Thomas Aquinas, Prokofieff, Scarlatti, and Henry Miller. Even beyond Henry Miller. They had copies of *The Communist Manifesto* and Mark Twain's *1601*. The University of Chicago seemed an elaborate kindergarten to prepare to be them.

My taste was tolerated with kindly indulgence. When I said I liked de Falla they played some for me and smiled witheringly while I squirmed. I nearly lost my girl entirely because at the dinner table I defended Plato against Aristotle. Somehow the argument came round, as they saw it, to the point that pain proved the reality of matter; and months later mother pleaded tearfully with daughter not to marry me because I didn't believe in pain. At their house I could associate on an equal footing with Jews, Negroes, homosexuals, alleged Communists (by that time no one was a Communist any more; they were all alleged Communists), painters, musicians, and even a former anthropologist—a white-headed, grandmotherly man who was reputed to have lived among the Indians and, disillusioned, have given it all up to become a civil service drone. I admired people who had given everything up. On a James kick, I saw renunciation as the ultimate moral act. I wished I knew a defrocked priest.

But I began to rebel against the idea of taste itself. Taste, like the French Revolution, was one of the irrational products of the age of reason. The concept of taste as a faculty of aesthetic judgment did not exist before the late seventeenth century when, apparently, there was a need of some *je ne sais quoi,* some safety valve for the engine of Enlightenment. It has descended into a shell game, chiefly useful for brow-beating young men from the sticks. It is astonishing to me, now that I look back on it, that so many people of otherwise scientific and antimetaphysical minds believe so strongly in the existence of taste, that is, believe that finer sensibilities perceive intuitively that some things are, in an absolute sense, "better" aesthetically than others, that Yeats sits higher than Frost in Heaven, that this is what the knowing know, inarguably—that such people, relativists in every other respect, are oblivious to the whirligig of fashion, fad, and advertising that leads them, ahead of the pack, through the paperback galleries, Sam Goody's, and off-off-Broadway. But in those days I was a perfect victim and wept over my tastelessness as over body odor.

I hadn't really any folk culture with which to resist the civilization I was coming to absorb. In some moods I self-righteously insisted on some kind of virile, wholesome background of the open prairies which had nothing to do with life in Oklahoma City, Tulsa, and Houston (all quite metropolitan) as I had actually known it. I was not like the Tom of this play: I was worse. I wanted to rescue my beauty from the dragon's den of modern civilization, and yet I had nowhere to take her. When the events described in the poem, "Love, the First Decade," took place, I did not, like Tom, stand on the dignity of innocence maligned; like a busy mouse I took advantage of the indecent suggestion as quickly as I was able, all the while scorning those who made it. The button-button game of taste is won by the one who first sneers at the sneerers.

But mostly I tried to join, to take on the coloration of my future in-laws. I tried to believe in the Thirties, in matter, economics, city planning, smears as art, noise as music, and monotonous madness as poetry, in aquarium architecture, in the helplessness of the individual and repulsiveness of the mass (particularly to hate the gangrene of "mass communication"—and communication itself), in the heroism of Harry Bridges, in kippered herring, and the Manchester *Guardian*. In most of these efforts I succeeded—and became what was, to my mind, a fairly acceptable Jew.

Although there were some actual Jews among my heroes and models, the term, as I use it here, refers less to real people than to the image of intellectuality which developed in my mind. It seemed to me that as a young man advanced around the Monopoly board of taste he might aspire to become either a Negro or a Jew. You see, it was renunciation, such as makes young intellectual girls wear no make-up and keep their hair straight and stringy, which makes for beards and sweatshirts and vows of poverty. If I could have shed my white skin, my Protestant Christian heritage, my youthful look, my nationality, I would have done so to join the brotherhoods I admired.

It was much harder to become a Negro—what Norman Mailer has called a white Negro. This instinctual, inarticulate, jazzy, hip, junky group, digging the Bird, seemed to consist of those who won by surrender. They were the enormously successful Defeated. They were terrifying: with a slurred word and blank stare they could make you feel dirty for being washed, stupid for thinking, impotent for having children, tedious for interrupting their bleary silence, a failure for having succeeded, futile for doing anything at all. They were mystics, and unless one had the gift there was little point in trying to break in; or, as Louis Armstrong put it about jazz, if you had to ask you would never get to know.

There seemed to be more prestige in being a Negro, for even the Jews endured jazz, though it seemed to me self-consciously and uncomfortably. The ability to take jazz—that nerve-shattering, cynical antimusic—was the Knight's Ordeal of those of either group who wanted to be in. It was a Sacred Cow and had Civil Rights. I gritted my teeth and took it—but never hoped to aspire to more than Jewishness (wherein jazz may be relieved by folk songs whining out of Eastern Europe or thumping out of the Congo or twanging from the Weavers out of a New York hootenany).

My conversion was not to any religion, for few of the in-group had any, but to that clan aspiring to success, cultivation, knowledge, reason, collective order, scientific explanations, Danish furniture, and Bronx diet. Such people had little natural beauty or strength and felt at odds with the middle class. Perforce they had to beat this society with brains—and I, among the puny, adhered gladly to such values.

I saw that clan as a people whose religion was chiefly a resentment of Christian assumptions and holidays (with a refreshing objectivity about things like mercy, Christmas, and meekness) and a loyalty to delicatessens, where the only rye, pickles, balogna, and corned beef were to be found. Also cheesecake. I communed via borscht with sour cream and unleavened, unpalatable matzos crackers. I tried to believe that liederkranz was an edible substance. They were frank about their interest in prices and salaries, an exchange of information necessary to those united against the system. They were sentimental about a rich, subterranean heritage of Yiddish stories and sayings and would drink tea from glasses if they didn't prefer martinis. Above all, their intensity about the intellectual life was chastening for me, as I was more flaccid in my dedication to the higher things. They knew when all the concerts were on FM, when the foreign films were coming, who wrote what, who performed on which recording, who was exhibiting where, and which were the bargains at the Contemporary Furnishings shop on 57th St. They were liberated and enlightened; they never took a step without the guidance of Freud or Consumer's Union. And they had good humor about themselves—unless the criticism came from one not of their numbers. That solidarity (in spite of their contempt for the All-Rightniks and the people who went to temple) made me jealous, as I had no people to be loyal to. I envied their history and traditions. They were rigorous, clerical, tirelessly evaluating, indefatigably discussing great ideas. They carried the East about with them, like the sandalwood aroma of lox, and I yearned to approximate that condition, if possible without fish for breakfast. And they, in turn, yearned for Europe in one way or another. Europe, I was learning, was farthest East of all—especially Eastern Europe. And Italy. I wanted to be Italian too.

I imitated and resisted, grew nervous but not mature. I would never make New York. When I visited there it seemed that America was gathering in Manhattan, yearning eastward for some sort of wisdom, elegance, *savior faire,* vaguely Viennese —or, as though Ponce de León, having found that spring, having lost his beard and memory, swaddled now in charcoal grey, haunted the East River wondering where was the spring to restore his age. Punchy, they call him down at the ad agency. Quite a history. Knew Fitzgerald in Hollywood. Fought in the Lincoln Brigade, which somehow brought back a lost Spanish heritage. Collects Spanish art—stuff beyond Dali, beyond Picasso, even beyond Miró. See those dapper grey temples? That's white shoe polish—which some regard as affectation. A terror on the handball court. Makes a mean omelet. Ordered father-son matched Ferraris from the factory. Skindiver. You could run a factory on what he pays in alimony alone, and yet he doesn't look happy. I saw old Punchy there, his boyish chin lifted to the East, and knew that if I tried hard and got the breaks, became a real swinging successful well-preserved American, I could, at best, end beside Punchy on the dock. And I guess I gave up trying.

Lacking an image now of what to grow up to be, I wait with dormant glands, years passing unnoticed as satellites, and, in turn, transmit no image to the young. Aging comes, I believe, when we accept a mold and grow into it. A successful, brilliant (boyish) professor I had in graduate school invited a group of us to his country home, split-level, booklined, for a barbecue. There was nothing *wrong* with the picture, but I shuddered and turned again from the direction in which I was traveling. I cannot imagine myself at fifty, at sixty: I will accept no definition of what I want to be when I grow up, and so, of course, will not become it. Meanwhile, as I stand before my classes I am aware that none will want to grow up and be me. How could they? They would have to grow younger.

Perhaps it is better that way—to make oneself up as one goes along. But there are anxieties implied which we must learn to cope with. It is written that a little child shall lead them, but it isn't clear about where—and we can't be sure they will follow. As our boyish nation looks around and finds no image of mature

nations on which it can respectably form itself, and younger
nations show no great eagerness to grow up and be like us, it is
another verse of Isaiah which catches the freedom, the promise,
and the horror of our situation: "The child shall die an hundred
years old."

Back when there used to be traditions, people formed themselves on the past, but that no longer seems a viable alternative.
I sometimes think I wouldn't mind growing up to be Abraham
Lincoln, but the frontier, which once molded American maturity, has now gone off where robots fly. Whom do the young look
to on the current scene? Teddy Kennedy? Bob Dylan? Robert
Lowell? Jimi Hendrix? Janis Joplin? Joe Namath? Eldridge
Cleaver? Ralph Nader? Do they find the wisdom, humaneness,
commitment, vividness, completeness, happiness which might
inspire them to imitate the gestures and set of the jaw, the verbal
modes, the style? Shall the world be governed by Beatles? My
characterless face in the mirror refuses all options. I will grin
and be forgiven. No telling how much longer my arrogant
innocence will be indulged.

Axelrod, the only nominal Jew in the play, is rendered
affectionately, but he is a red herring. Actually, the play is
infiltrated by the surrogate Jews of my Chicago experience.
Calvin, in spite of his name and the fact that his father was a
minister, is one of them. Gertrude is more Jewish still—and
her objectivity about the ideals of the menfolk saves them all.
Lois cannot but have inherited the qualities of both. Tom finds
himself, as I did, in the world they made, the world which will
succeed because it ought to, because its values are stronger
and wiser than those he brings to contest them. He will become
an imperfect and resisting Jew, as I have become.

Though there is an element of history in the central incident
of the play, the characters are not modeled on real people,
except on me. There is as much of me in Calvin as in Tom—
and recognizable hunks of my flesh are in Horace, Lois, Gertrude, Sue, and Axelrod. My fun with the play was that of
reducing my own attitudes to absurdity, blowing them up and
puncturing. The person in the play I most admire is Gertrude,
but her wisdom is only dimly perceived here: I yearn for the

maturity to see people with acceptance and love, for what they are in spite of what they say, with the intuitive moderation and placidity I have tried to attribute to her. I hope that when and if I achieve that, I will be rewarded with a weathered face.

I also had fun with the versification. The pentameter—iambic, anapestic, or, most often, a mixture—is intended to be free-flowing and yet to preserve the emphasis and artifice of the poetic line. I mean it to be read rapidly and naturally, hoping the beats emerge where I imagined them to be. The problem of handling contemporary, conversational idiom in verse is a fascinating one: the least touch too much will make it seem pretentious, and yet the least slackness will make it all seem flat, the poetry gone. My fear of the first has probably made me err in the direction of the second pitfall, but still the experiment seems useful to me as a way of working toward a viable poetic drama. As in the other plays, I have included songs—but the play is not a "musical comedy"; there is no chorus of janitors and parlor maids. It seems to me that song can be a useful way of heightening lyric moments in drama which need not, therefore, become a full-scale musical production.

I cannot help loving everyone in this play—since they are all me; I would hope that in imaginary or stage production the satire would be tenderized. One of our burdens as human beings is to transcend our wit.

VII

Drums

ACT I

A*ny afternoon in June we discover the living-room and porch of a swank, upper-story, big-city apartment, all glassy, straight-lined, tiled, gleaming, sterile. The decor of the living room suggests a medieval chapel, characterized as it is by vertical dis-tortion, symbolism, austerity, and dedication to the pursuit of higher truths of intellect—certainly not conducive to living. The walls are booklined. A stereo hi-fi dominates a wall like an altar. Mobiles and pictures, nonrepresentational, remind us of agony and mortification of all human instincts. The textures—wood, burlap, leather, metal—punish the flesh. The floor is laid with serapis to trip or slide under the unwary, to chafe the nude or barefooted. Bullet lamps and other devices for defeating light maintain a spectral and chilly gloom. Sculpture, all points and edges of scrap iron, reminds one at every turn of the grotesqueness of this rusting world.*

The porch is a little more cheerful. The furniture, of aluminum tubing and plastic webbing, invites a more relaxed posture. There is a smoking charcoal burner, a box of cacti on the ledge, a glass-topped table set for dinner for four, a Buddha, and a beach umbrella. The sun is setting behind skyscrapers like a bleeding pumpkin fallen on spears.

Tom and Lois, in the living-room on a foam rubber couch, are engaged in an apparently endless kiss. Lois, in shorts, has a neglected cigaret in an ashtray beside her. She resembles her mother in her flightiness, her ability to see most serious matters in humorous perspective, and an accepting warmth half-way between geniality and sensuality, but these days she has taken on an unfamiliar earnestness owing to her love for Tom. He wears a tie and summer jacket which is short at the wrists and inadequate around the biceps. He doesn't quite fit in the civilized mold, and though he is intelligent, educated, he reverts belligerently from time to time to the manner of his rural background. She is twenty—he is a few years older. Gertrude, Lois's attractive mother, has an imperturbable good will which seems at times to result from her incomprehension of what is going on around her. She hurries in from the kitchen, looking at her watch, stands over the lovers a moment, puzzled, cocking an eye, tapping her foot, before she pleads:

GERTRUDE: Suppose you kids could finish that kiss on the porch?

(*Tom abruptly sits up and straightens his tie, but Lois, languorous, picks up her cigaret without looking at her mother.*)

LOIS: Oh, Gertrude, can it! Thomas and I are talking.
GERTRUDE: Calvin is due in ten minutes. . . .

LOIS: So we have
         ten minutes.
GERTRUDE: You have your watch on?
LOIS: Yes, Mother
                                                       dear.
GERTRUDE (*checking her own*): All right, you have ten minutes.
         Make it eight.

(*Gertrude has been unbuttoning her dress as she talks. Now,
pulling it off, she starts for the bedroom. Lois, with a swift look
at her watch, throws her arms around Tom's neck.*)

GERTRUDE (*from the bedroom*): Hey! Call the liquor store and
                      order gin.
LOIS (*absently*): Yes, Mother dear.
TOM: Let's move out to the porch.
LOIS: You want everyone to *see* us?
TOM: How?
LOIS: They use
         binoculars across there in that penthouse.
         I've seen them with my own binoculars.
TOM: What do you do on the porch they want to see?
LOIS: I sunbathe there—and watch them watching me.

(*Tom reaches for Lois's cigaret, puffs it amateurishly and
coughs, hands it back, gets up, pulling at his collar, brushes
against a jagged piece of iron sculpture and jumps back in
fright.*)

TOM: I'm getting it again, Lois—that city feeling.
LOIS: Take off your tie, dear.
TOM: That won't help at all.
LOIS: What is it this time, Tom? Me? My mother?
TOM: Oh, parents peeping, neighbors knowing, I
         can't put my finger on it. Like this party . . .
         Who *are* these people you've invited? Why
         do *they* have to know? Why do we have to tell
         anyone just yet? Especially Calvin? There—
         that's it: it's Calvin I'm upset about.
         He's coming any minute, and I feel

like in a fluoroscope, with visible juices,
a television ad for liver pills.
I cross my legs as though to protect my virtue.

LOIS: There you go with your barefoot boy bit, Tom.

TOM: I'm trying to stop it. I'm trying to laugh at myself.
This place brings out my hayseeds. Let's take a
walk. . . .

LOIS: We can't always be walking in the park. . . .

TOM: Listen—the way your voice gets patient, icy:
you want me to adjust, that's what you want!
Even you! So I'm surrounded!
(*Mocking himself.*)
                                                    Ya'll want
to get this mustang roped in the corral!

LOIS: If you really think that I'm trying to trap you . . .

TOM: Lois, I don't know what I think. I only
know that I'm nervous. Let's blame it on the city.

LOIS (*sings*): Oh, metropolitan living makes for loving
devoid of privacy and mysteries,
with every nosy neighbor speculating
upon the business of the birds and bees.

TOM (*whispers*): Especially your parents . . .

LOIS (*louder, intending to be overheard*):
Especially my mother!

She compensates for insecurities
with cynical, libidinous stares,
developing a bulge, hence
vicarious indulgence
in clinical dissection of affairs.

To innocent affection she is blind:
a Valentine, a posy,
a kiss in corner cozy,
alerts her gynecological mind.
She thinks love an alliance
in the interests of science—
looks on like a deodorant ad!

Without a marriage manual
by Bill Coo and Kinsey Daniel
she'd never have comprehended dear old Dad!
TOM: Give me a wide sky and a saddle.
Give me a gun and a rustler to jail.
Give me a tall white hat and a blushing grin
and a girl at the end of the trail!

Let me save the rancher's daughter
from the mortgage that is due.
Let her come to me in calico—
and let that girl be you!

Give me a lonesome night with coyotes,
no friend but my loyal horse,
then a hard chase through the mountains,
full of Indians, of course;

give me a half-breed villain to conquer
with you looking on, wide-eyed.
Let me carry you to the preacher,
take you home to Mother, my bride.

Wear your neck-line high and your hem-line
just sweeping the pasture path,
your hair hanging loose on your shoulders,
your face like a babe in the bath,

and I'll swing my dusty ten-gallon,
try to hide my wobbling knee,
and know when you kiss me on tiptoe
that you saved all your kisses for me.

(*Gertrude enters, in her hose, snapping the placket of a cock-
tail dress, her pumps under her arm. She sits in a sling chair and
painfully works her shoes on.*)

LOIS: Gertrude, you spoil everything! You crush
a man's manhood. How do you expect for me
to take Tom seriously when you come in . . . ?

GERTRUDE: I don't know what to make of this, dear.
           Just because you are hostile, you don't have
           to be sassy, do you? Did you call for liquor?
           It was your idea—the punch. I mean, if you
           are going to do the Electra bit right here,
           you might at least call off this silly party.
           Calvin will be outraged, anyway.
           Would one of you go and remove the ice
           from the martinis? And would the other, please,
           order the gin for the punch—if you still want it?
TOM: I'm going home.
LOIS: You're what?
TOM: I'm going home.

(*Gertrude, with frequent glances at her watch, is standing on tiptoes to see in a high mirror, touching her hair into place.*)

GERTRUDE: In that case we won't need the extra gin.
LOIS: But, Tom, the party! Dinner!
TOM: I just can't
           face any more analysis of us—
           like specimens of something! Electra complex!
           Now every time you kiss me, must I think
           you're using me for a Calvin-substitute?
LOIS: She didn't mean it—did you, Mother? She
           never means anything, you know that, Tom.
TOM: I doubt she did. So much the worse. Manure
           is spread unthinkingly, but it still stinks!

(*Gertrude has been arranging periodicals on the coffee table. Now she straightens.*)

GERTRUDE: Manure? To refer to an old Greek tragedy?
           It wasn't I who brought deodorants
           and gynecology into the conversation.
TOM: You taught her. . . .
GERTRUDE: You want her ignorant?
LOIS: Hey, I'm a grown-up girl. Tom, please don't fight.

TOM: Will you go out to dinner with me, Lois?

GERTRUDE: Impossible. I've got it cooked. You can
      have your huff after dinner. Would you go
      remove the ice from the martinis, and
      either call the liquor store or call your friends
      and tell them not to come? I think it would
      be sweet of you, Tom, to take her out this eve-
      ning. . . .

TOM: Look, Gertrude, I'm not trying to be sweet. . . .

GERTRUDE: I understand. But Calvin can't stand Horace
      and Sue. I think you ought to leave us out. . . .

LOIS: Mother, we *can't*. I told you this was special!

GERTRUDE: Then call. . . .

LOIS (*uneasily*):   Tom, would *you* call?

TOM (*glumly*):   *What* liquor
                                        store?

LOIS: Axelrod. Look on the wall above the phone—
      a little card with the number.

(*Lois leaves the room. Tom starts for the phone in the hall, but
is stopped by Gertrude's voice.*)

GERTRUDE: Tom, come here.
      You know you're making everybody nervous?

TOM: Everybody makes *me* nervous, Gertrude.

GERTRUDE: Tell me what's going on—this party tonight. . . .

TOM: I'd rather not say. It seems to be all off.

GERTRUDE: What happened, Tom? What really happened? This
      is surely not all just because I mentioned
      Electra. You haven't had a quarrel with Lois?

TOM: Hardly.

GERTRUDE: You stiffen up as though resisting. . . .

TOM (*flops onto couch*): Oh, Gertrude, I don't know what I'm
      resisting.
      Sometimes I think it's just intelligence.
      I think you all know something you won't let on—
      even Lois. Sometimes she seems so smug—as though
      she understood things I am not supposed

to understand—a fatted calf, fondled,
humored, protected from the truth. Well, I
think I'm entitled to a point-of-view.
Just don't be so damned sure you're always right. . . .

GERTRUDE: I'm hardly ever right. . . .

TOM: I don't mean you.
I mean, I mean all of you. It's the way
you always see *through* things. It's a kind of blindness.

GERTRUDE: I don't see through what you are saying now.
I don't even understand you. . . .

TOM: I mean, like love.
Even Lois sometimes behaves as though love were
a sort of magic trick, a sleight-of-hand,
and she is privy to the backstage facts,
that love is a kind of applied psychology. . . .

GERTRUDE: I know you have a psychological complex—
a complex about psychology, that is—
but you needn't make a *thing* of it. . . .

TOM: Why not?
I want to have it out. I want to know
whether love is merely something glandular.
If so, I'll take a pill and cure it. But
I happen to think there's more to it than that.
I'd like to convince Lois, too. . . .

GERTRUDE: You haven't?

TOM: I can't be sure. You know, Gertrude, you've spoiled
that girl. She leads me around just as she does
Calvin and you. Who *are* these people coming—
this Horace and Sue? When I ask questions, all
she wants is a kiss. In fact I find that Lois
is rather hard to talk to. When I explain
ideals that mean very much to me, she gets
this absent look—making her own plans. . . .

GERTRUDE (*smiling*): Tom, I am on your side. You're good for
her.
Frankly, I'd like to see her absorb a few
of those ideals. She won't—if you run off.

TOM: I simply want some time to clarify. . . .

GERTRUDE: Hush, Tom, and listen a minute. Let's not have
   a scene at five o'clock. Calvin will be . . .

TOM: Calvin! It seems that everything has got . . .

GERTRUDE: upset enough about the party without
    you carrying on as well. I'm sure that you
    and Lois can figure out all this about
    psychology, or love, and things, some other . . .

TOM: Gertrude, you weren't paying the least attention, were
   you?

GERTRUDE (*glancing at watch*): How could I, with all these
    things to do, and Calvin . . . ?

TOM (*shaking his head in surrender*): Yes, Gertrude. Relax. I'll
    go and order gin.

(*Alone a moment after Tom leaves, she puts a record on the
phonograph, turns it on to warm up.*)

GERTRUDE (*sings out*): Lois! You may pour!

LOIS (*appearing at door, in anxious whisper*): How many,
   Mother?

GERTRUDE (*winks*): Four.

(*Lois goes out. Gertrude now holds the playing arm suspended
over the record, her eyes fixed on her watch. Tom enters behind
her, in a better humor.*)

TOM: What's up with you and the liquor man, Gay Gertie?

GERTRUDE (*concentrating on watch*): Liquor man? Which liquor man? I can't imagine.

TOM: Axelrod. *He* appears to know *you* well
    enough: "Why, *yes,* Mr. Fielding," says he, thinking
    that I was Calvin. "I will give it *spec*ial
    attention. Tell the missus I have not
    forgotten. Give her a little peck for me!"

GERTRUDE: I can't imagine. I do my business with Tracey's.

(*Lois enters with a tray and four martinis. She gives one to
Tom, takes one, and leaves the tray with Gertrude.*)

TOM: Perhaps he meant some other Mrs. Fielding.
    His tone was so suggestive. . . .

LOIS: Whose tone, Tom?

TOM: Mr. Axelrod, the liquor man. He said
    to tell your mother he had not forgotten.

(*Lois starts visibly, blushes. There is the rattle of a key in the door.*)

GERTRUDE: Shoo!

(*Tom and Lois go out onto the porch and sit together inconspicuously. Gertrude lets the needle down on the record and the air is split by drums, accompanied by weird chanting, just as Calvin steps in the door. A lean, imposing man of incisive manner, he is habitually somewhat surly as a result of his conviction that everyone he encounters is sentimental, irrational, and slow-witted. A little realistic common sense and there would be no problems. On the other hand he is aware of the shock value of his iconoclasm: it is his variety of humor. Gertrude floats to meet him with the martinis. Calvin, brief case suspended, purses his lips sardonically to greet her, but at that instant Tom springs into the room from the porch, startled, blinking his eyes. Calvin smirks. Tom, seeing the record turning, realizes he is intruding and turns, shrugging, back to the porch, returning to Lois in subdued light. Gertrude sets down the tray, takes Calvin's hat, suit coat, umbrella, and brief case and disposes of them in a closet.*)

CALVIN: He here for dinner?
GERTRUDE: Yes, and a party, too.
CALVIN: Party?
GERTRUDE: They're having a kind of party later.
CALVIN: Can we go out?
GERTRUDE: The party is for us.
CALVIN (*with horror*): For us? The four of us? What will we do?
    Birdcalls? I'm damned if I'll sit around and listen
    to Tom make mating calls.
GERTRUDE: They may be mating calls,
    though not of birds. Lois said something about
    some sort of announcement.

CALVIN: Tell her to write it down,
and we will go out for the evening. I'm damned if I
will sit around and listen to announcements.

(*He has now taken a seat in the chair which is obviously his, is
loosening his tie and shoes. Gertrude is handing him a shirt-coat,
sandals. He is putting on heavy, black-framed glasses.*)

GERTRUDE: Well, it is surprising—ominous—that she
should have invited Horace. . . .

CALVIN: Horace!

GERTRUDE: Horace
and Sue. She's hardly spoken of him since
he married. She says she can't stand Horace, says
Sue is a shrew who's simply *ruin*ing Horace. . . .

CALVIN: Whom in the first place she can't stand . . .

GERTRUDE: Of course
she can't abide us, either: she seems to have
arranged the evening for our mutual punishment.

CALVIN: I'm damned . .

GERTRUDE: For instance gin. Lois aked me
to make that gin fruit punch. . . . Do you remember
the last time we had gin fruit punch? That New Year's,
really the first time she got whoopsy-doopsy. . . .

CALVIN: Ye gods, woman! Drunk!

GERTRUDE: It's as though she meant
to bring back all that dreadful year on purpose!
Since she's been going with Tom they've been on milk,
wool shirts, and folksongs, woody walks at dawn. . . .

CALVIN: Birdwalks!

GERTRUDE: Do you suppose they really look
for birds?

CALVIN: At dawn? What else is there at dawn?

GERTRUDE: Calvin, you really are very hostile toward
birds. . . . But, anyway, gin, Horace, parents,
Sue—we are all impure, especially Horace.

CALVIN: Ha.

GERTRUDE: You think she's jealous of Sue, but that's not it. . . .

CALVIN: No, I said "ha" because the thought of purity,
        especially in regard to Lois, especially
        in regard to Lois and Horace, is such an amusing
        thought. . . .

GERTRUDE: Horace symbolizes sterility . . .

CALVIN: Ha.

GERTRUDE: and moral decay of intelligence in a world
        of crippling disillusionment, cynicism,
        and desperate loss of value, I think she said,
        which Horace and his crowd, and even worse,
        gin and her parents. . . . How did I start that sen-
           tence?

CALVIN: This glass isn't chilled.

GERTRUDE: It *was*. You talk too much.
        You know why I think she hates Horace? Because
        he is repulsive.

CALVIN: Oh? He sure as hell
        didn't use to be repulsive.

GERTRUDE: Not to her.
        I mean he is ob*jec*tively repulsive,
        and she has come to see that.

CALVIN: Nonsense. When
        has repulsiveness repulsed our Lois? Look
        at Tom.

GERTRUDE: Hush, dear. They're on the porch.

CALVIN: I know
        they're on the porch. Lois hates Horace because . . .

GERTRUDE: Really, Calvin, hush. You don't want him . . .

CALVIN: Doesn't he *know* about Horace?

GERTRUDE: Good heavens, Calvin . . .

CALVIN (*sips angrily*): Well, he *ought* to know. A man should
        know the goods
        he's purchasing. . . .

GERTRUDE: Oh, really, Calvin, you
        don't understand men, especially idealists.
        You wouldn't want to know the history
        of everything you bought. . . .

CALVIN: But—second hand?

GERTRUDE: It's better not to know, I assure you, darling.

CALVIN: Oh *do* you? What, for example, is it better
        that I not know?

GERTRUDE: That would be telling, wouldn't it?

CALVIN (*sanctimoniously*): It's never better not to know. The
        trick
        is learning to live with what we know by knowing
        a little bit more, by seeing the fact in context,
        coming to know that what we knew doesn't mat-
        ter. . . .

GERTRUDE (*kissing him on forehead and then leaving*):
        If it doesn't matter, why bother to find out?

(*Calvin irritably shakes out his newspaper, settles grimly to
read, his head bobbing unconsciously to the rhythm of the
drums. Suddenly he leaps to his feet and sings:*)

CALVIN: Oh, missionary women in the jungle
        defeat good sense with their sweet reasoning lips.
        We go to them for medicine, religion,
        are hauled in chains upon their slaving ships!
        She comes all pink and gentle to the savage
        and by surrender seeks to conquer him.
        He climbs down from the tree and goes off with her
        to civilization—just another limb!
            Oh we forget, until at five
                the cocktail hour comes
            and then we throb with memory
                of those old jungle drums!

(*He circles the room in a war dance, rolled newspaper for a spear, making appropriate cries.*)

The office and the market and the bedroom
are governed right and left by politesse.
No wonder, then, with common sense unseated,
we find our inner urges in a mess.
To say exactly what you mean is crudeness,
you must forget you know the things you know,
until, at five, you can, with savage shrewdness
decide that civilization has to go.

> Oh we forget, until at five
>   the cocktail hour comes
>   and then we throb with memory
>   of those old jungle drums!

(*Gertrude enters with the pitcher as the last of this is going on. She sets down the martinis and joins the dance. He looks back at her war whoop startled.*)

GERTRUDE: So lift a glass and gulp down to the olive,
               my noble savage of the avant-garde;
               put on your horn rim glasses and your sandals,
               make up for a living soft by drinking hard.
         I do not want my mate as an accountant
         tied down by apron strings or by red tape.
         Oh, you may be a gentleman till sundown—
         but then be my sophisticated ape.
                   Oh we forget, until at five
                     the cocktail hour comes
                   and then we throb with memory
                     of those old jungle drums!

(*The noise of this brings Lois and Tom to the door, who look on in horror. Tom, at the end of the song, turns away in disgust and goes back to the seat on the porch. Gertrude catches the look, picks up the pitcher to run to his rescue.*)

GERTRUDE: Tom's sulking again. Quick, Gert, the gin!

(*She goes out. Calvin sinks in his chair, taking up his paper. Lois stands behind him, nodding her head to the music.*)

LOIS: Hello, Calvin.
           (*louder, over the music*)
               Hello, Calvin.
CALVIN (*feigning boredom*):   Hello, squirt.
         How goes the job?

(*Lois bends to kiss him.*)

LOIS: I quit it.

CALVIN (*under breath, wiping off kiss*): Stop, you've got
       Thomas all over you. You *what?* You quit it?
LOIS: Rebelled.
CALVIN: Let me tell you the story. Tom
       rebelled as well, turned in his sample case,
       decided our economy was based
       on persuading people they should have what they
       are better off without—and both of you
       refuse to participate in such a swindle,
       especially as sales personnel. . . .
LOIS: Wait, Calvin. . . .
CALVIN: The two of you have joined the Peace Corps which
       has given you a special assignment to sponge
       off me and rehabilitate your home
       with friendly parties for the elderly
       industrial accountant set. My wealth
       will thus be redistributed among . . .
LOIS: You know Tom never quit anything in his life—
       and never will. . . .
CALVIN: God help him.
LOIS: *I* quit because
       selling perfume is so . . . so phony.
CALVIN: No doubt.
       But isn't everything phony in this world?
LOIS: Perfume is such a dumb thing to be phony *about.*

       (*She turns down record player, grimaces.*)

       Honest, Calvin—that stuff is so *prim*itive!
CALVIN: I see. What isn't phony is primitive.
LOIS: It's phony to be primitive when you aren't.
CALVIN: Drums relax me.
GERTRUDE (*entering*): You've got to hear it to feel it.

       (*She turns sound back up again.*)

LOIS: I feel it, I *feel* it.

(*Lois pouts and leaves, returning to Tom on the porch.*)
CALVIN: I am beginning to disapprove of Lois.
GERTRUDE: You disapproved of her before she was

conceived. She disapproves of *you,* I'm sure.
She has a benign and holy look these days . . .
a cow-like calm. . . .

CALVIN.   As she sips her gin.

GERTRUDE.   Some kind
of fuzzy superiority to reason,
indifference to mortality. She walks
with Thomas hand in hand—like immigrants
to the golden world, like missionaries, like
people at ends of movies, dope addicts,
children in toyland. . . .

CALVIN (*going back to his paper*): Like when she was pregnant.

GERTRUDE (*sloshing her drink*): What? Good lord, *yes!* Oh,
Calvin! Not again!

CALVIN: Don't be absurd. Thomas!

(*Laughs. Stops, then laughs harder—in a forced
manner.*)

Thomas!

GERTRUDE (*decisively*):   Thomas.

CALVIN: If Tom were capable I'd be relieved.

GERTRUDE: But this party—just like the old days. They are
going
to make *some* kind of announcement. She wants us
inebriate and amiable: I know. . . .

CALVIN: No. No. No. No. We are not going through
with that idiocy again. You don't invite
company for such announcements. Look, Gertrude,
if there is anything I can't endure . . .

GERTRUDE: I can think of several things you can't endure. . . .

CALVIN (*drawing her to him*): it's a child-centered home,
especially when
the children are over twenty-one. . . .

GERTRUDE: How do
you feel about a grandchild-centered home?

(*Gertrude kisses him and leaves for the kitchen. Calvin settles
down beneath his bullet lamp, and as the sunset is becoming
richer and fuller outside our attention shifts to the porch. We*

can just see Calvin, bobbing his head slightly to the beat of the drums. Lois, who has been sitting on a chaise longue, rises and shuts the door, muffling the music considerably, but it throbs quietly in the background. She sits beside Tom and worms into his arms. In a coordinated movement they bring their glasses to their lips and sip.)

LOIS (*sings*): Here we sit on our verandah . . .
TOM: of our bamboo house by the Amazon. . . .
LOIS: That record, in fact, was made in the Congo. . . .
TOM: I don't care if it's a tom-tom or a bongo,
        on the Tigris or Euphrates, Whang Po or Rubicon.
        These are the jungles of ancient Ampersanda.
        Man-eating Hieroglyphics are screeching in the trees.
        Hark to the message of the war-drums. . . .
LOIS: It's a chant for washing clothes . . .
TOM: . . . for mobilizing
        chimpanzees!
LOIS: But we have each other . . .
TOM: Supplies for a week . . .
LOIS: And no word from Mother . . .
TOM: who eloped with a sheik. . . .
LOIS: Have we insect repellent?
TOM: That is crude and irrelevant. . . .
LOIS: Are there snakes?
TOM: Who cares?
LOIS: Or earthquakes?
TOM: There's a moon in the mist from the river.
        There's aroma of strange jungle flowers.
        This may be our last night together.
        Those drums have been beating for hours.
LOIS (*interrupting song*): It says on the record jacket . . .
TOM: That is precisely the trouble with your family.
        You are all educated by record jackets—
        with a smattering of languages picked up
        from anchovy cans.
LOIS: I promise never to read
        another record jacket. . . .

TOM: Nor *New Yorker,* except
for cartoons. Nor attend another Scandinavian
film with nude women. . . .

LOIS: Harpsichord recitals?

TOM: Out. Also sour cream and bouillabaisse. . . .

LOIS: Especially together. . . .

TOM: You shall deny
yourself existentialism, all things called
New Wave, all tranquilizers or any other
adulterating pills, must never suspend
yourself in any chair made of wrought iron.

LOIS: I shall avoid abstract expressionism.

TOM: This above all: nothing further in your life
shall be abstract or expressionist. You shall
wear long hair, with a permanent, and make-up. . . .

LOIS (*dubiously*): Well . . .

TOM: Hold hands with me in the park, and marry me
before a preacher in a church. . . .

LOIS: A church?

TOM (*with self-satire*): Oh, I am no frequenter of churches, but
I am a Sunday School lover. I oil my hair
and send flowers. I court on the porch swing,
and keep a passionate, innocent diary,
respect the flower of womanhood and do
as Mother taught. I am milk-fed. I eat
popcorn in movies. I give ladies seats
on buses, and, to stray kittens, saucers of cream.

LOIS (*sings*): Here we sit on our verandah . . .

TOM: In the wilds of Ampersanda . . .
dreaming of a love that is pure—
of the heroes in the stories
who rode out committing glories
in the name of a maiden demure . . .

LOIS: dreaming of a clean romance—
of violins and roses,
holding hands and rubbing noses,
a corsage for the Country Club dance . . .

TOM AND LOIS: dreaming of lost gallantry,
            of courtship and of wedding
            (and eventual double-bedding) . . .
LOIS: with mystery . . .
TOM: and chivalry,
            an innocent and true romance!
LOIS (*speaks*): I mean, like a wholesome relationship.
TOM: A book of verses underneath a bough . . .
LOIS: Oh, please, Tom, not the Rubaiyat!
TOM: Why not?
LOIS (*distressed and embarrassed*): It's just that I hate it. Don't
            ask me why.
TOM: Because you hate the nineteenth century.
            Nothing for you but Allen Ginsberg. Well,
            Lois, my dear, I adore the nineteenth century,
            every last Tennysonian rumble of it.
LOIS: It isn't that at all, Tom. Tom . . . we want
            to be honest with one another, don't we? I mean . . .
            about everything?
TOM: Everything.
LOIS: (*with a touch of panic*):   *Everything?*
TOM: It's the only way. I've been around a lot,
            but there is nothing, Lois, about my past
            I wouldn't have you know. For example, the Army.
            You know what goes on. Well, you couldn't know.
            Anyway, I admit I tried to bum
            around on overnight passes with the fellows—
            but, Lois, my heart wasn't in it. Somehow I
            always ended sleeping at the Y. . . .
LOIS: It's not *your* past. . . .
TOM: You know, I kept my mother's
            picture in my footlocker. I am the sort
            of guy who got a bang from a game of checkers
            with a Red Cross Girl, doughnuts and cider after.
            Old-fashioned? Sure. But I've decided to stop
            apologizing for it. Sophistication,
            I've found, is nothing but loss of character.

LOIS (*miserably*) : That is so true.

TOM: And character is what
I stand for. I ask, what is wrong with all
of the old virtues: courage, honesty,
hard work, and thrift? What's wrong with those as
    goals?
It's getting so you feel you should feel guilty
for being simply decent, especially
in this household. . . .

(*He sips defiantly.*)

LOIS: Ideals are very inspiring—
but, Tom, a little terrifying. I mean,
if one expects too much . .

TOM: Well, that's the problem,
exactly. People are afraid of the rigor—
so rationalize away the virtue. Love,
even love. People like Calvin and Gertrude would
prefer avoiding the term, replacing it with
a symbol indicating carnal union.
The word *love* sounds too mystical for them.

LOIS: They've never known what it means.

TOM: Lois, it *is*
mystical. Supernatural. It is the birth
of angels and the ocean to which prayer flows.
It is the stuff of visions, ecstasies. . . .

LOIS (*innocently*) : Exactly. Even Freud said that.

TOM (*hitting the roof*) :   He *what?*

LOIS (*timorously*): Said sex caused all our visions, ecstasies. . . .

TOM: Who said anything about sex?

LOIS: I tell you, *Freud.*

TOM: I *know* he did. He caused the whole damned mess!

LOIS: But, Tom, they had it—in a primitive form—
even before Freud.

TOM: Freud! Let's not talk Freud.

LOIS: He *is* rather nineteenth century, I guess. . . .

TOM: Lois, what *are* you trying to do? Play dumb?
To make me out a prig? Nothing is easier,

you know, than to pick away and sneer a man
to silence. Sometimes I believe that you
are really of your parents' party, that
you take all that stuff seriously. . . .

LOIS: Like sex?

TOM: Oh, hell, it's hopeless!

LOIS: What is hopeless, Tom?

TOM: Could you, for just a moment, entertain
the notion that perhaps love isn't sex?

LOIS: Not *any* of it, Tom?

TOM: Don't be a fool!
What have I got to do, Lois? Wear a sign
saying I'm in favor of sex? Look, I'll tell you
who takes sex seriously: your own dear Tom—
though I think it no particular distinction
to have the urges everybody has.
I guess that I could get a certificate
if you're in doubt. Like maybe you think I kiss
to exercise my embouchure? I'm not
ashamed of sex, nor do I underrate
its fun or force or its necessity.
Okay? We clear?

LOIS: Oh, Tom, I didn't mean . . .

TOM: The hell you didn't! Not that I blame you.
Your parents undermine my love like termites
munching the oak. I feel I should perform
some sexual athletics just to prove
to Calvin that I'm not incompetent.
Manhood. Calvin. Think of your father, Lois,
and ask yourself just what you want from manhood.

LOIS: Tom, I was trying to kid . . .

TOM: Now, I suppose,
I lack a sense of humor.

LOIS: I didn't say . . .

TOM: Or now I'm too defensive. Isn't that
what you are thinking?

LOIS (*swelling to angry tears*):   No. Just that you are
impossible! I'm trying to tell you, Tom . . .

TOM (*grimly repentent*): You're right. I know you're not the
                 one I'm fighting.
         I *am* impossible. And what I want
         is impossible, too. The world has jacked us up,
         drained out our psyches and replaced them with
         psychology, as though we behaved by laws.
         Lois, I stand for unlawful human behavior.
         I think that love is more than a disposition
         to breed. It transcends flesh. It may be all
         the evidence we have of soul—but when
         I kiss you, soul is palpable. I know,
         exactly then, when most in grip of glands,
         how little glands explain. Why, rational
         magicians would stop the show aghast if they
         could but kiss you and learn the truth of magic.

(*A long kiss.*)

LOIS (*ambiguously*): I see what you mean.

(*They lift their martinis again in their coordinated movement, their glasses tinged by the last rays of the sun. In the living-room Calvin is pouring his own glass full again. The drums throb. The lights go out.*)

ACT II

(*Dinner is over; the music is off. Gertrude and Lois are carrying dishes off the porch. Calvin is semi-reclined on a lawn-chair, sipping brandy. Tom is sitting uncomfortably on the balustrade.*)

GERTRUDE: You *did* call the liquor store?
TOM: I told you I
         had quite a little talk with Axelrod.
GERTRUDE: Because I can't face Horace . . .
CALVIN: Who   can   face
                                     Horace?
GERTRUDE: Suppose he has our address mixed up with some
                 other Fieldings? You better call again.

TOM: You want to, Lois?

LOIS: I'll help clear. Why don't
you order from Tracey's this time, Tom?

TOM: Because
I wouldn't want to miss the fond reunion
of Axelrod and Gertrude. Would you, Lois?

(*Lois grimaces, quickly goes out through the living-room with
dishes. Tom follows to the telephone.*)

CALVIN (*imitating*): "I wouldn't want to miss the fond re-
                  union. . . ."
What the hell is he talking about, Gertrude?

GERTRUDE: I can't imagine. But, Calvin, you must try
not to make fun of Tom. What's he done wrong now?

CALVIN: Oh, nothing, nothing! It's simply that I can't stand
his prissy compound of pomp and purity.

GERTRUDE: The boy has a right to his purity.

CALVIN: He's hardly
a boy, and has no such right. Besides, I am
sarcastic only behind his back. How polite
do you want me to be?

GERTRUDE: To be exposed
to a little innocence will not hurt Lois.
It might rub off on her.

CALVIN: Innocence, Gertrude,
you don't acquire. You start with it. You lose it.
Like an egg shell. Once out, you don't crawl in.
Thank God. If there is anything which would
increase the anguish of my remaining years
it would be for Lois to regain her lost
innocence.

GERTRUDE: I mean the influence. Tom has
principles, character—you must admit you were
talking principles and character to her
three years ago.

CALVIN: Egg shells. Egg shells.
       (*Sings:*)
When the white snow falls, we shovel.

> When the green grass grows, we mow.
> When the fruit hangs ripe, we pick it.
> When a girl matures—heigh ho!
> Get a little, give a little,
> love a little, live a little,
> and when the anchor drags, heave ho!

GERTRUDE: When the rose bud blooms, we pluck it.
> When the wheat stands tall, we reap.
> When the barrel fills, then drain it.
> A fresh girl will not keep.
> Get a little, give a little,
> love a little, live a little,
> and there's lots of time to sleep!

CALVIN: Oh, you don't grow younger,
> you can't go back.
> From glut to hunger
> is a one-way track.
> A fast won't numb it,
> so eat your fill.
> Beyond the summit,
> it's all downhill.

CALVIN AND GERTRUDE: Oh, the horse breaks to the saddle,
> and the field folds to the plow,
> and steaks are broiled for knives, and
> the sea accepts the prow—
> so get a little, give a little,
> love a little, live a little,
> the time for life is now!

CALVIN: Egg shells are nice to have when you have them, but
> a damned relief when they break. A fellow Tom's
> age has no right to principles and character:
> to retain them beyond a certain age is rather
> like spoiling in the shell. He must know life. . . .

LOIS (*entering behind him*): Which boy-oh-boy my daddy
> *knows* . . .

CALVIN: All right,
> Miss Smarty, you tell me the difference
> between innocence and helpless ignorance.

GERTRUDE: Where's Tom?

LOIS: He finished phoning. I think he
went down the hall. . . .

CALVIN (*mock shock*):   Committing an indelicacy?

GERTRUDE: Did that man have the wrong address?

LOIS: Who?

GERTRUDE: Axelrod.

LOIS (*grimly*): Oh, no. I'm sure he had the right address.

TOM (*entering*): A curious place to keep Krafft-Ebing.

CALVIN: That
is where I am usually curious.

LOIS: Calvin. Gertrude.
Before the others come, I think we ought
to tell you what we're celebrating.

CALVIN (*belligerently*):   Well?

(*Lois nods to Tom to make him speak.*)

TOM (*firmly*): Lois and I are going to be married.

CALVIN (*firmly*): Lois and you are doing no such thing.

LOIS, GERTRUDE (*while Tom and Calvin stare each other down*):
What!

LOIS: Calvin, don't be an ass.

TOM (*shocked at both*):   Lois! Really!

GERTRUDE: Are you drunk, dear?

CALVIN: Not exceptionally.

LOIS: We weren't, you know, asking permission—or even
your opinion.

CALVIN: I noticed. And I was giving neither.
Merely a prediction. . . .

LOIS (*her toughness breaking*): Then, Calvin, would you
please . . .
Calvin, what in the world are you talking about?

CALVIN (*looking steadily at Lois*):
How well do you two . . . well, ah . . . *know* each
other?

LOIS (*tears break and are stifled quickly*):
Mother, can you make him stop it? Just shut up,
Calvin, will you? Will you just stay out of this?

CALVIN (*injured*): *Out* of it? I *started* it!

TOM: Sir, I will have you
                                                             know . . .

CALVIN: Sir who? Sir me?

TOM: that I have been completely open with Lois.
          There is nothing about my life she may not know.

CALVIN: *Your* life?

TOM: Sir?

CALVIN: I wasn't referring to
          your lordship's life, sir. But, sir, I would inquire
          precisely how far you have experimented
          with this relationship. . . .

TOM (*devastated*):   Sir?

CALVIN: Calvin.

TOM (*automatically*): Calvin.

CALVIN: Well?

TOM: I really can't see that that is any of your . . .

CALVIN: Look here, Jack Armstrong, whose daughter do you
                think
          she is, for you to be experimenting . . . ?

TOM: I assure you I have not nor would I think . . .

CALVIN: If you wouldn't think of such a thing you may guess
          why I predict so little success for your
          engagement.

LOIS (*still not quite crying*): You are embarrassing him, Cal-
                vin.
          He means . . .

CALVIN: Damn it, I know what he means.

LOIS: You
          can't . .

CALVIN: Stop you? I wouldn't dream of it. You may
          do what you please with your pretty selves, but I
          will have an opinion on my daughter's marriage!

TOM: I can see you have great love for your daughter, Calvin,
          but I assure you . . .

CALVIN (*imitating*): "But I assure you. . . ." Tom, what do you
                do
          to make ordinary English so offensive?

GERTRUDE: Calvin, you're not being very clear about
        your objections.

CALVIN: No? All right, I will be plain.
        Lois keeps quitting jobs and running home—
        she has not come to terms with the world at large,
        and seems rather unlikely to adjust
        to that most primitive and phony job of all,
        marriage, especially with Tom. And Tom . . . Tom,
          are
        you sure you would be able to sleep well
        in a double bed? Would you assure me, sir?

TOM (*bitterly*): I might consult Krafft-Ebing on the subject.

CALVIN: Will you grant me one condition, out of what
        you might term natural respect for my
        parental concern? Not such an ordeal I am
        prescribing, either, I shouldn't think. Will you,
        Tom, wait to marry her until you have,
        as it were, become, well, better acquainted?

TOM: If you mean . . .

LOIS (*nobly*): Calvin, that is against all Tom's ideals—
        and mine, too!

CALVIN: Yours!

GERTRUDE: Calvin, that is enough.

LOIS (*with gracious condescension*): Tom has taught me what
        love really is.
        I doubt that you can understand that, Calvin—
        but part of real love, real tenderness,
        is strength of character, restraint, reserve. . . .

GERTRUDE: There's something in what she says.

CALVIN: And not a word
        of it is honest. Well, Tom—can you take it?

(*The doorbell rings and everyone freezes—Tom, Lois, and Gertrude in various poses of dismay and alarm.*)

CALVIN (*calmly*): Your party, Lois.

LOIS: Very clever, Calvin.
        A fine engagement party *you* have made it!

(*Gertrude goes to door.*)

CALVIN: Some men I know would not be so appalled.
Tom, we can have a pleasant evening if
you agree to my condition. Do you? Well?

(*Lois looks to Tom, imploring, embarrassed. Gertrude is opening the door and admitting Horace and Sue.*)

TOM: If that's what Lois wants, but, nonetheless,
I resent this, Calvin. The whole thing is indecent.
CALVIN: That's as you choose to make it. I do hope
it proves less unsavory in performance
than it appears to you to be in prospect.

(*Horace, Sue, and Gertrude come onto the porch. Horace and
Sue are in their late twenties—a thin, hollowed-looking man,
the sort who holds a cigaret as though it were heavy, all teeth
and heavy eyelids, and a muscular but pretty girl, with a swift
and brittle manner. They are received by Calvin, Lois, and Tom
with forced good humor, distractedly. Horace makes himself at
home, slumping into a chair.*)

HORACE: If you've been fighting, we are going home.
LOIS (*artificially*): Fighting?
HORACE: I can't bear any more fighting. Sue
and I have scratched and kicked one another all eve-
ning.
SUE: I did not kick.
HORACE: We came to escape each other.
SUE: This slope-shouldered serpent, this lizard Lothario . . .
CALVIN: Please, Sue, don't tell us about it. . . .
SUE: It will amuse you.
It amuses me. In fact I find this Horace
a professional entertainer, handy-home-jester.
I laugh so hard my ribs are black and blue.
Here, let me show you.

(*She starts to do so.*)

HORACE: Calm down, Sue.
SUE: Calm *down*?
I am limp, insensible, pulp, as empty
as a wind sock. You blow, it goes right through me.

LOIS: And Horace always had such notions that
      he would be a model husband!
SUE: Oh, he's a model;
      he models right and left for one and all.
      But, as you may remember, Lois, he
      performs best extramurally. At home

(*Lois covers her reaction.*)

      he is a theorist. On household duties,
      for example, he has very clear-cut rules.
      "You do the woman's work," he says, "and I'll
      do the man's work." The woman's work consists
      of cleaning house, preparing dinner (after
      I get home from work), washing dishes, keeping
      accounts, taking out the garbage, writing
      letters to *his* damned mother. . . .
HORACE: You don't have to. . . .
SUE: To keep her from visiting us I do. I sew,
      mop, shine his shoes, buy his clothes, wipe . . .
HORACE: If we don't write her, maybe she'll forget us.
SUE: . . . the dishes, mend the light cords, squiggy that rub-
      ber . . .
HORACE: The plumber's helper.
SUE: . . . when the john sticks, which
      it invariably does. . . .
HORACE: Do you write your mother, Calvin?
CALVIN: I never had a mother.
SUE: . . . although the super
      claims it is fixed for sure. And *now* he wants
      a child, or, as he puts it, a son, as though
      he might perpetuate himself. . . .
CALVIN: Oh, he might!

(*Lois reacts unobserved.*)

SUE: Over my dead body. Well, do you know what
      a *man's* work is? Each Friday evening he
      changes the kitty litter.

HORACE: Tom, do you
          write *your* mother?
TOM: Yes.
SUE: Also he sharpens pencils.
          The other evening there he was on the stoop
          whistling like the barefoot boy incarnate
          and taking thirty minutes to a pencil.
          "There's something basic about this—whittling," he
               says.
          He frequently discovers things that are basic.
          "Something about the feel of wood and a blade—
          the shaping spirit. . . ." So, he got out all
          the pencils in the house and left them each
          a two-inch stub. . . .
HORACE: But sharp!
SUE: My knife about
          as sharp on the blade as on the handle. "Here,
          Deerslayer," I said—and handed him the whetstone.
          "There is something basic about sharpening a knife—
          the honing spirit." Says Horace, "Woman's work."
HORACE: Do we get drinks?
SUE: To*night* he comes home from
          the office and announces he is going
          fishing. *Fish*ing! My latter-day Ahab. If
          he met a guppy in his bath he'd think
          he'd sloshed the onion out of his Gibson. The only
          fish he has ever caught was kippered—and,
          at that, he cut himself on the can. But now
          the boys—he has taken to talking about "the boys"—
          were going out for the weekend to some lake.
          Comes Isaac Walton home with forty dollars
          worth of equipment: boots, creels, crawlers, creepers,
          sinkers and spinners, reels, rods, and such retinue . . .
HORACE: Also sun lotion . . .
SUE: and about four thousand
          yards of this tapered, waxed, spliced, wind-weight
               dacron
          string . . .

HORACE: Line, dear. Line.
SUE: which has to be soaked in the sink
            (after tossing my hose in the tub) while we have a
                drink.
            While I cook dinner he begins to stretch it—
            from the sink tap to the shower nozzle to
            the towel rack to the bedpost to the mirror
            to the refrigerator handle to
            the cuphooks, lampstand, andirons .. .
HORACE (*with growing self-satisfaction*):   and back again.
SUE: All this, you understand, half-crocked, and reciting
                imperfectly remembered passages
                of "The Big Two-Hearted River."
TOM (*seriously*):   Horace, are you
            a casting-rod man or a fly-rod man?
HORACE: Depends, Tom. Weather, condition of water, time
            of day. For your murky day and clear water, now,
            you want your fly-rod, dry-fly, no spinner. For
            your dawn fishing, or riffles, in rain or haze,
            your casting-rod is the surer bet. Consider
            the fish's point-of-view.

(*Horace gets down on his stomach to demonstrate, Tom squatting beside him.*)

                            Say water-level
            is here, and you are under a rock, like so.
            It's been raining, see, and the water is muddy, full
            of flotsam, leaves and stuff, paper cups, beer cans.
            Turtles are on the prowl. Comes a fly on the water,
            skipping along with a nervous little jerking.
            What do you do? Nothing. You can't even see it.
            A plug comes scooting past your nose. Well, now!
TOM: I follow.

(*Horace gets off the floor, brushing his knees.*)

HORACE: Of course it's entirely different for gravel bottoms.
            On your gravel bottom . . . well, no telling what
            you do on your gravel bottom. Don't we get a drink?

LOIS: In just a minute. First, though, Tom and I
    would like to make an announcement. . . .

CALVIN (*in panic*):   I didn't say
    you had to announce . . .

LOIS: Not that. The other, Calvin.

HORACE: Is it a *long* announcement . . . ?

TOM: Lois, let's fix
    some drinks.

LOIS: We can't make punch until that man
    delivers the gin.

HORACE: Our old friend Axelrod?

LOIS (*pointedly*): I can't remember ever having met him.

TOM: Well, let's see if there's anything which might
    tide Horace over in the meantime, Lois.

(*She gets his signal and follows him into the living-room, where
the light follows them while the others remain talking quietly
on the porch. Lois throws her arms open for a kiss but Tom
walks past her to the couch and sits down.*)

LOIS: Is something bothering you, Tom?

TOM: *Both*ering me!

LOIS: It was terrible—but just like Calvin, Tom.
    You've been so jumpy all evening. They are just
    the way they've always been. It needn't mean
    anything about *us*.

TOM: I wonder, Lois, if
    we ought to announce our engagement to them to-
      night.
    I think we need some time to talk about it. . . .

LOIS: I've had a wonderful idea, Tom.
    Calvin and Gertrude are leaving in the morning
    to spend the weekend in the country. We
    could, well, if you would come to dinner after
    work, and we had the apartment to ourselves. . . .

TOM: *Here?* I suppose with drums in our ears and those
    chicken deposit paintings swimming in
    our eyes? No thanks. That wouldn't be my notion
    of playing house. . . .

LOIS: We could go wherever you say.

TOM: I tell you, Lois, we need time to talk.

LOIS: We could talk and talk—all weekend. . . .

TOM: I find the whole
    idea—of being together under his leer—
    repugnant. We mustn't let ourselves be forced
    to spoil something that ought to mean so much. . . .

LOIS: I've *got* it. We can *lie!*

TOM: Lie?

LOIS: Yes, lie.
    You know—say that we, well, sort of have—
    to make him happy. . . .

TOM: What a mess! I should
    report to the father of my fiancée
    that I *have* . . . when I haven't . . .

LOIS: Or, if you want, we *can* . . .

TOM: You mean, you *want* . . .

LOIS (*cautiously*):   Oh, I'm . . . indifferent. . . .

TOM: In*diff*erent!

LOIS: I mean, well, not indifferent, but . . . well. . . .
    Oh, Tom, what do you *want* me to say?

TOM: Hell, I
    don't know. I don't mean to pick on you. This is
    exactly what I mean, though, Lois. Who
    can have a simple response? Who can know
    what he wants or what he feels? What happened to
      love?
    Why can't we love each other simply, cleanly?
    Is it asking too much to want to court you, love you,
    respect you, respect our wedding? Does he think
    I'm not . . . ? Oh, God knows what he thinks! Who
      cares?
    Why do we have to pick and analyze
    a feeling natural as the flowers in spring?
    And how can I make love with Calvin watching . . . ?

LOIS: Oh, we wouldn't let . . .

TOM: Figuratively. I'll sense
    his eye, the eye of reason, like the eye

of God, on the bedroom wall. It's not that I
don't *want* you, Lois: I want you weekdays and Sun-
    days,
openly (in private), free and unashamed.
Hasn't this been our dream—and hasn't he wrecked
    it?

(*Lois has begun crying softly.*)

Lois! What is it, dear?
LOIS: I'm just afraid
I won't be all you imagine me to be.
TOM: Imagine? You think I don't *know* you?
LOIS: You don't—
and I'm . . . afraid to tell you. . . .
TOM: Afraid? Of what?
LOIS: Of that dream. Tom, there are facts. . . .
TOM: Now that sounds like
your father's daughter. Facts. Is love a subject
one studies in a book? Love happens, Lois,
outside our verifiable sphere: it *is*—
like courage, kindness, loyalty, or fear.
The facts of life are irrelevant to love.

(*Lois starts to protest but Tom draws her to him, stops her with
a kiss, and then rises to sing, exploring Calvin's library.*)

Can you make love on a budget?
Can a diary record,
a photo album verify
that you are hereby adored?
Can you put it in a history?
Is it a laboratory fact?
Is there a law without a flaw
defining our contract?
LOIS: Look it up in the
latest Britannica
or take a crack at the almanac.
Perhaps the librarian

　　　　or unabridged dictionary can
　　　　put you on the track.
TOM (*picking up Calvin's discarded paper*):
　　　　I'll try the Evening News,
　　　　under vital statistics. . . .
LOIS: They say some lovers use
　　　　advice of professional mystics
　　　　in the astrology column.
　　　　It says what will befall 'em.
TOM: Is love among the sports?
　　　　The travel news?
　　　　At those resorts?
　　　　The women's page?
　　　　On screen or stage?
LOIS: Perhaps you'll find it Classified.
　　　　Don't leave a single page untried.
　　　　It may be anywhere!
TOM: I finally flip
　　　　to the comic strip
　　　　and fail to find it there.

　　　　Oh, do I love you?
　　　　How can we ever know?
　　　　I say I love you.
LOIS: Can we be sure?
　　　　You say you love me,
　　　　but is it really so?
TOM AND LOIS: How can we certify
　　　　our alleged amour?

(*They are in an embrace, interrupted by a cry from the porch.*)

HORACE (*shouts*): Drinks! Drinks!
LOIS (*shouts*): I can't find any! We will have to wait.
GERTRUDE (*shouts*): Look on the pantry shelf for that Mason
　　　　　　jar
　　　　with my cooking bourbon in it.
CALVIN (*rises, to go to bathroom*):　　　Krafft-Ebing time.

(*Lois has gone to the kitchen. Tom, on the couch, disconsolately watches Calvin cross the room, stopping him just before he goes into the hall.*)

TOM: Well, Calvin, you may congratulate yourself.
         You stuck your finger in a dream, and it turned
         to powder.
CALVIN: Can't have been very substantial then.
TOM: Love never has stood very close examination.
CALVIN: Oh balderdash.
TOM: We love one another, still—
         but love is rather ugly, stripped of honor.
CALVIN: You're welcome to your honor, but you can't
         have it and Lois too.
TOM: What do you mean?
CALVIN: Just trust me. I know Lois fairly well—
         and whatever kind of pap you are giving her
         will not sustain her long. Dreams have, you know,
         a way of existing only in one head.

(*Calvin goes into the hall. The doorbell rings and Tom goes to admit Axelrod, who is a rotund, downright sort of man with a sack under his arm.*)

TOM (*calls*): Hey, Lois, never mind. The liquor's here.

(*Lois enters, catches a glimpse of Axelrod and, ducking her head, hurries to the porch.*)

AXELROD (*calling after her, pushing past Tom*):
         Oh, Mrs. Fielding! Please to let me deliver,
         impersonal, this gift to you and the Mister. . . .

(*Gertrude, hearing this, looks up expectantly as Axelrod moves onto the porch, ignoring her except for a general grin and nod of his head to the others. He goes straight to Lois, sets down his sack, takes her hand and Horace's.*)

         You don't remember—but you changed my life!
HORACE (*jerking his hand free*): Hey, just a minute . . . !
AXELROD (*imperturbably reciting*):

Come, fill it up, and in the fire, fling
Your winter garment. And no repenting. Spring
    Has birds with hardly time to flutter around
For birds do it on the wing.

You remember that? It changed my life. I put
it on a sign with sparkles. Very pretty.
Very popular.
HORACE: I think you are mixed up.
AXELROD: Oh no, Mr. Fielding. Listen. You will remember.

A jar of herrings underneath a bough,
A jug of wine, some cheese and matzos: wow!
    With only you there in the wilderness.
Oh, Wilderness is Paradise. And how!

Just like you taught it me. And you sat there
(*explaining to others*)
right there, with the missus, newlyweds, I bet
my dollar bottom. A Saturday morning. The sun
on the porch and taxis honking like ducks below. . . .
Just three years past. My life was changed. Just like
the poem says, "And how!" Remember now?

The Moving Finger writes, and having wrote,
Quits. And you will lose your wits. I quote:
    What once is wrote in black and white . . .

(*to Horace*)
How does that one end up?
HORACE: I wouldn't know.

(*Calvin enters, stands by porch door eavesdropping.*)

AXELROD: Ah, *then* you did, Mr. Fielding, nibbling each
itsy finger tip of the missus' hand. Eleven
in the morning, both in your pajamas, sweetings.
"Ah, Vintner," you said. "No, sir," I said, "my name
is Axelrod." You laughed to shake your teeth up.
"Have a drink," you said—and I said I never drank.
You understand, folks, I was an earnest fellow,

never drank my goods with a ten-foot pole, kept all
the records straight for the auditor, fetched meat
at the store for my wife, and curbed her yappy little
rat terrier according to the city
ordinance. Yappiest dog I have seen in my life,
and she loved that mutt more than she loved myself.
Would you believe it, the only human being
I ever knew could yap and percolate
on the curbstone at the same time! And the world
passing me by, like I was standing still.

CALVIN: And then Mr. Fielding changed your life?

AXELROD: I live
to say it. "I often wonder what the vintners
buy with the money they get for this stuff they sell,"
he said. I had to have it explained how I
was a vintner. Now you should see it on my store:
MARVIN AXELROD, VINTNER, and under it,
in lights: "I often wonder what the vintners
buy half so precious as this stuff they sell."
(*to Calvin*)
I give it some thought, sir, and I didn't know.
Since then, as the poem says, impersonal:

(*proudly*)
I have done my credit in the World much wrong,
Have drowned my Glory in a shallow cup,
And sold out my Reputation singing a song.

Marvelous! He quoted me whole chapters, and
when I got back at the store I wrote it down
just as he said it. From that moment I
was rehabilitated stem to stern.
In the back room I poured myself a shot.
I set it on a case of Scotch, and like
a ceremony I saluted it.

The Wine of Life keeps oozing drop by drop,
The Leaves of Life keep falling down one after an-
        other.

Down the hatch! Another. Down the hatch!
A merchant, you know, has to believe in his goods.
In the selling racket the only thing that counts
is sincerity. Before that moment, I
was a hypocrite. A stinking hypocrite!

CALVIN: And now you have more faith in your merchandise?

AXELROD: Not so much money—but faith I have. And more.
Happiness. Look. I drink too much. My wife
leaves me, and *takes* the dog. Marvelous!
Business drops off. I got fewer worries. Friends
desert me. Marvelous: I had friends like
that yappy dog had fleas. Now Herman and me
sit in the back and play pinochle, drinking,
discussing world affairs, and when the bell
rings at the door I peep out through a slit
to see if it looks like the type of fellow
can appreciate the wine of life. If not,
Herman goes out and says some verses to him—
like that one about the fellow so
potted he couldn't find the pot, or the one
about the willy-nilly water—which I forget.
Marvelous. Customer goes away, and maybe
Herman has changed his life, for all we know.
Now here is a gift. Three bottles London gin—
no charge, except I want to know the name
of that poem.

HORACE: I never heard of it in my life.

AXELROD: Mr. Fielding, you play jokes. Please, Missus, tell
the name of the poem. It is my law and creed.

(*He has pencil and paper ready.*)

LOIS (*carefully*): The Rubaiyat.

AXELROD (*writing*): The Roo? By Mr. Yat?

LOIS: No, no. By Omar Khayyam.

AXELROD: By an Arab! Who would think it?

(*Axelrod stuffs his paper in his pocket and, nodding goodbye, leaves in confusion. Calvin is laughing heartily. Sue and Ger-*

*trude appear distressed while Horace, Tom, and Lois look off
studiously in three directions.*)

GERTRUDE: But *no!* Omar was a Persian, wasn't he?

(*Lights out.*)

ACT III

SCENE 1

(*Later, company gone, Tom is stalking up and down before the
couch where Lois lies weeping. On the porch Gertrude and Calvin can just be seen, shoes off, feet on the balustrade, punch
bowl between them.*)

TOM: You should have known that that was not the time
        to announce any engagement!
LOIS: I'm sorry, Tom.
        I had to think of something to say. It was
        so awkward after Axelrod . . .
TOM: Absurd!
        Hadn't we just decided that perhaps
        we ought to wait and talk the whole thing over?

(*Silence a moment as he paces and Lois weeps. Suddenly he
stops and reluctantly announces a new decision.*)

        I think I'll ask for a transfer to the West Coast.
LOIS (*sitting up, encouraged*): Oh yes, yes, Tom. To start all
        over! Get
        away from them all—where we can properly
        be married, start a decent home in peace. . . .
TOM: I'm sorry, Lois. That isn't what I mean.
LOIS: You wouldn't. . . .
TOM: Maybe I should. . . .
LOIS: How *could* you, Tom?
TOM: Would, should, could . . . ye gods! How should I know?
        I simply know that I'm not ready for marriage.
LOIS (*newly wailing*): Oh Tom!
TOM: I feel like a hick being bilked by sharks!

LOIS: You don't mean *me?*

TOM: Lois, I love you, I think—
but if I have to think to love, how can
I think . . . ? Well, there it is again, you see?

LOIS: I don't see anything!

TOM: If you had just
been honest with me, Lois! Wasn't I
perfectly open with you about everything?

LOIS (*wails*): You didn't have anything to be honest about!

TOM: But knowing, and knowing, especially, that you
didn't *want* me to know. . . .

LOIS: I was only seventeen!

TOM: But, Lois—with Horace, of all the ridiculous people!

LOIS: I didn't *know* anyone else!

TOM: Oh Lord!

LOIS: I mean . . .
Oh, Tom, I *want*ed you to know. I really did.
I've changed—but it's a change that needs explain-
ing. . . .

TOM: Hasn't there been opportunity to explain?

LOIS (*timidly*): Not really, Tom. Do you know that you are
sort of a difficult person to talk to?

TOM: Me?

LOIS: You are, Tom. You don't really listen to . . .

TOM: You're right. I'm fighting, aren't I, Lois? I
feel awkward, ignorant, among you, and
defend my ignorance like a trapped beast.
Whatever civilization is, I don't
want it. I'm scared of it, and half suspect
I'm right in being scared. I guess I shut
my ears because I don't want to be trained. . . .

LOIS (*tentatively*): Tom . . .

TOM: But I don't mean *you.* I realize
that at times I forget that you're not one of them.

LOIS: Tom . .

TOM: But I'm fighting for my soul, you see.
Soul! What a round, empty word! Or is it?
Soulology. Imagine such a thing!

If I keep picking on psychology
it's because that seems to be the central disease
of the city. A city is a place where every
man on the street can tell by the twitch of your nose
your secret desires, deducts your toilet training
from table manners. I'm naked. People can tell
my defense of defense is defense because I needed
more sucking experience as an infant. . . .

LOIS (*smiling a little*):   Tom . . .
Yoo hoo! Are you ready to listen a minute, Tom?

TOM: I did it again, didn't I, Lois? Well . . .

LOIS: Do you know what happened with me and Horace, Tom?

TOM: Axelrod caught you here on a Saturday morning. . . .

LOIS: Caught us? We ordered the liquor. He simply came.

TOM: Well, anyway, you were here. . . .

LOIS: In pajamas.

TOM: Yes.

LOIS: Suppose it rained. We were wet,
and Gertrude was in the bathroom, ironing our clothes.

TOM (*hopefully*): *Was* she?

LOIS: Suppose that we saw that Axelrod
mistook us for married—and carried it off as a joke.

TOM (*trying to smile*): You *did?*

LOIS: No, we didn't. But suppose. Would you
prefer to have it that way?

TOM: Good lord yes!

LOIS (*furiously, crying*): Then have it!

(*Calvin is entering. Lois sees him, hides her tears, and runs out
to Gertrude on the porch.*)

TOM: Lois! Lois!

(*Calvin passes through to the bathroom as Lois runs by.*)

LOIS (*hugging Gertrude*):   Oh, Mother!
I'm not going to marry Tom!

GERTRUDE (*patting her consolingly*):   Of course not, dear.

LOIS (*wails*): Oh!

GERTRUDE: I mean you may—but it's touch and go with that
       sort of fellow. . . .

LOIS: What sort of fellow?

GERTRUDE: Tom's sort. He
       is very much like Calvin was at that age.

LOIS: But everything he believes . . .

GERTRUDE: Believes? You can't
       set too much store by what a man believes.
       The important thing is the way that he believes it.
       With Calvin it was a kind of religious fervor
       that we should go to bed before we married.
       He argued so that I could tell he wanted
       to prove a point more than he wanted me.
       I'd have none of it. . . .

LOIS: You didn't!

GERTRUDE: Not on your life!
       He said I was unreasonable, and I
       determined to prove him right. I don't want him
       to get me mixed up with ideas, to be
       only a piece of evidence! He walked
       out more than once—and how I cried! For I
       wanted to go ahead, you know, except
       it didn't seem to me the sort of thing
       you do to prove someone's abstract idea.
       He hasn't gotten over it. I think
       maybe that's why he's being so stubborn now.

LOIS: But, Mother, you had it easy. To make Dad see
       you as you were, you only had to refuse. . . .
       Now what am I supposed to do? Accept?
       I mean, it seems like a kind of . . . well, a rape!

GERTRUDE: No, that won't do. You need some kind of test
       that needn't take place in bed, and yet will make
       him *see* you, primitive, the person beneath. . . .

LOIS (*laughs painfully*): You mean like drums.

GERTRUDE: Like drums?

LOIS (*collapsing, sobbing, on Gertrude's bosom*): Those God-
       damned drums!

(*Calvin is re-entering the living-room where Tom sits pouting.
He stops and studies him.*)

CALVIN: The marriage is off, I gather.

TOM (*angrily*):   Calvin, you snoop!

CALVIN: Who needs to listen? I guess you know that from
      my point-of-view that is rather good riddance?

TOM: Doubtless.

CALVIN: But Lois, I am convinced, loves you
      more than her wits, which are, I hope, against you.

TOM: I'm very sorry to hurt her. I'll always love her.

CALVIN: Do you know why you want to leave her now?

TOM: I haven't said I want to leave her, but
      in view of this affair with Horace—or
      not so much that, but her lying about it . . .

CALVIN: Or
      neglecting, or being unable, to tell?

TOM: Whatever. Anyway, I see very little
      foundation now for trust and happiness.

CALVIN: Do you know why she never told you about
      Horace?

TOM: Because she was ashamed, I suppose.

CALVIN: Of what?

TOM: What do you mean, of what? Did she
      or did she not have an affair with Horace?

CALVIN: You don't know?

TOM: She implied that maybe it
      was innocent—and then ran out. She won't
      be straight about it. In this house she has learned
      sophistication—which gets in the way.

CALVIN: Look, I am as sorry as you we didn't provide
      her with enough discrimination concerning
      her relations with males. She is, in fact, a little
      scatterbrained, rather sensual, superficial. . . .

TOM: I resent your saying that. . . .

CALVIN: Poopoopeedoo!
      She's a better person than you are likely to know.

She is frank, sweet, spontaneous, bright, amusing—
and above all honest, or what you call "straight."
If she has not been straight with you it was
because one can't imagine saying anything,
*any*thing to *you* that really matters. You
haven't sufficient interest in Lois or
anyone outside yourself to want to know
or make any effort to understand. You were
buying a pig in a poke, proposing to Lois—
but through no fault, I'm convinced, of hers. It happens
the pig was quite a piece of pork—but you
have let her go. That's just as well, for her.

TOM: I *haven't* let her go; I mean it's all . . .
Damn, Calvin! Now all I can think about is pigs!

CALVIN: You'll let her go as soon as you know about Horace.

TOM: *What,* for God's sake, about Horace?

CALVIN (*calls*): Lois, come here.
Tom wants to know about Horace. Come, girl. Facts.

LOIS (*enters with swollen face, Gertrude behind her*):
Tom isn't interested in facts.

TOM: Oh, Lois,
don't take their side!

LOIS: Whose side am I to take?

TOM: I haven't the curiosity of your father
about other people's sexual affairs.
You needn't tell me anything. I can
decide whether I love you or not without
a public confession.

CALVIN: Sorry, Lois. I thought
I had him ready to talk—or, rather, listen.

TOM: You're ganging up on me, Calvin. Would you please
stop torturing us? Just look at Lois. Do
you really enjoy making her suffer like that?

LOIS (*quietly*): It wasn't Calvin, Tom, who made me cry.

CALVIN: Lois, do you mind talking about what happened
with you and Horace three years ago?

LOIS: No.

CALVIN: I mean right here, with all of us. Would you rather
            Gertrude and I weren't here?

LOIS: It doesn't matter.

TOM: You've been brain-washed, Lois. Don't let them make . . .

LOIS: I've talked about it with them many times.

TOM: But our affairs . . .

LOIS: Oh? Do we have affairs?

GERTRUDE: Oh, let's do talk about everyone's affairs.

CALVIN: You have objections, Gertrude?

GERTRUDE: I agree with Tom.
            It seems rather silly dragging it all out here.

CALVIN: Okay, I won't insist. I'd just as soon
            the engagement never happened anyway.
            It's clear they'll never marry as things stand.
            It's clear they'd never marry if Tom knew.
            So why bother? It seems to me that I
            have made my contribution. I'm off to bed.

(*Calvin leaves. The others sit and look at one another uncomfortably. Tom lifts his chin unassailably.*)

TOM: If I knew what? By now I assume you had
            relations with Horace. So? People have relations.
            It's not that I want all the cuddly details.
            The only thing I still don't understand
            is why Lois should have hidden it all from me.

GERTRUDE: There are several things, Tom, you don't understand.
            Go on and tell him, Lois. I'll go to bed.
            He's got himself in a state—too proud to ask.
            But he'll have a thing about it, now, unless
            he knows. And, as Calvin says, it seems there's nothing
            to be lost anyway. You're not ashamed. . . .

LOIS: Ashamed? That's not the point. I was too scared
            of what he'd say to force him to listen, but
            it wasn't shame. I think I wanted him
            to want to know—know *me*—to love enough
            to want the truth and to accept it in me. . . .

TOM: Okay! Okay! Right here before your mother,
please tell me, step by step, how Horace took
advantage of you when you were too young . . .
on this couch, the bed, the porch, in which hotels,
his habits, his persuasive arguments,
how his breath stank, teeth bit, his scrawny back
bent to his work! All this is sure to make
me love the *real* Lois, which I have failed
through egotism to take into account. . . .

LOIS: Thanks. I'm beginning, at least, to understand
the real Tom. You can take your rural ideals
and feed them to the pigs!

(*She starts to stalk out down the hall, but Calvin, who has been
listening, pushes her back into the room.*)

CALVIN: Tom is touchy
about pigs this evening. Try another tack—
or, better yet, let Daddy supervise.
What happened with Horace, Lois?

LOIS: I loved him.

CALVIN: Why?

GERTRUDE: Calvin, we *know* all this!

CALVIN: But you have seen
how far they get discussing it alone.
Let's get it out in court. I want to see
that the right questions are asked—and nothing
skipped.

LOIS: Who knows why people fall in love? I was
excessively typical as a high school senior;
he was a verbal, unpopular college boy.
The very fact that Horace was repulsive
inclined me to try to find him otherwise. . . .

GERTRUDE (*to Calvin*): You see, I told you she . . .

CALVIN: Lois, go on.

LOIS: That isn't fair to Horace. He was witty,
accepting, willing to be silly like
the gang of girls I ran around with. He
would sit in the drugstore with us, Horace and

a half a dozen girls, the harmless center
of attention. I was envied because he chose
me to walk home. He seemed, at least, no threat.
I let him in. We kissed. In this respect
it seemed that I could teach him something. He
was no seducer. When, eventually,
we went to bed, he sort of apologized.
He suffered in the act and whimpered after—
sleeping like a survivor of a shipwreck.

CALVIN: Did he love you?

LOIS: He loved tenderness: he licked
the hand that gave him tidbits. He loved to be
seen with the girls, to have an audience.
I don't think he ever knew who was inside.

TOM (*stiffly*): This seems to be a favorite theme of women!

CALVIN: Shut up. Be educated. Did he want
to marry you, Lois?

LOIS: I think he thought he did.
We tried it out that week you were away
and he moved in. He smoked a pipe and read
the evening papers. He broke one of the drawers
in your dresser, trying his hand at carpentry.

GERTRUDE: So that's what happened to . . .

LOIS: He drank too much
and wept and told me stories of how his mother
liked to watch him bathe. I had a bellyful. . . .

CALVIN: Even then?

LOIS: That wasn't what I meant, but I
suppose I had that, too. That week was the end
of my affair with Horace.

CALVIN: Whose idea
was the week alone? Did Gertrude and I approve?

LOIS: It was my idea. You didn't know about it.

CALVIN: I approve retroactively. Tom, do you approve?

TOM: It sounds disgusting.

CALVIN: Exactly. Without it, I
might have had Horace for a son-in-law.

LOIS: You have a grandchild for a souvenir.

TOM: He *what?*

CALVIN: I approve of my grandson, too, except
I see too little of him. Tom shows some
interest in this grandson. Tell him about him.

LOIS: He lives with an aunt in Ashtabula, Tom.
I went there through my pregnancy, and then,
since I wanted to work, to be independent, to find,
I hoped, a husband, to make a home for Georgie—
that's the boy—it seemed a good idea to leave
him there, at least awhile. But now it's been
over three years. That's much too long. I have
to find a way that we can be together.

GERTRUDE (*enthusiastically*): He doesn't resemble Horace in the
least!
He's chunky, mesomorphic like his mother. . . .

CALVIN: Why didn't Horace marry you, Lois, when
he knew that you were pregnant?

LOIS: He never knew.
I hope he never knows he has that son.
I'm glad, Tom, you have never known him, either—
that you decided not to marry me
as I decided not to marry Horace,
without the complication of Georgie. He
is a heart-breaker. . . .

GERTRUDE: Oh, they surely can
do something about correcting those crossed eyes!

LOIS: I don't mean that. I mean he's just the sort
of kid you'd sacrifice your happiness
to make a home for.

TOM: Lois, I haven't said . . .

LOIS: Well, I will say it for you. After this,
marriage is out. I wanted to explain,
and tried, I thought—but I guess not hard enough.
And now it comes out all wrong, doesn't it, Tom?
I was too cowardly. I'll know next time.
Golly, I want to go to bed, unless
you think that other facts are relevant.

TOM: Lois, I . . .

(*He sighs and sinks back helplessly.* Lois *watches this—then quietly leaves the room.* Calvin *and* Gertrude *watch* Tom *a moment, then* Calvin, *with a shrug and a wave goodnight, goes off down the hall.* Gertrude *sits watching* Tom.)

GERTRUDE: You want a pillow, maybe?

TOM: This modern world
    goes out of its way to create ugliness!

GERTRUDE (*laughs*): Modern-schmodern. The world must al-
    ways have been
    about the same in all important respects.
    You can't call Georgie ugly. Even his eyes
    are kind of cute. . . .

TOM: I mean the labels, the planning,
    the probing and naming and cold-blooded experi-
    ments. . . .

GERTRUDE: Well, *Hor*ace's blood may have been cold. But, Tom,
    I think *you* just object that people now
    have better means for finding out what they
    are dealing with. I, now, find it confusing—
    but a confusion of riches. People talk
    too much. Calvin, especially. But there's
    no *harm* in it. It's sort of fun. And it's
    surely the same underneath—when talking's done.
    (*Sings:*)
    When I wake up in the morning on foam rubber,
    look out my picture window at the street
    and see the traffic throbbing at the stop-light,
    feeling the radiant heating at my feet,
    and walk on nylon carpet to the bathroom,
    where fluorescent lighting modulates the space
    and air-conditioning controls the atmosphere,
    my mirror, tinted, polaroid, reflects, I fear . . .
        the same old face.

    When the predigested bread is in the toaster,
    and instant coffee heats on infra-red,
    when television has announced the temperature,
    I must get the same old husband out of bed.

I hear the buzz of his electric shaver,
I hear the slosh of his new dentifrice,
I get a whiff of scent which makes him masculine,
and, at the breakfast table, something genuine:
    the same old kiss.

It's the same old world, though they make it out of
    plastic.
It's the same old world, in high fidelity.
It's the same old world, though it often seems fan-
    tastic.
It's the same old world, or a good facsimile.

They say the earth abides beneath the concrete;
they say behind the highway signs are trees,
that weather still occurs in backward countries,
and they have not quite conquered all disease.
They say that lovers quarrel still, and sometimes
kiss and make up, in the old-fashioned way.
Though many things have been explained, it seems
    that
they never will be quite explained away.

Transistorized and synchronized,
sans nicotine, and on wide-screen,
electrified and dripped and dried,
fluoridated, desegregated,
polyphonic, supersonic,
art abstract and vacuum-packed,
homogenized and pressurized,
this weary planet, wired for sound,
still by love is whirled around—
it's the same old world.

TOM: Sure, Gertrude. It's the same old world, but I
    don't see in it the same respect for marriage . . .
    or maybe there was never respect for marriage,
    but back home, parents, at least, didn't plot to make
    marriage a mockery before it began.

GERTRUDE: A mockery? How have we done that?

TOM: If marriage means anything, it means you can't . . .
    until you are, and then not with anyone . . .

GERTRUDE: Oh, I see marriage as a positive thing,
    not just a lot of limitations, Tom.
    I see it as a kind of a release,
    like maybe then you can relax a little. . . .
    Tom, I think maybe marriage means a lot
    more to Calvin and me than it does to you. We want
    a realistic basis, so it may
    endure without chains to hold a pair together.

TOM: You call this orgy with Horace . . .

GERTRUDE: Good   grounds   for
    parting.
    That's why I'm worried about your going off
    in a huff. You don't really know. You haven't
    good grounds.

TOM: I suppose I should try first, and then
    go off? Didn't you learn a thing from Horace?

GERTRUDE: Well, Calvin felt, I'm sure, that what you needed
    was some close conversation, and thought he
    was quite imaginative about how that
    might be achieved. . . .

TOM: Imagination, you call it?

GERTRUDE: Well, Calvin thinks for you to unbend there must be
    extraordinarily disarming conditions. . . .

TOM: Calvin! Calvin! He's got you brain-washed, too.

GERTRUDE: Not quite. He's an absolutist, Tom, like you.
    He's strict in his ideals, and forgets
    the same things cannot work for everyone.
    His father was a minister, you know.
    I don't know what would work for you and Lois—
    but you'd have to find that out—and I agree
    it'll take some conversation. Calvin and I
    are going away for the weekend. Would you like
    for us to leave her here—or take her with us?

TOM: She doesn't want to see me. . . .

GERTRUDE: Then we'll take her with
    us.

TOM: Although I owe it to her to explain . . .

GERTRUDE: Oh, I think she understands. You can write a letter.

TOM: I mean more intimately—if she would
agree to see me, say, just one more time.

GERTRUDE: Well, this is painful for her, Tom. If she
would come with us to the lake she'd be distracted.
Why don't you wait and talk to her next week?

(*Tom walks around the room a moment, scowling. Suddenly he stops over Gertrude and looks down angrily—then suddenly breaks into a defeated grin.*)

TOM: If I were to marry Lois I think I would
develop an Oedipus-in-law complex!

(*He kisses her on the forehead, stands to go.*)

Suppose you could persuade her to invite
me for a dinner date tomorrow night?

GERTRUDE: I'll try. She's stubborn, once she has made up
her mind. She can call you at the office tomorrow?

TOM: No, I'll just come. And if she's here, she's here.

(*He kisses her again lightly and waves goodnight, leaves through the front door. Calvin and Lois immediately pop out of the hall, both dressed for bed.*)

LOIS (*anxiously*): Did he *go?*

GERTRUDE: He grows gregarious. I think
by tomorrow he'll be skeptical of the stork.

(*Lois shakes her hands in a sign of victory, then goes off to bed. Calvin and Gertrude begin clearing the porch and straightening the house, with occasional yawns.*)

CALVIN: You handled that well, dear.

GERTRUDE: Were you listening?

CALVIN: Oh, inadvertently.

GERTRUDE: But you didn't want him . . . ?

CALVIN: I think Lois may be good for him.

GERTRUDE: No doubt.

CALVIN: Good head on the boy, in spite of his ideas.

GERTRUDE: I think he may be good for Lois.

CALVIN: No doubt.

Lois and I have been having quite a talk.

Gertrude, you say you really . . . wanted to . . . back then?

GERTRUDE: Oh yes! But I thought you wouldn't respect me.

CALVIN: Hmm.

GERTRUDE: Do you think you would have?

CALVIN: Times are different now.

GERTRUDE: You mean I was right?

CALVIN: You made me awfully angry.

GERTRUDE: But wasn't that just because of ideas, Calvin?

CALVIN: *Just* ideas! Of course it was ideas!

GERTRUDE: Well, then it didn't matter, did it, really?

CALVIN: I seem to have adjusted to your terms.

Listen, why did you turn me down? Wasn't that ideas?

GERTRUDE: More a reaction, like. Just tit for tat.

CALVIN: That's rather a misleading way to put it.

GERTRUDE: But you can't decide for others, can you, Calvin?

I mean you can't arrange their love life for them. . . .

CALVIN: Ha. You arranged them pretty well tonight.

GERTRUDE: We didn't really *trap* him, did we, Calvin?

He was rather uneasy, he said, about being trapped.

CALVIN: It's only fair to help them along a bit.

It takes so long to learn to love.

GERTRUDE: That's it.

(*She comes to him and takes his hands.*)

It's much too complicated for the young. . . .

CALVIN: They're inexperienced and too high strung. . . .

GERTRUDE (*sings*):

I hope they learn to love as we have learned it—
The way to get along and make it do,
to take it easy, and, when they have earned it,
woo as the wise old owls have wit to woo.

CALVIN: When they have our years may they be as happy. . . .

GERTRUDE: May she love him as well as I love you. . . .

CALVIN: And may their children learn from their grandpappy
    how wise old owls still have the wit to woo.

CALVIN AND GERTRUDE:
    Fine wines grow all the finer as they mellow.
    Golden is the sunset hue.
    The harvest comes when leaves are growing yellow,
    and in the winter, owls have wit to woo.

    With faces fresh and feelings green and tender
    may youngsters take a clue from me and you—
    that after dark the owl achieves his splendor,
    under the moon he has the wit to woo!

(*Lights out.*)

SCENE 2

(*The following evening Lois is alone in the house, standing on tiptoes in her hose to put lipstick on before the mirror. She whisks around, much as Gertrude did the evening before, putting on heels, fetching a tray with two martini glasses. Finally she takes her position by the record player. There is a knock on the door. She does not answer. Another knock. Still she waits. The knob turns tentatively and Tom cautiously sticks his head in. Lois sets down the needle and drums boom out, causing Tom to jump back, startled, and slam the door. Lois waits. Finally the knob turns again, softly, and Tom looks in, sees Lois, enters, and closes the door. He takes her shoulders fondly, holding her at arm's length. At last his head begins to bob to the rhythm of the drums.*)

VIII

Barefoot Boy as Courtly Lover:
Notes on *The Glass Mountain*

THE ALCHEMIST

Your touch would Midas Midas: a daffodil
instantaneously in your palm is golder
trumpeting than bloom has been or will.

Your fingers release perfection: older
are antiques handled thus, newer new shoots,
shier the shy at your touch, and the bold bolder.

Higher the tree struts, curling its roots
like toes and digging: you, the cause,
leaning and loving there, stir attributes

of bark that stiffens stiffer, quicker draws
sappier sap up from the soul of soil.
The me of me wakes up and gladly gnaws

when I am brushed by but your eyes. I coil,
grow serpentine, when just your fingertips
trace the cheek of my cheek. My petals toil

to be touched. Change me, oh palm, that casually slips
into my handy hand! Oh, gold and shrill
be the trumpeting of silence! Touch my lips.

The Glass Mountain is obviously the other side of the coin
from *Drums*. I like to imagine them being played by the same
seven people on the same evening as a deliberate contrast—

one a fairly conventional drawing-room comedy, the other a
fantasy; one dealing with a reluctant lover and one with a lover
who is too importunate; both exploring the assumptions of
courtly love which still complicate relations between the sexes
in the Western world.

In one way or another the lady is always in the tower, proud
and useless, the hero always below, dedicating himself and his
deeds to her in hope of favors. Love itself is worshipped as a
god, and an exacting and irrational code governs the rites of
its celebration. This love is invariably pre- or extramarital. We
avoid it like a disease, and when we fall into it our friends laugh
at us. We suffer paralysis, fever, and chill. It has very little to
do with affection or lust; in fact, it has very little to do with the
lady in the tower, who may be Rosaline or Juliet indifferently.
It is an obsession, something like what a pupa must go through
in metamorphosis, which transforms the worm into a silly bright
creature, capable of giddy flight. Once one is *in* love his object
is to achieve sexual release, like the lancing of a boil, which
cures the disease.

I can give a classical illustration from those religious days I
have already described. I was attending what passed in Houston
for a high school when the arrow of Eros struck my heart, just
at the moment I was looking at a bony beauty with long caramel
curls named, I believe, Shirley. It is significant that I am not
certain of her name although I remember very well a variety of
girls with whom I had friendships or sexual intimacy. I hadn't
fallen in love with them. Love is something, specifically, which
happens to the lover. I came down with a fever; I vaguely remember day after day writhing in my bed, slipping in warm and
chilly waves from dream to wakefulness and back again. My
fantasies were elaborate, usually having to do with a desert island and very little to do with sexual activity, except, perhaps,
for an occasional ceremonious kiss.

Surviving the initial coma, the lover moves on to perform his
derring-do. The next crisis is that of letting her know that she
has been chosen as the beloved. I had only one shirt with which
I could wear my single tie. The collar was too tight, it was short
at the wrists, a pale green. I wore this daily (if I could persuade

my mother to launder it when she came home from work), and so went to school in my coat of mail, face red, eyes bulging, arm-pits cut and wrists exposed, tie awkwardly tied. My idea of announcing my love to Shirley was to sit in class dressed in this manner, fingering my tie and combing my hair frequently. She did not seem to catch on. While I had no difficulty talking to other girls, I could not bring myself to say a word to her, and, in fact, would gaze abstractedly in the other direction if she seemed to notice me. She probably thought I had developed some irrational hatred for her, if she had any speculations about me at all.

This obstacle requires the dangerous next step of the intermediary. To tell a male friend was unthinkable, embarrassing, and too great a risk, for he might prove a John Alden. My Cressida had no Uncle Pandarus that I knew of. Nor had either of us a wily servant. I got on well enough with a fat little girl who was clearly out of it and who could in a friendly manner indicate my interest to Shirley. When I knew that the message had been delivered, the affair took on a whole new excitement. I began wearing a sweater with a clover flower or other decoration, a tie clasp. Then, when I sat in the classroom ostentatiously looking the other way, gagging on my collar and blinking what I hoped were sensitive lashes, I *knew*, I just *knew* she was looking at me, curiously, considering.

It would have been fortunate at this time if I could have gotten in a fight with someone or been spectacular at touch football during gym period (when she, in her bloomers, with brittle brown legs, flew after a soccer ball in a neighboring field), but I did not dare and was unable. I slew dragons in secret, performing a variety of lone feats on a rope swing in the woods along the bayou, on my bicycle, on my paper route. I was up at four every morning, took an icy shower for Shirley, engaged in imaginary conversation with her as I rolled my papers, and imagined her following as I rode the dark streets sailing the papers expertly thirty feet to clunk to rest by the dark doorways. The kind of girl I want to marry, I told myself, was one who would go around with a fellow on his paper route. At school I slept through all classes except those Shirley attended. Was my heroism making any noticeable difference in the size of my muscles? in my bearing? I wondered, looking away. When we passed in the hall I gave her a casual, almost condescending smile—and imagined I heard her giggling as she and her girl friends walked away behind me.

The first Favor was granted at a party, under the sheltering guise of one of those Post-Office-type kissing games we used to play. After mischievously dodging me most of the evening she finally let herself be tagged (or whatever), and her forfeit was to walk around the block with me. We set out stiffly, Shirley setting a brisk pace. I reached for her hand, and she let me hold it, or, rather, used mine to drag me after as she sailed along. It *was* a rather chilly evening. But at some point I dug in my heels and pulled her around to me, shaking, teeth chattering, embraced her hard frame, stood on my tiptoes, and kissed her cheek. She let me! She *let* me! I released her hand and danced down the sidewalk ahead of her back to the house.

But, though we had not yet exchanged any words, the romance had taken a serious turn. She knew through the intermediary that I was her declared lover. Our silent exchanges had confirmed that I was interested in Shirley and that she was at least watching me—with amusement and curiosity. I had touched her, held her hand, and kissed her cheek. Ahead lay the perils of writing her a note, speaking to her, and kissing her lips. I quaked and despaired and spent another feverish night.

Of those necessary next steps, writing notes seemed least terrifying; I began composing long ones on green-tinted notebook paper (green was becoming my pennon color; I was practicing fancy signatures as an armorial device); some of those notes I even permitted my fat friend to deliver. I don't remember ever getting any reply. But a crisis could not be postponed indefinitely. At the end of the semester, worse than grades, came a Dance. If I did not ask her, someone else would. And yet I didn't know how to dance, particularly couldn't dance with Shirley (who had several inches on me), and could hardly imagine the succession of horrors involved in (1) asking her, (2) getting an answer, (3) if she accepted, dressing to go, (4) sending or taking flowers, (5) picking her up—on foot? on bicycle? (6) talking to her through an evening, (7) deciding whether or not to try to kiss her—all this beside the problem of staying up until nearly midnight and still managing my paper route the next morning.

Brash youth that I was, I *did* ask her, though—and in person. It was by her locker in the hall. I just stopped, cocked my head, grinned suavely, and said, "Shirley, would you go to the Junior-Senior Prom with me?" It was crudely, impetuously done. It was treating her just as though she were a person. And this error undoubtedly was the factor which brought the romance to disaster. She said she would let me know—but day after day she did not. I passed her more notes—directly now, without the intermediary, so callous I had become. I grew cocky, reckless (e.g., riding with no hands on a busy street pretending to read a book), self-confident in bearing: had I not, after all, asked my girl for a Date—indeed, to a Dance? And I waited for her reply with a sickening dread. When she received my notes she passed them around, I knew, hearing them giggle—and I bore my punishment with desperate dignity.

I can see now that she was waiting for another invitation. When her note finally came it was in Latin class, and the folded notebook paper, elaborately blotted with very distinct lipstick impressions of a passionate mouth, was passed back down the row to me, all eyes, like those of lines of courtiers in the presence of the Queen, following its progress until I took it in my trembling hands. It was perfumed, written in purple ink, the i's dotted with o's. It said she was very, very (with many underlinings) sorry that she could never, never feel about me the way I seemed to feel about her. Obviously, though it was intended to look casual, it had been prepared with great pains the night before, perfumed and blotted. My blood rushed from my face and I folded like a fish de-boned.

A true knight would not have been deterred. This was simply one more terror after the dragons. But it finished me. By the end of the hour I had loosened my tie, rolled back my sleeves, unbuttoned that strangling collar, and wadded that note into a ball which I rolled around and around in my fingers. (They were pink and scented until I washed them in the boys' room.) Going

down from the third to the second floor I flipped the ball off my
thumb up to an inaccessible, wide, marble window sill, where
to my knowledge it still remains (eastern stairwell, Austin High,
Houston). I whistled off-key and went back to the fellows. From
time to time thereafter, in passing, I looked up at that window
sill with a self-satisfied smirk. Boy, had I fixed Shirley!

In over two decades of marriage, as I have become a professor and studied courtly love in medieval books, watching
with increasing objectivity the coeds in their dormitory glass
mountains and chevaliers trooping out of their barracks in noisy,
happy groups, until one of their number gets cut off from the
pack, the arrow striking as he stands alone, helpless without
cohorts, suffers the secret agonies, falling behind in his work,
doing push-ups in the gym, it all seems so inevitable. And yet
a Chinese friend tells me that romantic love is unknown over
there. The strong emotion in their literature is, for example, the
loneliness of parted friends or mates, grief at the death of a
loved one, or the serene happiness of being together. He says
there is little of this obsessive torment about the beginning of a
relationship.

THE SUPERIORITY OF MUSIC

Lang has no lovewedge. The world forgot
such courtly praise for neon eyes
as roused their hurricano sighs
in knightly years. I am not
like a yacht, nor dare I to
a harbor resemble thee. My tears
gully no landscapes. I have no fears
of chill disdain, nor wanly woo
pent in pantameter. My verse is ill
with marriage and commonsense
constraining conceit and elegance.
Shall I sonnetize the Pill?

Nay, wife, I still with clapper tongue
proclaim that you, like any she
belied with false compare may be
with hyperbolic baubles hung:
I root my ropy route among
your petal hills; I pioneerly boar

my sow of despond, salty shore,
or, as spring from pikespeak sprung,
twist down melodically and clear.
I lick the jewels from corners, halt
midair nijinskywise. I sault
summerly and slobber, bucking near,

for you, my satin-saddle, gra-
vey grave, my scorching wine, my squirrel.
I love you like boiled onions, girl,
buttered. You suck my spine away,
soak me. You tenderize my twigs.
I think in orange. My tongue twitches
till sundown. You invent my itches.
You look like music and taste like figs.
You are to be virtuo-solely played,
sweetly and with pizzicato,
ad libitum and obbligato,
my straddle-various, my fiddled maid.

No go. The mind in praise ties knots.
Yet when you lie there like a long smile
brownly smiling at either end a long while,
moon glazing your gullied landscape, thoughts
circling and settling like evening birds,
and you turn and stroke my skin with eyes
like tonic chords, and silence lies
as gently over us as music without words,
I would not then restore to love its tongue.
You are not like anything. No poet imagined you.
You are dreamed by the earth, wordless. You
are not to be described, but sung.

But ridiculous as courtly love may be, it seems to me to have
a number of things to recommend it. It gentles a man, causes
him to transform the virtues of the battlefield to those of the
drawing-room and boudoir, teaches him manners, brings out his
eloquence, and stimulates his imagination. As "The Alchemist"
says, it transmutes, ennobles, and vitalizes. We may owe to it
the stamping out of dragons. But I can see no advantages for
the girl—and that is what this play is about. In both *Drums* and
The Glass Mountain, idealistic fathers try to create conditions
of love different from those they experienced, different from
what they really wanted for themselves. This seems perverse if

not dishonest, but is, I imagine, fairly normal parental practice. Love is hard enough on young people without parents contributing obstacles. And except for the exercise and transformation of the male as he leaps against the kennel wall, everyone loses. The girl, high-heeled, long-nailed, powdered, painted, skirted, curled, corseted, ruffled, and perfumed, is as effectually removed from service to herself and society as if her feet were bound at birth (and what about that, my Chinese friend?). It is expensive for the parents and painful for the daughter—not the ennobling pain her lover suffers but simply a hollow, passive frustration. Moreover, when she finally *is* brought down from her glass mountain, she has very little way of knowing how they live down there on the plain, and, particularly, knows very little about this male who will share her life. Many mutate backwards from butterfly swain to husband worm.

With changing mores (I expect the Pill soon to be dispensed with the orange juice in college cafeterias), the courtly rites may be doomed to total obliteration, but I doubt it. I think our peacock antics are as biologically based as are those of the peacock—who, after all, finds his hen on no father-reared glass mountain and never gives a thought to birth control. Courtship seems to produce erratic and unnatural behavior in most species —and I don't mean the unreason of lust but that of preening and dancing and ritual, all of which deny as they promote passion. It may be glandular after all, but if so the glands are bewildering enough to serve as an example of Mystery. Perhaps, with the aid of pills and key clubs and other devices to liberate behavior, we can get the purely physical problems of sex licked, and courtship may flower even more beautifully than it does on artificial glass mountains. With sexual license rapidly increasing, sales of articles such as men's perfumes have boomed suddenly into multimillion-dollar businesses. I think people will become more selective when they have more possibility of selection. My ordeal with Shirley discouraged me about the whole process— and I developed a resistance, if not total immunity, to love. To the extent that love is such torture, we encourage the male to prowl opportunistically, hoping to discharge his urges without contracting the social disease of infatuation. He will hate women—who cause such pain and demand such attention. And perhaps one way he will take out his subconscious revenge on the whole sex is by incarcerating his daughter on a glass mountain.

I think the Pill will level a whole range of glass mountains, and more power to it. That other, less innervating love, which replaces the sickness of courtship, liberates the spirit and can induce a more lasting transmutation. My desire to be a hero for my wife and children is a much more serious and profitable motive than anything I ever felt for Shirley. Romantic love, secret and jealous, specializes the heart, and as it grows pointed it grows limited. This other love, an amiable cross between Eros and Agape, enlarges one's capacity to love others. It fertilizes and forgives. And, if you work it right, you don't have to go to dances.

Of the plays in this collection, *The Glass Mountain* is my favorite. Whether or not readers will share my preference, I would like them to know the qualities which attract me to it. First is what I would call its objectivity: I feel that I am no longer expressing myself here, but making; the characters, though they seem real and individual enough to me, hardly retain shreds of the flesh from which they were torn. Second, I am attracted by its neatness: proportion, pace, liaison of scenes, variety, and coherency are all worked out more successfully here, I feel, than in the other plays. Third, I find I read the verse with more pleasure: the interweaving of rhymes and the metrical variations seem smoother, more flexible, and yet more orderly and consistent than in the other plays. The same medium would not work, of course, for other kinds of material, but form and content seem to me to coalesce better here than, except for moments, they have ever done in my plays before. Fourth, I am pleased with the combination of specificity and universality. It has a kind of UN decor—with English Don John, Mediterranean Carlo, Central European parents, etc.—and takes place spanning the stone age and modern times. Yet it is not as abstract in idiom, character, or situation as, even, *Drums* or *Candle in the Straw,* both of which would seem to demand much more realism and specific setting. Now, all that may not work the way I imagine it, but I spell out those criteria for what use they may be in helping you understand what I am working toward in this and the other plays.

In its one stage production, we used a black plastic-covered cone for the mountain, with a wide, slippery board out of sight on one side for the characters to climb and tumble on. In my imaginary production, where the mountain glistens crystalline and the white charger paws and snorts, Shirley, though the braces are now off her teeth, never gets to the dance—and I am not Carlo or the Prince, but that drunk who mutters "the day would come when women needed men."

IX

The Glass Mountain

The stage is dominated by a glass mountain, preferably black
obsidian, perhaps twelve or fifteen feet high, with steep, sloping,
irregular sides, fairly far forward on the stage and to one side.
On top of the mountain sits a pink boudoir of elaborately
feminine decor. Its walls are transparent and there is a large
window-frame facing us. In the boudoir is a large four-poster

*bed, skirted in voluminous sheer pink fabric—as is the vanity
table, over which hangs an enormous mirror heavy with scrolled
wood frame, painted ivory. The curtains and all other decorations are like spun sugar in their richness, prettiness, and delicacy.*

Scene 1

(*Princess is sitting before the mirror abstractedly powdering her
face with a giant puff. She wears a billowing, sheer gown of
modern design, but in keeping with the decor of her room—a
softly beautiful girl with long, loose golden hair down her back.
She has graceful, innocent movements, a young, sweet voice—
an incarnation of all female loveliness at the first blush of maturity. Papa, a balding, paunchy, little middle-aged man who
speaks with a slight German accent, is dressed in carpenter's
overalls, with a hammer and carpenter's rule in his hand. He has
built this room and now is finishing the last of the windows. He
bangs at the frame a little and then tries the sash to see that it
works freely. He leaves the window open.*)

PAPA: It works good now.
PRINCESS: Was that the last?
PAPA: Ja, all is done.
PRINCESS (*sighs*): Done so fast?
PAPA: Why, Princess, is it sighing now?
PRINCESS: No, Papa, I am pleased—but vaguely hating
            to see it done, to see you go,
            to find myself here, waiting.
PAPA: Oh, not so long to wait! Why, when
            I was a youngster . . .
PRINCESS (*teasing gently*):   . . . and men were men?
PAPA: Ja. It wouldn't take so long.
PRINCESS: Ah, you were strong!
            From the wheat field, from the summer haying,
            working the long day through when men were men.
PAPA: Ja, I was thinner then.

PRINCESS: And how you must have ridden up that hill—
    as you were saying. . . .
PAPA (*modestly*): Oh, not *so* high. . . .
PRINCESS: As high as this?
PAPA (*contemptuously*): Oh, *this!*
    It's like a pimple to that other hill.
PRINCESS: How scared you must have been—on glass so near
    the sky!
PAPA: Not of the hill so much. But your mama, ach!
    She had an eye
    that made a fellow wish he could skitter home.
    (*Thoughtfully*)
    Princess, *you* should look that way.
PRINCESS (*joining him at the window*): But why?
PAPA: Ah, you should not seem to want them. Comb
    your long soft hair and look away. . . .
PRINCESS: But, Papa, tell me why!
PAPA (*morally*): A man should think he is a worm to want you:
    he is a fool even to try.
PRINCESS: But if they *shouldn't* want me, Papa, why am I here?
PAPA (*evasively*): Like bees they'll swarm: they'll haunt you—
    but they should climb up in fear
    like for your mama dear I climbed—
    (*with increasing dramatization*)
    the hooves of the horse clattering on the mountain,
    foam on his neck, his head plunged down,
    his eyes like bursting pods,
    glass splintering under his feet and showering
    like a wicked fountain,
    dead suitors in the crofts like fallen gods—
    and the last long blinding slope like a bulge of ice,
    when the horse fell and I was flung
    from him grappling for some hold on the slick
    and hung,
    watching my horse slip, twice
    kicking to stand again, sliding, then,
    helplessly, heavily, over the ridge
    and out of sight.

Ah, I clung panting, my fingers desperately
digging in fright,
my belly pressed to that cold high knob,
and I started to climb like a slug.

Then, Princess, I saw her, your mama,

(*Taking pose of cool disdain, with one haunch on the
window sill.*)

like this, at the window . . .
and I shivered and gave that chill hill
a loving hug.

PRINCESS (*wonderingly*): What makes a man keep going?

PAPA (*tragically*): Too soon, Princess, you will be knowing. . . .

PRINCESS (*guessing*): Afraid to go back?

PAPA: You never go back,
though you would: you would like to go home—
but like vines on the wall you grow
upward and upward only,
or die.

PRINCESS (*almost crying*): You said it was beautiful, grand and
ennobling. . . .

PAPA: Not I.

PRINCESS: Then why should I stay, Papa? No!
I will climb down with you. . . .

PAPA (*hurt*): Ach, Princess—so pretty, this room, with its pink,
so soft are the curtains. Just think
of your bed like a cloud, and your mirror, perfume,
and then think of the slide and the tumble . . .

(*Puts leg out window, carrying tool kit.*)

you won't want to leave your room.

PRINCESS (*frightened*): Oh, Papa, stay *with* me! I'll be scared
and lonely. . . .

PAPA (*tenderly*): Maybe. But someone will come. There always
is one.
There surely is one for you. . . .

PRINCESS (*more frightened*): But what will he be?
Papa, what will he do?
I don't want him, Papa, but you, but *you*. . . .

PAPA (*regretfully, but firmly, as he climbs out*):
>   *That* you can't do. . . .

(*Once out of the window he becomes very frightened, holding the window ledge and letting himself slowly onto the glass side of the hill. Suddenly, with a short, terrible scream, he lets himself go, the tool kit flying and spilling, the tools clattering, as he slides in an awkward tumble to the bottom. Princess watches this in horror, leaning out of the window. At the bottom, Papa groans for a few moments and then painfully hobbles away.*)

PAPA (*waving back*): That son-of-a-gun, she's high!
PRINCESS (*waving*): Goodbye, Papa. . . .
PAPA (*tenderly*): Princess, goodbye.

(*Princess watches him hobble away and then turns despairingly from the window, walking around picking up objects and putting them down, bored and restless. She sings:*)

PRINCESS: They didn't tell me
>   what a girl should do . . .
>   all done up in crinoline, all coiffured,
>   just sit and hope that something will be lured,
>   just hope the fairy stories
>   are true.

>   (*Picking up hairbrush as weapon.*)

>   Oh no one told me
>   what I should expect.
>   No telling what invisible beasts or boys
>   climb hills like this and fetch girls for their toys!
>   Well, I will strike at anything
>   erect.

>   They told me what I mustn't do.
>   They told me what was just too, too.
>   But in between the don'ts—
>   what *is* a girl to do?

>   My papa told me . . .
>   nothing much to do.

>   (*Languorously brushing hair.*)

I don't know what I'm fixing myself up for—
or if these arms were meant for peace or war.
My Papa didn't say what
men do.
My Papa didn't tell me what
to do!

(*Carlo, an adolescent, enters riding a burro, an unconscious parody of the Knight in Shining Armor. Although he is Latin, his clothing is of no specific nationality or time—simple peasant garb. He is barefooted. He is volatile and vulgar in his movements and speech, very agile, very animal. Princess doesn't see him at first—but he sees her brushing her hair by the window and whistles in spontaneous sexual appreciation. He heads the burro for the mountain. Princess hears the whistle and watches him in timorous fascination. At the base of the mountain the burro stops. Carlo excitedly gets off and pushes, to no avail. He gets in front, a step or two up the slippery side, and pulls, but the burro will not budge. Carlo drops the lead rope and takes a run at the hill, but falls and slides back down on his stomach. He jumps to his feet, undaunted.*)

CARLO (*calling*): Hey, lady, up there! How do you get up?
PRINCESS (*afraid*): Oh, I don't think you *can!*
CARLO (*outraged*): *What* is this? You can't get down or up?
PRINCESS (*vaguely*): I . . . I'm waiting for a man.
CARLO (*frankly*): Boy! I sure would like to get up there!
          (*new thought*)
          For *any*one? Or for *some*one?
PRINCESS (*timidly*): Oh, you can *try* to climb it. I don't care.
CARLO: Man, it don't make *sense!*

          (*Scrambling unsuccessfully at the hill.*)

I sure like to get a little closer—
so we can really talk.
Makes a man feel silly just to stand down here
and gawk.
PRINCESS: A man? How old are you?

CARLO: Old enough, you bet. I got my own
    chickens. I'm raising
    my own bull calf. I can lift him, just like that.

    (*Demonstrates by putting arms under the tail and
    neck of the burro.*)

    Of course, when he's a bull . . . but it's amazing
    how strong a guy can get, if he stays *at* it.
    (*confidingly*)
    You think if I lift him every day while he grows
    I still can do it when he's a bull?

PRINCESS: Goodness knows!

CARLO: I don't think so. . . . I'm Carlo. I live right by
    the stream—
    my father's place now, but, man, when he dies . . .
    I have this dream . . .
    of making millions on chickens! Man!
    I want to be *so* rich . . .
    or maybe drive a racing car. I don't know which.

(*Papa enters with a walking stick. He stands by to observe.*)

PRINCESS (*intending to close conversation*): Well, Carlo, I
    am glad you came,
    although you couldn't climb my mountain. . . .

CARLO (*backing off for another run*): Shoot, man! I
    didn't even try!

PAPA (*gesturing behind Carlo's back*): Not this one, no
    not this one, honey!

(*Carlo makes a long run up the hill, coming to an undulation
where he can just barely keep his footing, barely out of arm-
reach of the window sill. He hangs there, panting.*)

PRINCESS (*terrified*): What does he *want?* Oh, Papa!
    What makes his eyes burn with a sullen fire?

CARLO: Give me a hand up, lady?
    I just can't run any higher.

PAPA (*loud whisper*): The look, Princess. The look!
    Gaze coolly at the sky . . .

CARLO: Hey, lady, can you hear?

PAPA: . . . and brush your hair!

(*Princess nervously brushes, trying to look away from Carlo, but watching him with fearful glances.*)

CARLO: Hey, lady, can't you help a guy?
You don't know what you're missing . . .
how we could smooch on that plush bed!
Do you go for cuddling? kissing?

(*No answer.*)

I think this frilly room went to your head!
I say, wind up the world and let it run!

(*Jumps a little, catches sill with one hand.*)

Don't that sound hot?

(*Pulling himself up, as Princess in fear lifts her brush.*)

Well, I'm for all that stuff, even if you're not!
If sheets are silk or muslin, it's all the same—

(*His face now in the window*)

and I like what you do there, never mind the name!

(*Princess puts her hand on his face and pushes him back. He slips down the hill, Princess unconsciously wiping her hand on her gown in repugnance. Gretchen runs in, a pretty girl in peasant dress, voluptuous, exceedingly warm and direct, and rather coarse. She screams to see Carlo fall.*)

GRETCHEN: What's happening here? How did this poor fellow fall?

PAPA (*calm acceptance*): The Princess pushed him. It's what I'd call
a risk of the game. In my day all
us fellows fell from time to time.
Ja, bruises were the mark of a man in his prime.

GRETCHEN (*indignantly*): What kind of girl is this—who shoves her lover
down a hill?

(*Going to Carlo and kneeling beside him as he rubs his thighs.*)

        Ah, it is Carlo. . . .

CARLO: I don't know you.

GRETCHEN: Gretchen. I live in the forest cottage—by the well.

CARLO: Sure! I see you always in the clearing there,
        always a hoe in your hand, pine shadows blue
        at the field's edge, and you, your feet bare
        in the soil, at work in the sun, the sun
        on your back—and a scarf, for the sun, on your hair.

GRETCHEN (*rubbing his thigh*): Some dame up there, eh?

CARLO (*contemptuously*): Ha! Her! A lousy cheat!
        She talks nice from the mountain—but just get close
        (*Laughing.*)
        and blam! She knocks a fellow off his feet!

PAPA (*instructively to Princess, who is leaning out of the window fascinated*):
        You see—this affection—these people? Very gross.

(*Mama enters as Carlo is getting to his feet with Gretchen's aid. She is a thin, weary woman of Papa's age, her face having once been beautiful, but now, browned and lined, merely withered and weathered. Carlo and Gretchen go out, arm in arm, leaning together. Mama, her hands folded, watches with the cocked head of pleasant memory.*)

MAMA (*warmly, to no one*): Ach, isn't it darling, darling—
        how they go, and leaning
        one upon another so.
        Such a day have I seen—such weaving walking
        along the woods, and hardly talking . . .
        but no sense grieving.
        (*Collecting herself.*)
        How is it, Princess? Do you like your little house?

PRINCESS (*amazed*): Mama, did you see that boy and girl?
        How softly they met and blended . . . ?

PAPA (*quickly*): Ach, that is not for you. . . .

MAMA: I saw them, ja. It was a picture, very nice.

PAPA: But not for Princess, Mama!

PRINCESS (*obliviously*): . . . and for a moment I pretended . . .

MAMA: No, darling. Not for you.

PRINCESS: Where is her hill? Did she fall off her hill?

MAMA: Who can afford hills? Most never have . . .

PAPA (*quickly*): Hush, Mama, now! Such talk is not for Princess.

MAMA: Papa, you cannot hide what she can plainly see!

PAPA: Just think of her position—the role she has to play!
Our princess can't be bothered night and day
with what goes on down here. It should not be!

MAMA (*reluctantly*): Ja, I guess you know the proper way.

PAPA (*to Princess*): If only you knew how your Mama has
worked . .

MAMA (*to Princess*): Your Papa, how he worked . . .

PAPA: Late in the evening, sewing by the lamp . . .

MAMA: Day by day out in the field,
hot sun—or cold and damp . . .

PAPA: Peeling potatoes for twenty years . . .

MAMA: Poor man, to live on soup and bread . . .

PAPA: How wearily she sagged into her bed . . .

MAMA: How often life brought my strong man to tears!

PAPA: All that is past: it was for you, for this.

(*Waves at boudoir.*)

Princess, if you are happy, we are paid.
We want fine things for you and high regard:
no ugliness of life, no working hard;
but each day airy, bright, arrayed
in gossamer—no salt of sweat and blood,
no wrinkles from a frown. . . .

MAMA (*without irony*): Ja. Until some Prince comes and brings
you down.

PRINCESS (*moved*): Thank you, Mama, Papa.

PAPA (*starting off*): Coming, Mama?

MAMA (*calling as he leaves*): A moment, only.
(*to Princess*)
Darling, are you eating well?
Each day a piece of fruit?

PRINCESS: Yes, Mama.

MAMA: Each bedtime you will say a little prayer?

PRINCESS: Yes, Mama.

MAMA: And not so much of reading—for your eyes.

PRINCESS: Yes, Mama.

MAMA: Nor too much sunshine—so your skin stays fair.

PRINCESS (*beginning to weep*): Yes, Mama.

MAMA: Ach, then. Is it my darling baby cries?

PRINCESS (*wiping tears*): No, Mama. I will be happy. I promise
      you.

MAMA (*satisfied*): Sure, sure you will. What else is there to do?

(*Curtain.*)

SCENE 2

(*A year or so later. Princess has aged a little, looks harder, more
certain of herself: she has become dynamically rather than pas-
sively beautiful. She is standing before the mirror, swirling her
skirt—any modern, attractive dress. She takes a pose then, hands
on hips, legs a little spread, looking very jaunty, and sings:*)

PRINCESS: I'm getting better and better
      at doing less and less,
      at saying no to more and more each day.
     So whether I'm in a sweater
     or in a skimpy dress,
     I leave them having less and less to say.

     My eyelids flutter and flutter,
     my lips invite a kiss,
     my long arm holds them off with such a skill,
     the boys all turn into butter
     beneath a sun like this
     and sadly drain themselves away downhill.

     I've learned to live without them,
     and what they have to give.
     Now all I have to learn, it seems,
     is simply not to live.

(*Bitterly*)
I'm growing older and older—
and wish I would get wise:
I'm having to say no, now, less and less.
My heart is starting to smolder—
smoke drives away the guys.
I hope I have a chance, still, to say yes.
I wish these coals
would catch on fire—
and I would finally say yes!

(*Don John enters, dressed as an eighteenth-century dandy—a middle-aged man with a seasoned, lecherous face. He looks up at the window; the Princess promptly takes on a delicate, disdainful air of perusing her beauty in the mirror, her hand touching at her hair. Don John silently surveys the mountain, sighting, pacing, estimating. He takes out a paper and pen and writes down measurements, all with a businesslike air—glancing only now and then at the Princess, who, in turn, steals an occasional glance at him. Abruptly he leaves. Papa and Mama enter, she leaning on his arm, he on his walking stick.*)

PAPA (*calling up*): This week, how does it go, Princess?
PRINCESS: Just three this week, Papa. On Sunday a scholar
          who said he hadn't much time. His horse was grey
          like dirty snow, his suit was out of fashion,
          there was a fringe of age around his collar.
          Poor man, he was shy, and hadn't much to say,
          but ran at the hill, awkwardly riding,
          sitting his horse like a grasshopper, sliding
          back off the saddle, though the horse came on.
          I reached right out and touched the horse's nose—
          but the man was sprawled, tight in his suit, face wan
          with fright, at the bottom. That night, late, a noise
          at the window woke me: a drunk was fumbling
          the shutter. He had clambered up without the aid
          of any other beast except himself. I said
          he shouldn't come at night and huddled in my bed,
          afraid; but he stayed there, mumbling

the day would come when women needed men.
Finally he fell: I heard him grunting, tumbling.
Monday I was a wreck—he had upset me so.
That afternoon a pansy wandered by, you know,
(*imitating him*)
just for a chat, he said, as just then
he was rather bushed, you know, but still,
he said, looking up lewdly, I will, one day, try that
    hill.
He much admired the fabric of the curtains, the de-
    sign
of the window frame, the roof's low line—
and left the way he came. No one since Monday.

MAMA: And have you been crocheting?

PRINCESS: Oh, Mama, I get bored with that. . . .

PAPA: Then solitaire you're playing?

PRINCESS: I can't stand cards.

PAPA (*disappointed*): You used to play.

PRINCESS: When one gets older, one regards
    it as absurd to sit and worry
    over problems self-inflicted,
    to stick to silly rules, to bury
    discards in the deck and start again.

MAMA: You telling Papa how it is, this getting older?

PAPA (*to Mama*): She means not *that* much older. When
    you come around to playing games again,
    I guess, you have outgrown maturity.
    I confess that solitaire means much to me.

(*Don John backs onto the stage, directing someone behind him.
A long board appears, and Carlo, carrying it on his shoulder.
Mama, Papa, and Princess look on in amazement.*)

DON JOHN (*to Carlo*): Just set it here.
        (*studying base of mountain thoughtfully*)
    Let's see . . .

(*Carlo leaves. Matter-of-factly, to Princess*)

    Have you out of there in a jiffy.

PRINCESS: But who are you? Why is he bringing all that lumber?

(*Carlo enters with a ladder and boards to make a triangular base for it. He begins erecting the ladder, fastening pieces on the side so it will stand up straight alone.*)

DON JOHN: Don John's the name. I won't encumber
    you now with architectural details,
    but, briefly, these are the joists, the beams,
    my man, here, will erect. The work entails
    some hammering and noise—so if it seems
    too ghastly, say the word; I'll have him build
    it in the woods and bring it in intact.

PAPA (*protesting*): But what are you building? This is not
    a place to build a house! In fact,
    this land is all restricted for the wooing
    of my daughter. . . .

DON JOHN: Ah! You're the father!
    (*considering tactics*)
    Hmm.
    (*suddenly*)
    Have you seen the fair?

PAPA: The what?

DON JOHN: The fair—down in the village. Some freaks are there,
    and animals from jungles round the world.
    They have a gadget so you can be twirled
    like a painted top, a ferris wheel, a carousel,
    the largest pumpkins and prize-winning stock
    from all the farms of the county. Also, beer.

PAPA (*to Mama*): We *haven't* seen those cows and pigs. . . .

DON JOHN: I have a pair of tickets here. . . .

MAMA (*to Papa*): But what is this he's building?

DON JOHN: A temporary scaffolding: it will not mar
    the mountain or the view.
    Quickly it goes up—and quickly down.

PAPA (*taking tickets*): Come, Mama. . . . Let's us go down to
    the town.

MAMA: (*acquiescing*): Ach! I should think it's a better show
    right here.
    But you go, I go, too.

(*They leave.*)

PRINCESS: But you must tell me what all this is for.

DON JOHN: To get you out, of course. You won't be scared
to walk a narrow plank?

PRINCESS: You act as though I cared
for getting out. . . .

DON JOHN: Of course you do.
Why should a healthy girl want to be stuck
up on a mountain in a chiffon-lined room?

PRINCESS: I . . . I . . . like the view.

DON JOHN: Bah! View! You're desiccating in a pink tomb!

(*Carlo has erected the ladder now, a few feet from the base of
the mountain, sticking straight up. During the following dialogue
he has to put a board across from the window sill to the ladder,
to make a platform so that one can walk across. He rests one
end of the board on the side of the hill, then takes a run up to
a position where he can stick, while he pulls the end of the board
up higher, and begins climbing toward the window sill.*)

PRINCESS: You have to scale the mountain properly. . . .

DON JOHN: What in the world *for?* If I were up, we
would still have to get the both of us down.
Besides, exercise bores me. Do you really *like*
to see a man come clambering like a clown?

PRINCESS: Some men ride with grace,
do feats of daring, climb with style. . . .

DON JOHN: In that case,
you must enjoy the show. But I'll
save grace and style for feats that two
can do.

PRINCESS: I am waiting for a man of honor—
heroic in his bearing and his mind. . . .

DON JOHN: Oh, some *do* make a ritual of love.
But those who get it done are of a different kind.

(*Carlo, at this point, has pulled himself up to the window sill,
making Princess jump back in surprise. He pulls the board up
and places it so that it makes a bridge between the top of the*

ladder and the window. Casually, he gets up on it and walks across, coming down the ladder.)

PRINCESS: Plain naked competence is almost alarming!
DON JOHN (*sings*):
> I am the one
> who gets it done.
> I've loved ladies who were crippled with arthritis,
> and those who were protected by their aunts,
> and those who think men beasts and try to fight us,
> and even those addicted to the Dance.

> I have loved them though they had their hair in curl-
> ers,
> or at parties talked of novels of the day,
> the gossips and the knitters and the pearlers,
> gum-chewing girls and girls who played croquet.

> In some matters I'm fastidious
> but in girls my taste is hideous,
> though I am particular about my food and wine.
> But no obstacle detains me
> when a woman's love enchains me:
> I think they are the best thing offered in that line.

> So no matter if their husbands never travel,
> or their brothers are professionals in crime,
> or their fathers lay the law down with a gavel,
> I have got to them all in very little time.
> I am the one
> who gets it done
> every way and every time.

(*During this song Carlo has descended the ladder, the Princess has looked on it with increasing dread. Just as Don John finishes, Gretchen enters with a lunch basket for Carlo, and the two of them sit to eat, more or less ignoring the others.*)

PRINCESS: Take that thing down.
DON JOHN: Don't be absurd. Now hoist your gown
> and walk across, like Carlo did.

PRINCESS: I want a hero or nothing.

CARLO (*his mouth full*): Some kid, this kid.

DON JOHN: A knight in shining armor, I suppose,
    an athlete with an income, whose
    golden shield is crusted with his pedigree.
    I see.

PRINCESS: Your mockery
    is the snarl of a dog whose teeth are bad—
    you hope to fight with noise.
    No. Some tall lad
    with muscle in his thigh,
    in whom a true love blooms, whose heart enjoys
    the ceremony and ordeal, the kiss, the sigh,
    glad agonies of love and grand endeavor,
    whose love will last past tempests of the glands,
    whose love no mood nor distance nor even death
    can sever. . . .

DON JOHN: The sort of love a statue understands . . .

PRINCESS (*angrily*): The words of love turn sour on your
                 breath!

DON JOHN: I suppose I ought to inscribe them on a scroll
    and have a page
    come running ahead
    to let you know I want you in my bed,
    but at my age
    I have outgrown that folderol.
    (*after a pause*)
    You won't step out on the plank?
    (*after a pause*)
    Then I'll come over. If I break my neck,
    young lady, I'll have you to thank.

    (*Wearily and awkwardly he begins climbing the
    ladder.*)

PRINCESS: I warn you! Stop!

(*When he reaches the top she pulls her end of the plank, so
that it comes free of the ladder and falls—leaving Don John
foolishly standing on a ladder in midair.*)

DON JOHN: Now why the deuce did you do *that?*

(*Looks down and sees Gretchen for the first time.*)

Carlo . . . ah . . . we seem to have dislodged
a crucial slat.

(*Climbs down and Carlo, in disgust, leaves his lunch to replace
the board. Don John approaches Gretchen, who is sitting
demurely by the picnic basket.*)

GRETCHEN: Such a fancy suit to wear wooing.
DON JOHN (*proudly*): Rather splendid, is it not?
GRETCHEN: I'd think it would get in the way
     of . . . what you're doing.
DON JOHN: Oh, rot!
     It *does* come off, you know.

(*He sits beside her.*)

GRETCHEN (*looking him over*): I don't see how.
DON JOHN (*modestly*): Well, buttons and the usual thing.
     (*catching on*)
     I could show
     you exactly in a jiffy.
GRETCHEN (*innocently*): I'd really like to know.
DON JOHN: Oh, *would* you now?
GRETCHEN (*losing nerve*): I didn't mean just *now.*
     (*to change subject*)
     Are you very rich?
DON JOHN: Yes, very.
GRETCHEN (*affectedly*): It must be such a bore.
DON JOHN: Oh, no, I find I'm always wanting more.
GRETCHEN (*touching his waistcoat*): I *thought* you must be
     rich—
     the way this waistcoat's covered with tiny pearls
     and decorated with a golden stitch. . . .
DON JOHN (*disinterestedly*): That's all hand-done, you see.
GRETCHEN (*pouting*): I think such clothes look better worn by
     girls.

DON JOHN: Oh, would you like to have it, dear?
Let's . . . ah . . . take
a little walk off in the brake. . . .

(*He stands and offers to help Gretchen to her feet.*)

GRETCHEN (*protesting mildly*): Won't this look sort of queer?

DON JOHN (*pulling her up*): I'll show you how it's done.

(*as they go off*)

You know, I don't give waistcoats just to anyone. . . .

(*As they leave, arm in arm, Carlo, who has laboriously climbed the mountain again, pulling the plank up after him, is at the window-level now. He sees them and angrily throws the plank back down the mountain. Princess has been watching the whole scene from the window. She jumps a little at the noise of the falling board.*)

CARLO: Shoot, man! Look at that!

PRINCESS (*instinctively puts a hand on his shoulder to console him*):
Poor fellow! She wasn't very kind to you. . . .

CARLO (*looks at her disgustedly*): Man, she was *kind*.
But I just as soon she wouldn't be kind to Don John,
too.

PRINCESS (*withdrawing hand in embarrassment*):
I guess she means to wind
the world up tight and let it go. . . .

CARLO (*climbing down the mountain*): Man, you think I don't
know!

(*As he carries off the plank, Princess falls miserably on her bed.*)

(*Curtain.*)

SCENE 3

(*A day or so later, the ladder has been removed. By light of dawn we see Princess tearfully packing up a little bundle to leave. She has on a traveling cloak with a hood tied under her chin. She brings her bundle to the window and sets it on the sill, then starts to climb out. As soon as she puts a foot on the glass she realizes that high heels are not appropriate—so she flings them down ahead of her and, barefooted, stands on the glass, holding the sill, then looks down. She is frightened. She makes a few tentative reaches with her foot for another place to step below—but hasn't the nerve to let go the sill. Finally, crying more now, she climbs back in, hurls the bundle in a corner, and falls on the bed. There is an offstage clatter of horse's hooves—at which she looks up and comes hopefully to the window. As the sun is stronger, Prince enters on a snorting white charger. His golden armor and that of his horse glint in the dawn light. He is handsome, young, and has an innocent look and manner, as Don John suggested, "an athlete with an income." He ties his horse to a tree, appearing to be lost, and wanders across the stage, more or less stumbling on the base of the mountain, and looks up. Princess immediately remembers herself: she throws back her hood and looks coolly, disdainfully off into the sunlight, making a properly radiant spectacle of beauty.*)

PRINCE (*in croaking tones*): Fair lady, art thou the fabled
           princess of the hill,
      disdainful, cruel maid to whom the way is strewn
      with bodies of the knights who died for her love?

(*Pause. The Princess does not turn her head. The Prince is sweating a little. He wipes his forehead with his hand. Resuming manfully:*)

      Methinks that thou art she of the golden tresses,
      languishing still
      upon her crystal hill all hewn
      by the hooves of steeds, enshrined above
      the heroes of the kingdom, deaf to their addresses!

(*Pause. Still no response. The Prince is getting very nervous, pulling now at his mail collar and wiping his head again. He drops to one knee—and, in doing so, discovers one of her shoes. Delighted:*)

      But what is this?

PRINCESS (*glancing down, startled*): My shoe!

PRINCE: A favor dropped from thy gentle hand!

> (*Picks up shoe, holds it worshipfully.*)

> Ah, Princess, this sign doth renew
> my sinking hopes—an eloquent command
> to me, your slave, to sally forth and do
> high deeds of nobleness to earn the other shoe.

> (*Rises, kissing shoe.*)

> My heart cheered so, I will away—
> and not return for one year and one day. . . .

PRINCESS (*gasping, before she thinks*): Oh no!

PRINCE: What's that, my beauteous princess?

PRINCESS (*embarrassed*): I . . . I mean, the other one's down
there someplace.

PRINCE (*jarred*): Huh?

(*He looks around, finds it, and stands holding one in each
hand, very puzzled.*)

PRINCESS: You see, I . . . I kicked them off, when I . . .

> (*Stops in confusion.*)

PRINCE: Then these are not a token . . . ?

PRINCESS (*simply*): Oh, no. Just shoes.

PRINCE (*crestfallen*): Ah, must I leave without a pledge—
the words of bondage left unspoken?

PRINCESS: Well, usually they try to climb the hill. . . .

PRINCE (*newly inspired*): But yes! I'll mount my steed
> I've tied to yonder tree
> and fly to thee
> with wingéd speed. . . .

PRINCESS (*shielding eyes from sun to look at horse*):
Oh, has he wings?

PRINCE: Only the airy wings of my heroic, loving heart.

PRINCESS: In that case, I think you'll find it easier on foot.

PRINCE (*dubiously*): Is that within the tournament rules?

PRINCESS: My papa, when he
> put me here
> was not so clear

as to the tools
or means or what decoy
men of renown
might fittingly employ
to get me down.
I will not smirk
at anything that will work.

PRINCE (*reluctantly*): Thou art certain it is not demeaning
to come up on my hands and knees?

PRINCESS: I know only that those who insist upon careening
upon that glass on horseback reap
nothing but broken heads from their sprees.

PRINCE (*noticing shoes in his hands*): What should I do with
these?

PRINCESS: Well, could you toss them up?

PRINCE: My duty is to do what thou mightst please.

(*He tosses shoes and she catches them. Putting them on she
regains some of her dignity.*)

PRINCESS (*grandly*): Now you may climb the hill and kiss my
hand.

PRINCE: Your pleasure is my will.

(*He tries ponderously to climb, but, as his feet are encased in
sollerets, he slips ridiculously.*)

PRINCESS (*concerned*): I think you'll have to take a run.
The whole course must be planned:
if you can make it to this indentation just below
the window, that's step one.
From there the climbing's rather slow.
(*Hesitantly*)
Could you take off those metal pants
and shoes?

PRINCE (*shocked*): Ma'am?

PRINCESS (*businesslike*): You see, the way this mountain slants,
you'll slip. You know, you might use
a rope. Did you happen to bring a rope?

PRINCE: Fair lady, I should hope
    a knight might scale that steep in full attire. . . .

PRINCESS: Well, usually they flop
    miserably: it is higher
    and more slippery than it looks.
    One boy can make it to the top
    with ease—but he works
    barefoot. . . .

PRINCE: That's not by the books!

(*Gretchen enters, wearing Don John's waistcoat over her peasant dress. Prince backs off for a run, then clatters toward the hill, getting up a few feet and beginning to slip. Gretchen comes up behind him and tries to help him by shoving. Prince looks around and nods thanks, his feet running ineffectually on the glass—but still can make no progress. Finally Gretchen lets him slide back down.*)

PRINCE (*panting, to Gretchen*): My thanks, fair maid of the
    dell. . . .

GRETCHEN: No, I live in the forest, by the well.
    You get there by the path along the creek. . . .

PRINCESS (*desperately*): Wait! I'll tie bedsheets!

PRINCE (*obliviously, to Gretchen*): Methinks I need a cup of
    milk,
    cooled in an earthen crock,
    to renew my vigor for this grand ordeal.

(*Princess ties one sheet to another and lets an end dangle down.*)

GRETCHEN: Come, then, to my place,
    only a moment's walk,
    for milk—and then see how you feel.

(*They leave. Princess sadly hauls in her rope of bedding.*)

PRINCESS (*sings*): Don't worship me
    and leave me lonely.
    Please don't confine
    me in a shrine.

Don't love me from
a distance only.
My heart is weary
of being only mine.

Don't honor me
with adulation.
The hot stars die
in their cold sky.
Oh, love demands
a close relation—
the blossom bends to
the settling butterfly.

Glass mountain, glass mountain,
you've served your purpose well.
You've made me sublime and
my life an empty Hell.

I want from you
more than adoring.
My lips are more
than metaphor.
Not only words
have they been storing.
Let tall waves crumble
upon this lonely shore—
and I will worship *you*
for evermore.

MAMA (*entering*): Well, Princess, has he come yet, any Prince
    Charming?
PRINCESS: Yes, Mama—come and gone.
MAMA (*shocked*): What is this? He could not climb the hill?
PRINCESS: I'm afraid, Mama, such a paragon,
    even, as was this shining prince, is still
    not man enough—that men aren't men
    the way they were back when
    Papa rode, strong in his stirrups, to
    your lofty room and captured you.

MAMA: Such a story! What makes you think
       I could afford such richness when I was a girl,
       a gorgeous room upon a brink
       of glass!
       Alas,
       my father was no Earl—
       nor is your Papa, though
       by hard work he has made it so
       that *you* can be
       aristocracy.

PRINCESS: You mean he scaled no mountain to take you away?

MAMA: Ach, no—unless it was a summer's mound of hay.
       When I was milking in the evening he would come
          round
       and hang about the barn—a pudgy, clumsy boy
       from the place down the road. He pulled my braids
       and made me angry. I picked up my stool, nearly
          crowned
       him for his teasing. I made him finish the milking!
       That's what *he* got for toying with the maids.
       But he was sweet about it, carried the bucket
       side by side with me to the door. Then ran for fear
       my Papa would thrash him. Oh, my dear . . .
       how we had stolen meetings in the fields, the lofts,
       for nearly a year. My Papa scoffed
       at the notion I had of getting married—until
       your oldest brother began to show.
       Ach, no . . .
       no hill!

PRINCESS (*starting to cry*): Oh, Mama! The lie he told me!

MAMA (*calmly*): Now, did he?
       I'm sure he meant it for the best,
       thinking, maybe, you would be depressed
       up here alone if you thought
       your Mama wasn't caught
       like the best of girls.
       (*after pause*)
       Maybe your prince will come again?

PRINCESS (*with new tears*) : Oh, Mama, he's a pompous fool!
MAMA (*philosophically*) : Ja, that's the way with men.
PRINCESS: How much of that should women allow?
MAMA: Who has a choice? Well, I must go
    tell Papa that
      at least a prince has come and doffed his hat.

(*She leaves. Princess walks back and forth in growing frustration. Finally she ties one end of the rope of bedsheets securely to the windowframe, tosses her shoes down again and heaves herself out of the window, walking down the glass barefooted, holding to the sheets. At the bottom she picks up her shoes and starts to put them on—but thinks better of it. She pitches them back through the window of her room and runs off barefooted, calling:*)

PRINCESS: Carlo! Carlo! Carlo! Where are you now?

(*Curtain.*)

X

Alcoholic: Postscript

Sometimes when I hold my cigaret in a particular way, not out at the tips of my fingers but back close to the knuckle, letting most of it project, just a bit available to my lips, so that as I draw I can clasp my whole chin with my open palm, caress my jaw as I pull the cigaret away from my mouth, it is my father's face I feel under my hand. His cigarets (in his last years,

Wings) always seemed to have gotten battered in the pack, so
that the white tendril hung wilted and exposed; and he smoked
it like making love, with an amorous suction combined with a
sensual, lingering tug of the cheek flesh. I now suspect that the
habit came from the drunk's need to test his skin sensations, as
one touches himself, particularly around the lips, for that
tingling, swollen feeling that tells him how far gone he is; but
Dad claimed he used cigarets to give himself time to think.
While he took a good long draw of smoke and leisurely exhaled
it, he could, he said, generally think up an answer. It was a time
out—such as others take by polishing their glasses.

The thirties were his time of life. He was twenty-five (and I
was three) when they began, and his life was substantially over
when they ended, though, of course, it is the seven years he
lived into the forties that I most clearly remember. Searching
for an early image of him I see the two of us parked all night
in a grassy field a couple of hundred yards from an oil derrick,
lights strung up it as on the tower of a ferris wheel. We watched
the tall pipes swing as, endlessly, the crew was pulling stem to
change a bit, then lowering it again, length after length, and
finally we would hear the tension-building growl of drilling,
water churning into the slush pit, brine and oil in the acrid air.
On chilly nights Dad would periodically idle the motor, letting
the car heater rasp out its hot breath, and I would doze with the
gleam in my eyes of the resplendent rig and, in the car, like a
hearth, the soft light of the radio dial, the bubbling melancholy
of Bing Crosby: "Come to Me, My Melancholy Baby," "Stormy
Weather," "Tea for Two," "The Lady in Red," "Smoke Gets
in Your Eyes," "Sonny Boy," "Peg-o-My-Heart," "Mighty Lak
a Rose." We were waiting for the moment the teeth would cut
the critical cap of limestone and the well would come in. Usually
Dad had no more financial interest in the well than a few acres
of royalty on a neighboring lease. He just liked gushers, those
wild earthy orgasms, and had infinite patience as he waited in
hope of seeing another. I believe I liked to be with him, though
all such memory is tinged with sweet terror.

I catch glimpses of him still in old movies—in the gestures,
tones, expressions of Jack Oakie and Leslie Howard, of Clark

Gable and Jimmy Stewart. (I see his business associates, as in bad dreams, like James Cagney, E. G. Robinson, Wallace Beery.) Fred Astaire seems to me most fully to evoke my young father, though there was little physical resemblance, and Dad had nothing of Astaire's sophistication. Perhaps I associate them only because I remember that *Top Hat* was one of the few films he could sit through. (He had a few favorites he would see over and over; unless the film were one of these, he would stalk up the dark aisle after fifteen minutes and wait for us to see it through; we would find him smoking and pacing in the lobby.) "Dancing Cheek to Cheek" was one of those songs that kept recurring to his lips. He was sentimental in Astaire's gay dry way—and, like Astaire, swiftly brittle. He was a thin man with no hips, long-jawed, nervous, with cynical, watering, hurt eyes, full of heavy, exaggerated winks (you betcha!). Crooning, always crooning—as he shaved, as he drove, as he bent over maps on his high drafting table, or as, foot on the marble sill, elbow on his long knee, he gazed thoughtfully out of his office window down at the traffic of Oklahoma City, drew deeply on his cigaret, then, with a sharp flip, sent the butt sailing into the summer air, watched it fall to the alley, hawked, cutting off his song, spit, watched that arc down the shaft of grey air, then went back to work, cocking an eye, winking his slow, mocking wink at me when I asked a question. He had style. Fred Astaire with maybe a little of Bob Burns and his bazooka.

But—as I find myself crooning more often these days—that was long ago, and hazy as Stardust. Back before television. Back before plastic. I think of my father learning to laugh with Will Rogers and Marie Dressler, of my own values forming to the harder, emptier voices of Fred Allen, Charlie McCarthy (those long, rich Sunday evenings with the radio), and of the young man who now learns the wincing laughter required by insights of Bob Newhart. I think of Mark Twain as a giant in the earth. The past always seems so much more humane, so much more Deep Purple.

And "Tiger Rag." They had invented drive-ins, miniature golf; and by the building shaped like a giant rootbeer mug we sat at the long picnic tables eating watermelon and spitting seeds, then back into the car in time for Burns and Allen, driving high on a bridge over the dried red mudflats of the Canadian River, which had been reduced to a trickle by the drouth, and the no-man's-land of the riverbed was now all a sprawling Hooverville. And soon past the lights and under the stars, the bugs spatting on the windshield, nerves rubbing like straining hawsers as we swung out and in like a tail behind the tall, red-lit, swaying rump of a truck, then whined around it, the road now stretching empty and black ahead off toward Tulsa, Dad's cigaret coal sparking on the easy breeze, his sandy tenor rising to compete with the radio's version of "Dinah."

I piece it together as former lovers search backwards for the good times, the bad times, the old feelings, trying to remember what it was they had and where it all went wrong, just when the quality of life turned from bittersweet to sour. The good times are hardest to remember. He loved still rivers at dawn, the mist lifting and the bass hitting in the deep holes under the trees, and as we drifted up in our old green canoe he would whip the long rod back and forth, the line lengthening in somnolent arcs in the sweet fishy air until he dropped the fly in under the branches, just over a projecting stump, made it skate right and left with little jerks of his wrist (fifty feet away!), then whip it up to sail in long arcs again, whispering out, the ratchet of the reel drilling like a little cricket in the great humid silence of the Oklahoma woods.

ON MOUNTAIN FORK

discipline: the whispering S of line
above the canoe, the weightless fly thrown through
a gap in the branches, spitting to rest
on the still pool where the bass lay,
                                    wrist true
in the toss and flick of the skipping lure.

love: silence and singing reel, the whip
of rod, chill smell of fish in the morning air,
green river easing heavily under, drip
of dew in brown light.
                        At the stern I learned
to steer us—wavering paddle like a fin.

art: tyrannous glances, passionate strategy,
the hush of nature, humanity slipping in,
arc of the line, ineffectual gift
of a hand-tied bug, then snag in the gill, the snap
and steady pull.
　　　　　　　His life was squalid, his

temper mean, his affection like a trap.
I paddled on aching knees and took the hook.
My father shaped the heart beneath my skin
with love's precision:
　　　　　　　　　　the gift of grief, the art
of casting clean, the zeal, the discipline.

Or, driving through a highway cut in the Arbuckle Mountains, he would impulsively stop the car to look at the twisting formations of old rock and would excitedly explain to me how the angled projections of rock in the field indicated a prehistoric arch, would show me the parallel structure in the cliff sliced by the highway, and, a few miles down the road, would find the corresponding rocks projecting back the other direction, creating for me a vision of that ancient mountain washed away. I would be able to see the prehistoric ocean covering Oklahoma, the life swimming in it, now all skeletons in limestone from the crushing weight, packing down, the bulging up of some hot subterranean force, the cooling peaks, the centuries of weathering that left these tilted tombstones obstructing the plow. He was reputed to have been the best surface geologist in Oklahoma City—all his knowledge gleaned from night studies (he never finished high school) and from roving the land with love.

Looking for money. He thrilled with the romance of the old earth contorting and subsiding, but he knew that that subterranean dome, parallel to the surface structure, trapped gasses from life decaying in the buried sea, and that if a deal could be made, the dome could be punctured by a long drill stem and rotating diamond teeth, so from the black belly under the red earth of Oklahoma would erupt the slick, stinking stream of rotten life, fountaining up through the derrick, ripping all before it, scattering the boards of the derrick platforms a hundred feet into the air, sending the roughnecks diving for shelter, clouding the sky with a gold, gassy sheen, and splashing black money, money, money, all over the wasted Oklahoma fields.

He never accumulated any, but we lived comfortably enough in what seem to have been a dozen different houses, first in Tulsa, then in Oklahoma City, renting, moving, the country storing its grapes of wrath but the oil business booming, a pool discovered right inside Oklahoma City and derricks going up in back yards, even on the capitol lawn. In a second-rate office building Dad had a suite of several rooms—a rambling, long place with bare wooden floors and a private toilet in which was a cupboard with a bottle and glasses. He was heady with success.

Alcohol began to change its function from that of providing naughty fun on fishing trips to that of lubricating the oil business. Alone or with another couple or two they used to bundle me, months old, into the car at midnight and strike off for the Kiamichi Mountains. So it still was when, old enough to remember, I would wake to black night in the moving, crooning car and catch the thrilling scent of pine, hear the rustle of water. I could sleep on the shelf under the rear window—or on someone's lap in the rumble seat of the little green Buick coupe as it ground around the twisting gravel roads, canoe tied on the roof with ropes to front and back bumpers. Such memories bring into focus the later ones—of Dad, drink in hand, drawing geological formations on the white enameled kitchen table-top, passing the bottle with a lease owner out in the field, under the thundering rig, or, again, waking to find myself in the Kiamichis, now become a wilderness for recuperation or for finishing off a bender. Mother would be driving—as though in flight—and Dad, with bare feet sticking rudely out the window, sleeping in the seat with his head on her lap. The Kiamichis are on the Arkansas border, and Arkansas was wet. If you've got to have it you might as well avoid bootleg prices.

Recently in our Ohio village two-chair barbershop, where a tiny radio whines all day the songs of yesteryear and the noise of now and the announcers carry on an unconscious dialogue with the white-headed barber, the radio said, as it frequently does, "Remember, alcoholism is a disease. It can be treated." The barber snorted, "Hell it is. It's a damned bad habit!" Those

are roughly the views of science and religion—and I believe my
father foundered in the gulf between them.

According to the barber and to most of us in some moods
(certainly according to Mother when she was dealing with Dad),
a person has will. He is responsible for his choices. If he drinks
excessively—to the injury of himself and others—that is wrong.
Not sick, but wrong. You help him by trying to awaken his conscience, hoping that he will feel guilty, exercise will power, and
be good, or moderate his drinking. He must sense a duty to himself and others—and perhaps his sense of duty will help him
break a bad habit which he has slipped into through moral las-
situde.

All such terms have very little scientific content; they are, in
fact, religious because they assume a soul independent of con-
ditioning. Mother was certainly no church-goer, but her thinking, like the barber's, like even Dad's, rested on some old-fashioned religious assumptions—such as that there is a right and
wrong way of behaving, that a person has the capacity for knowing the right and adhering to it, that life has meaning and purpose and values which it is a sin to destroy.

Mother's moral view sometimes erupted in violence. You fight
with a man you think is bad—and could be better—not one you
think is sick. No one would treat measles with a spanking—and
if we assume that alcoholism is a disease, even a therapeutic slug
on the jaw must be administered without value judgment, like
an aspirin. That was not her spirit as she cracked the crockery.
I would be awakened at night by doors slamming, dishes breaking, and, in the hall, find them slapping and wrestling, weeping
and shouting. Finally, having borne it for several terrible years,
she took decisive steps. In 1936 and '37 she moved out with my
brother and me, got a divorce, resettled in Houston, and began
to support her family. Dad was, of course, unable to give the
support stipulated by the court as he was making little pretense
of holding his business together. Mother worked as a secretary
and made ends meet.

Perhaps she was wrong, perhaps her whole view was wrong:
her model of the human psyche did not coincide with or account
for the evidence. The litany of the radio in the barbershop sug-

gested quite a different model and different terms. A doctor would set aside such concepts as sin and will and conscience and repentance, would say the man was sick or maladjusted. His antisocial, unhealthy behavior should be treated by reconditioning. No soul—just a malfunctioning nervous system. Without blame, those of us who know what health is, who are functioning properly, will attempt to bring the deviant into line. Bearing already an intolerable freight of guilt, the alcoholic needs not judgment but sympathetic treatment. You know the line.

Only in the case of alcoholism, science has not yet been as successful as the religiously oriented Alcoholics Anonymous. Of course Dad would have nothing to do with AA simply because it *was* religious. He shuddered to read the "twelve steps." He feared the claptrap of church, the superstition of prayer, sanctimoniousness and self-righteousness, even the humility and cloying compassion of those who have "found the way." Of course he might not have found those qualities in AA if he had given it a fair chance, but the mere mention of the organization would send him streaking for the bootlegger. Probably he feared, above all, any force which might cut off his addiction—and he rationalized his fear with belligerent atheism. Typically, he was too proud to admit he was the slave of drink and was damned if he'd be a slave to a "Power" (in the terms of AA) or a psychiatrist. He would not admit dependency.

When Mother granted him independence from his family, his response was to try to drink himself to death, an inefficient form of suicide. He holed up in a cheap hotel on Oklahoma City's Skid Row ("down on deep Reno Street"), paid the porter to keep bringing the gin and fruit juice (the latter nourishing as the former destroyed), and for some weeks drifted up to consciousness only to slug himself under again (using a towel around his neck to brace his hand as he brought the glass to his lips). Somehow he wound up in a sanitarium. There, waking with knotted intestines, head drifting in clouds of paregoric, focusing on birds on the lawn in hard sunlight beyond the barred windows, he thought things such as that he "had nothing to live for" unless he had a family, which "gave life meaning." Had anyone told him his meditations were "teleological" he would, after looking the word up in the dictionary, have thumbed his nose, with both hands, and sputtered a raspberry—a form of argument he frequently resorted to.

Perhaps a year later he showed up in Houston hoping to get his family back, but apparently the emotional impact of seeing his children (Mother was at work when he arrived) upset the sobriety he had vowed and uneasily maintained. Somehow he managed to take my brother (who was five or six) off to the zoo. They were not back when Mother came home from work, not back at dinner time, not back as darkness fell and the night wore on. I prayed and prayed, finally, desperately, promising God that I would never do again what I was in the habit of doing with an adolescent girl named Florence if He would just bring back my brother. I wrote that promise on a piece of paper, burned it, and put the ashes between some significant pages of the Bible. Shortly afterwards, around ten, a cab arrived with my brother and I was stuck with my promise.

Dad was in the cab, too, half-conscious and surly. He got out with his suitcase, expecting us to put him up for the night. That ended with Mother calling the police, who took him away to sober up.

When he returned a few evenings later to talk things over, he was rational, pale, soft-voiced, and gentle, bearing gifts. We children were shunted off to the bedroom, and the peaceful, intent voices of our parents came drifting under the door. I was old enough, eleven, to have a vision of family life with them—if he were only to be always as he was that evening—and I cried in hope for it. They were lovely people. Mother was a trim, beautiful, dark-haired secretary in those days—with a roundness and warmth and full-throated resonance and humor which gave her beauty depth. She was—and is—a woman of strength, character, and wisdom, not so sentimental as Dad, but able to feel, able to love. Dad, in this good moment, angular, hollow-faced, moustached, seemed thoughtful, honest, earnest. I remember his saying (through the door) that he had been wearing his heart on his sleeve, an image I was intrigued by. That phrase does describe his problem and his most winning qualities—a raw vulnerability which made him irritable, self-pitying, and weak, but also made him easily impressionable, easily moved, quickly understanding, imaginative—and unpredictable. I knocked and asked if I might do a marionette show for them; they permitted me to set up my stage in the doorway and perform, congratulated me, and sent me back to wait with my sleeping brother. Of course Mother could not trust his promises. Next day he was drinking again, proving both of them right, and I saw little of him for the next couple of years.

Dad apparently fought the fight out the hard way, in and out of the sanitarium, piecing together the remains of his oil royalty business in his sober periods, lettering and selling maps of oil plats. I must digress to tell about those maps. They were mostly simple checkersquare plats of leases traced off on the incredibly geometrical landscape of Oklahoma and Texas. The lease owner was identified at the bottom of each little square, holdings of major oil companies shaded in with pale colored pencils. But Dad had the neatest lettering hand of anyone I have ever known. He produced an infallible, delicate italic which reproduced perfectly even when the map was photographically much reduced in size. The lettering was tiny enough on a map three by four feet, but when it was reduced to six by eight inches the lettering would still be legible. Moreover, Dad could make corrections on those tiny maps when property changed hands—and the new printing (as on the head of a pin) could not be distinguished from the old. He sold these maps for a few dollars apiece; then his buddies in the oil business would keep bringing them back for corrections, since no one else in town could hope to make them so neatly. Dad would be out of the office on a drinking bout for a few days and return, nervous, very sober, to find a pile of those little maps which had been left in the office during his absence. Well, he would reason, since I can't concentrate on anything else right now, I'll work on the lettering, which is good therapy anyway. He would hone his miniature drafting pens, hunch over his table, and make a blot. Too shaky. He would curse and stew—and then figure that just one glass of beer would steady his hand. Just one glass. . . .

Earlier, during the depression, he made a little money tying dry flies (which sold on printed cards at the sporting goods store: "Ralph's Hand-Tied Flies"). I remember him working over the dining room table with tiny little hackles and pieces of fur, winding the thread in a perfect, tight coil to make an insect body, lacquering, trimming with tiny scissors, tiny pliers. Miniatures. Steady hand. Perfectionism. Grace and beauty. He was also chronically constipated.

His second wife was a noble, gaunt, big-boned girl, raised in bleak exposure on farms in the panhandles of Texas and Oklahoma, durable in body and character, yet tender, loving, childlike in her milk-fed and long-footed way. She was quiet, with a girlish, innocent wit, incredibly patient, understanding, accepting —and yet not indulgent. In every way she was the perfect mate for a recently rehabilitated alcoholic. She knew that alcoholism was a disease. She had been a secretary in the oil business in the big city for some eight of her twenty-six years. She knew what men were like—and that they couldn't help it. When I think of her sweet clarity and shy, gangly, colorless but loyal love, I wish her life had been uncrossed by my father's tragic shadow. Some half a dozen years she gave him: her season in Hell.

They married on $50 and a car, rented half of a duplex and a good office address, and began putting a life together. When their marriage was but months old, my brother and I were invited to come up to Oklahoma City for a visit.

Dad was beginning to take an interest in our intellectual development. His own intellectual heroes were Robert Ingersoll, Elbert Hubbard, Clarence Darrow, Arthur Brisbane, O. O. MacIntire, Robert Service, O. Henry, Mark Twain, Alf Landon, Will Rogers, Sir Rider Haggard. He was a steady reader. Like his own father, he wrote poetry—a rocking, dialect verse with much vitality, flavor, and wit as well as a mawkish strain derived from Edgar Guest. As I had recently undertaken my brief career of Methodism, I was probably a priggish pain in the neck. He loved clothes (which he somehow never was able to wear well) and bought a lot of them for us. He was enormously enthusiastic about whatever we said or did; I remember his giddy joy when he discovered that my brother (about nine) could play a little chess. It may have been sheer excitement which broke him down—or maybe I drove him to drink by eliciting from him a promise that we would all go to church on Father's Day. Father's Day he was drunk and remained so until we were hustled off to Houston.

For the next couple of years I knew him only by letters which came (to the resentment of my new stepfather) airmail—typed on his business letterhead: humorous, thoughtful, loving letters which began to form in my mind more of his earthy and philosophic style. He began to be a father to me, influencing my thoughts, helping me define myself as what I then believed I wanted to be—a journalist. He sent books and, in his letters, talked about them: made me begin to see books in a new way—as challenges, as ideas, as products men wrote for good reasons. When, my sixteenth summer, I moved to Oklahoma to enter the state university, I went relishing his love and wisdom. He engaged my intelligence more than any adult I had known.

His pattern at that time, I soon discovered, was of periods of unstable sobriety—sometimes lasting months—interrupted with increasing frequency in the next couple of years by sick benders, desperate, week-long attempts to find obliteration. The crises come back to mind as moments when he was too drunk to drive and would insist that his wife (or, later, that I) take him to the bootlegger's. Oklahoma's prohibition made liquor no less available but more expensive and more directly associated with crime and seediness. Dad could make us take him by threatening to go alone and weaving out the door with the car keys. His bootlegger operated from a clandestine bar up a flight of steps in a shabby building in the slums. My stepmother or I (or both) would sit out in the car, sometimes for hours, waiting for him to come staggering down the steep dark stairs of that hideous building, a bottle tucked in the pocket of his flapping, vomit-stained blue topcoat, and reel across the street.

Home again, and the long night interrupted by trips to the kitchen. Weekdays I stayed at the dormitory in Norman, twenty miles away, but I spent a good many weekends with them in their tiny house in the country (rented: my father, on principle, would not work for a salary and would not own property—except for a car). I hiked miles in the surrounding woods that year

chasing their cocker through the snow, dreading the house, the
long single room with a bed in a nook at one end and a kitchen
in a nook at the other. I slept on a trundle bed which pulled out
from under their bunk, so that he stepped on my mattress whenever he crossed to the sink. His wife never argued, protested
only weakly, in whispers, rarely cried or showed the incredible
strain, though some mornings I would find she had slipped
down to sleep beside me, on top of the covers, on my trundle
bed.

"What would you do if I came home drunk?" I asked him
once.

"Slug you."

"Suppose I should slug *you*, now?"

(To imagine the outrageous humor of this you must realize
that I titillated the scales at 100, a cocky little snot; and he,
though by no means a big man, was about nine inches taller,
with a ropy muscularity, unshaven now, with bloody-rimmed
eyes and a heavy slur, leaning against the refrigerator and drain-
board as in the corner of a ring. . . .)

"Go ahead and try it. Just try it, goddamn it. Try it!"

I lifted my chin proudly and did not stoop to fight.

Perhaps I should have, though. It would have done me good
to be beaten. But, of course, he would not have fought. He
would have cowered, as I saw him once huddling on the floor
in the back room of a bar, the bartender standing over him with
a lifted butcher knife, kicking him again and again, trying to find
out from Dad (who didn't know) where his cute little woman
had gone. I dragged Dad out into the car. True, the bartender
was a powerful fellow; but that was not the reason for Dad's
complete, submissive surrender. Innocent in that case, he somehow felt he was wrong, no matter what the circumstances—and
feeling wrong made him snap but not strike; his resistance was
verbal—sarcasm, obscenity, picking, sneering, snarling. And
even drunk he could talk rings around most arguments, slicing
away with cutting truth at one's personality in the process. But
he hated himself, wanted to be stopped, and would have wel-
comed, I think, physical punishment and restraint.

They call it looking for limits. We have suffered all the ills of repression, rigidity, of Victorian restraints, and seem to be moving into a period in which we suffer the ills of expression, of freedom without meaning, of permissiveness and indirection. These, too, can drive one mad. I would not claim, of course, that punching my father in the jaw would have cured his alcoholism. Mother had tried that long since, and it didn't work. But it is difficult to know how to be kind. Mother's way was dangerous: not for her, but for him—as she surely knew that by leaving him she was risking killing him. But her way at least cast him back upon himself and forced him to discover his resources if he was to live at all.

"You're insecure," I once informed him with collegiate glibness.

"You're goddamn right I'm insecure."

"Well, Dad, that's the sort of thing a psychiatrist can maybe help you with."

"You tell me how the hell a psychiatrist can make me secure."

"But it's not that you're *not* really secure. It's just that you *feel* insecure."

"Listen, Buster, I *am* insecure."

And of course he was, and however seriously I took my father it was never seriously enough to grant that his ruin had some meaning. Sober, Dad was one of the sanest of men—penetrating, tender, witty, albeit Elbert Hubbard and Arthur Brisbane did not, perhaps, provide him with enough ideas to understand his world—nor did his own boyhood, watching his own father and brothers undermined by drink and business. What he did understand was insufficient for the rich possibilities of his own sensibility. And through that gap ripped the currents he could not swim. His ethos had no use for his capacity for love and vivid response; rather, it demanded toughness and cleverness in pursuit of what it defined as success—a rather narrow definition, too: money. Whatever of his verdant being could not be sold for cash was left to rot on the vine or sour in the soil, to ferment and decay, to lie in darkness until some rotating bit cut through the cap and all spewed in a wild black fountain. Minds not permitted to answer dull themselves so that they will not question. Hearts that opened themselves have been ignored or injured. They wise up, get smart, and pickle the tender parts exposed.

Aside from his uneconomical personal habits Dad was also cursed with generosity and spontaneity. When we had little to spare he got drunk and bought out half a toy store for an emaciated little Negro boy he picked up out in the country (while trying to make a royalty deal on the farmer's patch of scabby cotton land). We ate steaks when there wasn't money to fill the gas tank—not because he liked eating (he, like most alcoholics, avoided food) but because of his sheer joy in good things and a pathetic urge to make up to his family the pain of enduring him. He was too soft to survive: he once was set off on a bender because, while his second wife was in the hospital at the birth of a new daughter, the cocker at home had pups. It was too much. Otherwise he would have been all right.

And the open heart, closing, clamps tight. He became vicious, sadistic, sneaky, cruelest to those he loved ("Ballad of Reading Gaol" was one of his favorite poems). He never got smart and didn't know anything else to try to be.

"But intelligence isn't a virtue," I told him prissily, fending a compliment.

"The hell it isn't," he said and told me an intricate story of how a friend had made a clever deal, substantially cheating the government, and cleared several thousand dollars. "Now I tell you," he concluded, punching his finger in my pigeon breast, "intelligence is a *virtue!*"

However, intelligence in that sense—the ability to outwit— he never really acquired. In spite of his outrageous selfishness, he never acquired a proper sense of self-interest, and his last act of charity was to weaken his condition sufficiently that virus pneumonia could, at last, relieve us of him:

> My father (didn't everybody's?) drank—
> the Dread Disease, plague of his generation,
> and we were patient, swallowed down his spite,
> and understood him as he thrashed and sank,
> and all forgave, with whining and evasion,
>
> and all refrained from saying wrong or right.
> We knew, in dry, bright Oklahoma City,

the only cure for drink was love and pity.
We knew the flesh was frail, with delicate breath,
and so indulged each other into death.

But when he dared me, cursing me, demanding,
and shuffling scrawnily down halls of the mind,
sagging his jaw, speaking with tongue gone blind,
should I have answered him with understanding?
He cannot help the things he does, we said.
(He grinned and snitched a ten and drove off, weaving.)
His heart, we said, is spotless—but his head
disturbed. (Late I would hear him: racketing, heaving.)

Years after he was gone I think I saw
how we insulted him, drove him along:
his spirit we called nerves, said nerves were raw—
denied his holy sanction to be wrong.
The sonofabitch (God bless him) drank and died
because we understood away his pride.

And now as I near the age he died he stalks my imagination:
perhaps my father is my picture of Dorian Gray. I look in the
mirror and see his face engrained in mine, emerging as I age.
Did I ever know him really? Have I only projected myself? Is
he a character in a play, in whom I have distilled my own sentiment and cynicism, temper, self-indulgence, resentment of authority, my refusal to be governed or helped?

When Shakespeare watched Iago walk the boards it must
have been with humble self-recognition. We create pieces of
ourselves and send them onto the stage of our imagination; we
hiss and boo and laugh at them, but at night they come home
and climb in bed alongside our Desdemonas and Falstaffs and
Juliets and Lears. Herb Gardner has used the figure of our various selves, like a thousand clowns, piling out of the miniature
car in the circus ring. Man, what a show! But in the darkness
after the set is struck and the posters peel in the cold wind,
those thousand clowns crowd themselves into our chest and head
and loins. It was a great relief to externalize and mock them. But
their prancing in the ring of fiction made them at last more real
and more difficult to absorb.

Goodnight, Dad.
Goodnight, Jud.

A Note on the Author

Judson Jerome has won several awards for his creative writing, including an Amy Lowell Poetry Traveling Scholarship and a William Carlos Williams Award in Fiction. He has published numerous articles, poems, short stories, and seven books: *Light in the West* (poems, 1962), *The Poet and the Poem* (essays, 1963), *The Ocean's Warning to the Skin Diver and Other Love Poems* (1964), *The Fell of Dark* (a novel, 1966), *Serenade* (poems, 1968), *Poetry: Premeditated Art* (a textbook, 1968), and *Culture out of Anarchy: The Reconstruction of American Higher Learning* (1970). In addition, he has written a monthly column in *Writer's Digest* since 1961. Mr. Jerome is interested in exploring new forms of education, and is currently director of the Center for Documentary Arts at Antioch College's Columbia, Maryland, campus where he is professor of literature.

UNIVERSITY OF ILLINOIS PRESS